Ami Pro™ 3
QuickStart

Suzanne Weixel

que

Ami Pro 3 QuickStart

Copyright © 1994 by Que® Corporation.

Library of Congress Catalog No.: 94-65142

ISBN: 1-56529-732-6

97 96 95 94   4 3 2

Interpretation of the printing code: the rightmost double-digit number is the year of the book's printing; the rightmost single-digit number, the number of the book's printing. For example, a printing code of 94-1 shows that the first printing of the book occurred in 1994.

Screen reproductions in this book were created with Collage Plus from Inner Media, Inc., Hollis, NH.

Ami Pro 3 QuickStart is based on Ami Pro 3.0.

Publisher: David P. Ewing

Director of Publishing: Michael Miller

Director of Acquisitions and Editing: Corinne Walls

Product Marketing Manager: Ray Robinson

About the Author

Suzanne Weixel is a self-employed writer and editor specializing in the technology industry. Her experience with computers began in 1974, when she learned to play football on the Dartmouth Time Sharing terminal her brother installed in a spare bedroom.

For Que, Suzanne has written and revised numerous books, including *Easy PCs 2nd Edition, I Hate Word for Windows 6, DOS 6 QuickStart*, and *Everyday DOS*. She also writes about noncomputer-related subjects whenever she has the chance.

Suzanne graduated from Dartmouth College in 1981 with a degree in art history. She currently lives in Marlborough, Massachusetts, with her husband Rick, their sons, Nathaniel and Evan, and their Samoyed, Cirrus.

Dedication

To my husband, Rick.

Publishing Manager
Charles O. Stewart III

Acquisitions Editor
Nancy Stevenson

Product Director
Jim Minatel

Production Editors
Phil Kitchel
Donald R. Eamon

Editors
William A. Barton
Danielle Bird
Lorna Gentry
Lori A. Lyons
Susan Ross Moore
Linda Seifert
Kathy Simpson
Nancy Sixsmith
Pamela Wampler
Phil Worthington

Technical Editors
Tich Nye
Lisa Warner

Book Designer
Amy Peppler-Adams

Cover Designer
Dan Armstrong

Production Team
Gary Adair
Angela Bannan
Claudia Bell
Kim Cofer
Meshell Dinn
Karen Dodson
Mark Enochs
Teresa Forrester
Joelynn Gifford
Carla Hall
Jenny Kucera
Bob LaRoche
Tim Montgomery
Nanci Sears Perry
Linda Quigley
Beth Rago
Caroline Roop
Dennis Sheehan
Carol Stamile
Michael Thomas
Tina Trettin
Sue VandeWalle
Mary Beth Wakefield
Robert Wolf
Michelle Worthington
Donna Winter

Indexer
Rebecca Mayfield

Composed in *Stone* and *MCPdigital* by Que Corporation.

Acknowledgments

I would like to thank my parents, Joan and Bernard Sudikoff, who are always willing to provide emergency child care, even when it means driving 30 miles in an ice storm.

I also want to thank everyone at Que who had a hand (or at least a finger) in the planning, development, and production of this book, especially Nancy Stevenson who somehow managed to make me believe that the schedule was reasonable and that the end was in sight.

Trademark Acknowledgments

Contents at a Glance

Table of Contents

10 Working with Frames 181

11 Using Draw 199

Introduction

Ami Pro 3 is a powerful *WYSIWYG* (what-you-see-is-what-you get) word processing software package that takes full advantage of the easy-to-use Windows environment. The program combines basic text entry and editing capabilities with sophisticated layout, formatting, and document management features. Ami Pro 3 is an ideal choice for beginners trying to produce a simple memo as well as for experienced computer users creating complex reports and presentations.

Ami Pro 3 QuickStart covers the fundamentals of using Ami Pro 3. The text is supported by step-by-step instructions, on-your-own exercises, and clearly labeled illustrations, all designed to get you up and running with Ami Pro 3 quickly and easily.

What Does This Book Contain?

Each lesson in *Ami Pro 3 QuickStart* is built around a set of related tasks. The lessons, and the sections within the lessons, are organized so you can use the information presented to accomplish the tasks that follow. In addition, the lessons are grouped into parts. You don't have to read the book sequentially, however, to learn to use Ami Pro 3. Feel free to jump around from lesson to lesson and section to section to find the information you want.

From beginning to end, the lessons move from the basics—such as creating and revising documents—through paragraph and page design, and then into more-advanced tasks, such as customizing and automating the program; incorporating graphics, tables, and charts into documents; and using Ami Pro 3 with other Windows applications.

The book begins with a Visual Index of documents you can create with Ami Pro 3. The Visual Index illustrates the wide range of projects you can produce with this program.

Part I: Creating and Editing Basic Documents

Lesson 1, "Learning the Basics," begins with an overview of Ami Pro 3's features. The lesson covers such essentials as starting Windows and using a mouse and a keyboard, then you move on to learn how to start Ami Pro, understand the Ami Pro screen, and get help.

Lesson 2, "Creating a Document," introduces you to style sheets. You learn how to start a new document and use Ami Pro's typing conventions to enter text. Finally, you learn how to save and print the document.

In Lesson 3, "Revising a Document," you learn how to open an existing document and use basic editing skills such as moving and copying text to make revisions. You learn how to correct mistakes by deleting text, using Undo to revert to a previous version of the document, and finding and replacing incorrect text. You also learn how to open multiple document windows and make multiple copies of a document.

In Lesson 4, "Proofreading Your Document," you learn how to use Ami Pro's three proofreading tools—Spell Check, Grammar Check, and the Thesaurus.

Part II: Formatting for a Professional Look

In Lesson 5, "Dressing Up Your Text," you learn how to use fonts and character attributes to format your text.

In Lesson 6, "Lining Up Your Paragraphs," you learn how to align, indent, and space lines and paragraphs.

Lesson 7, "Setting Up Pages," provides information on creating and modifying a page layout and describes how to use rulers to set margins, tabs, and newspaper-style columns.

Lesson 8, "Making Your Pages Pretty," teaches you some of the finer points of page layout and design, such as how to add decorative borders and lines, use headers and footers, and insert page and column breaks.

Part III: Customizing and Adding Nontext Elements to Documents

In Lesson 9, "Customizing Ami Pro," you learn how to make Ami Pro suit your own needs. You learn more about styles and SmartIcons, and you learn how to change Ami Pro program and start-up options.

Lesson 10, "Working with Frames," explains the concept of frames and describes how to create, format, and manipulate frames in a document and place a picture in a frame.

In Lesson 11, "Using Draw," you learn how to start Ami Pro's built-in drawing package and use it to create and edit a drawing.

Lesson 12, "Working with Tables," covers creating, formatting, and editing tables.

Lesson 13, "Working with Charts," describes how to use the different types of charts available in Ami Pro.

Part IV: Advanced Features and Integration

In Lesson 14, "Merging Documents," you learn about the merge operation and how to create a merge data file and create, print, and save a merge document.

Lesson 15, "Working with Document Notation," provides information about Ami Pro's document notation tools, including notes, revision marking, comparing documents, and inserting and finding bookmarks. It also discusses using document information to track and find documents.

In Lesson 16, "Working with Other Windows Applications," you learn the ins and outs of using Ami Pro 3 with other Windows applications. You learn to share and link data between applications, including the other programs in the Lotus SmartSuite series.

In Lesson 17, "Managing Your Files and Documents," you learn how to use Ami Pro's file management features, including those for finding and organizing your files. You also learn to manage longer documents by creating outlines and a table of contents and by inserting footnotes.

Appendix A: Installing Ami Pro 3

Appendix A provides instructions for installing all or part of Ami Pro, the Adobe Type Manager, and the WordPerfect Switchkit.

Who Should Use This Book?

Ami Pro 3 QuickStart is a useful guide for anyone who wants to use Ami Pro 3. The book presents enough basic information to get a first-time user started, then builds on that user's growing understanding by introducing more-advanced topics. If you're an experienced user, the book covers features and tasks to expand your knowledge and increase your proficiency. You can also use this book as a reference tool.

Where to Find More Help

After you master the features in this book, you may want to learn more about Ami Pro 3's advanced capabilities. If so, refer to Que's *Using Ami Pro 3*, Special Edition. To learn more about using Windows, you may want to consult Que's *Using Windows 3.1*, Special Edition.

Ami Pro 3 also provides extensive on-line help to answer many of your questions. To learn about getting help with Ami Pro 3, see Lesson 1, "Learning the Basics."

Lotus also provides customer assistance and support for registered users.

What You Need to Use Ami Pro 3

To use Ami Pro 3, you must have the following computer hardware and software:

- A computer with an Intel 286 microprocessor or greater, capable of running Windows 3.0 or higher.

- A minimum of 2M of random access memory (RAM).

- An EGA, VGA, SVGA, or Hercules Graphics video adapter and monitor, compatible with Windows version 3.0 or higher.

- Microsoft Windows version 3.0 or higher, running in Standard or Enhanced mode.

- DOS version 3.0 or higher.

- One 1.2M 5 1/4-inch disk drive, one 1.44M 3 1/2-inch disk drive, or one 720K 3 1/2-inch disk drive.

A Windows-compatible mouse is highly recommended, but not required.

Conventions Used in This Book

Ami Pro 3 QuickStart uses the following conventions to help you use and understand the information in this book:

- Text that you type appears in **boldface** type.

- Key combinations, such as Ctrl+Enter, indicate that you should press and hold the first key as you press the second key.

- Important words or phrases appear in *italics* the first time they are discussed.

- Menu commands appear like this: Choose **F**ile, **R**un, which means you use the mouse to click the **F**ile menu, then click the **R**un item on that menu. You also can press Alt+F, and then press R. (Using menus is explained in Lesson 1, "Learning the Basics.")

- If SmartIcon alternatives to menu commands are available, the icon appears in the margin of this book.

- *Notes* describe information that can help you avoid problems or accomplish the task in a more efficient manner.

- *Cautions* warn you of potential problems that could arise as the result of a particular action.

- *Keywords* in the margins briefly define new terms that you encounter as you read this book.

- *If You Have Problems...* paragraphs provide troubleshooting information to help you avoid—or escape—problem situations.

Visual Index

Ami Pro provides tools for creating a wide range of documents. This section illustrates some of the documents you can create using Ami Pro's built-in style sheets. Each sample has labels that briefly describe the relevant tasks and refer you to the appropriate sections of the book.

Text flows before and after the frame, "Changing the Appearance of Frames," p. 194

Title centered in a frame, "Entering Text in a Frame," p. 187

Headings with different emphasis, "Understanding Character Attributes," p. 98

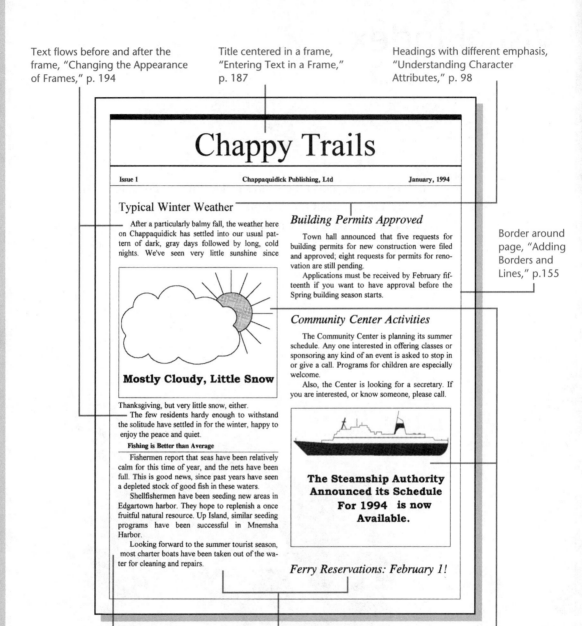

Chappy Trails

Issue 1	Chappaquidick Publishing, Ltd	January, 1994

Typical Winter Weather

After a particularly balmy fall, the weather here on Chappaquidick has settled into our usual pattern of dark, gray days followed by long, cold nights. We've seen very little sunshine since

Mostly Cloudy, Little Snow

Thanksgiving, but very little snow, either.

The few residents hardy enough to withstand the solitude have settled in for the winter, happy to enjoy the peace and quiet.

Fishing is Better than Average

Fishermen report that seas have been relatively calm for this time of year, and the nets have been full. This is good news, since past years have seen a depleted stock of good fish in these waters.

Shellfishermen have been seeding new areas in Edgartown harbor. They hope to replenish a once fruitful natural resource. Up Island, similar seeding programs have been successful in Mnemsha Harbor.

Looking forward to the summer tourist season, most charter boats have been taken out of the water for cleaning and repairs.

Building Permits Approved

Town hall announced that five requests for building permits for new construction were filed and approved; eight requests for permits for renovation are still pending.

Applications must be received by February fifteenth if you want to have approval before the Spring building season starts.

Community Center Activities

The Community Center is planning its summer schedule. Any one interested in offering classes or sponsoring any kind of an event is asked to stop in or give a call. Programs for children are especially welcome.

Also, the Center is looking for a secretary. If you are interested, or know someone, please call.

The Steamship Authority Announced its Schedule For 1994 is now Available.

Ferry Reservations: February 1!

Border around page, "Adding Borders and Lines," p.155

Narrow margins leave more room for text and graphics, "Modifying Selected Pages," p. 126

Two newspaper-style columns, "Modifying Selected Pages," p. 126

Clip art graphics inserted in frames, "Entering Graphics in a Frame," p. 188

Page numbering in header, "Understanding Headers and Footers," p. 145

Underlined title, "Understanding Character Attributes," p. 98

```
Nathaniel Evans - 1


Nathaniel Evans                                    34 Words
23 Jenison Street                                     Full
Newton Centre, MA 02159
617-555-5555                               © Nathaniel Evans
999-99-9999
```

<u>THE ART OF SNOW FORTS</u>

by

Nathaniel Evans

Children digging in a snow drift at the end of the driveway may not know it, but they are taking part in a tradition rich in history.

Humans have been building snow forts since the ice age.[1] Snow forts have served a variety of purposes. They have been built to provide warmth, to provide shelter, and, in cases such as the children mentioned above, to provide fun.[2]

Around the world and across the span of time, the requirements for snow fort building are snow and cold. But different cultures approach the fort in different ways,

---

[1] Paul Falk, *Life in the Ice Age*, 1977, Bunion Press.

[2] Alex Daniels, Shelter from the Storm, 1983, MK Press.

Footnotes, "Using Footnotes," p. 321

Double-spaced lines, "Setting Line Spacing," p. 113

Centered title,
"Aligning Text,"
p. 108

Tabs align text in the header and footer,
"Modifying Selected Pages," p. 126

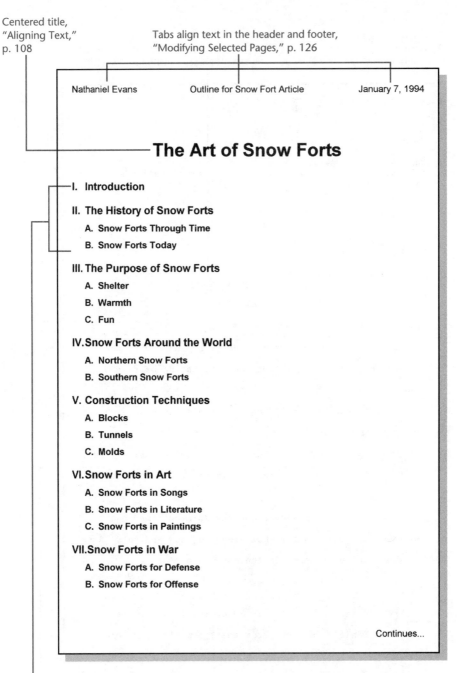

Nathaniel Evans   Outline for Snow Fort Article   January 7, 1994

The Art of Snow Forts

I. **Introduction**

II. **The History of Snow Forts**
   A. Snow Forts Through Time
   B. Snow Forts Today

III. **The Purpose of Snow Forts**
   A. Shelter
   B. Warmth
   C. Fun

IV. **Snow Forts Around the World**
   A. Northern Snow Forts
   B. Southern Snow Forts

V. **Construction Techniques**
   A. Blocks
   B. Tunnels
   C. Molds

VI. **Snow Forts in Art**
   A. Snow Forts in Songs
   B. Snow Forts in Literature
   C. Snow Forts in Paintings

VII. **Snow Forts in War**
   A. Snow Forts for Defense
   B. Snow Forts for Offense

Continues...

Outline levels and numbers are
built into paragraph styles,
"Using Outline Mode," p. 311

Different font sizes,
"Choosing Fonts," p. 97

Centered title and right-
aligned paragraph,
"Aligning Text," p. 108

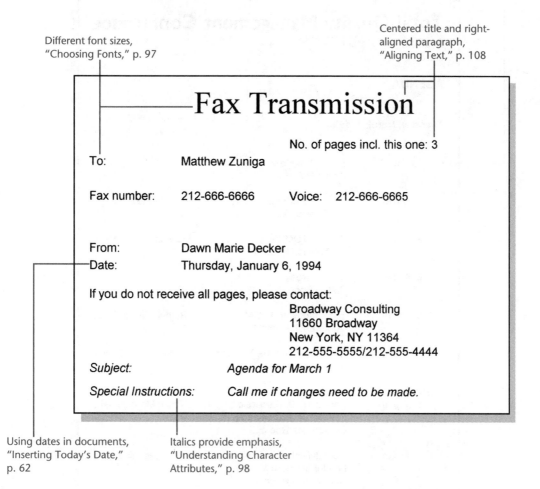

Fax Transmission

No. of pages incl. this one: 3

To: Matthew Zuniga

Fax number: 212-666-6666   Voice: 212-666-6665

From: Dawn Marie Decker
Date: Thursday, January 6, 1994

If you do not receive all pages, please contact:
                        Broadway Consulting
                        11660 Broadway
                        New York, NY 11364
                        212-555-5555/212-555-4444

Subject: *Agenda for March 1*

Special Instructions: *Call me if changes need to be made.*

Using dates in documents,
"Inserting Today's Date,"
p. 62

Italics provide emphasis,
"Understanding Character
Attributes," p. 98

Decimal tabs align times, "Modifying Selected Pages," p. 126

Different fonts and font sizes, "Choosing Fonts," p. 97

Total Quality Management Conference

Hyatt Regency, Maui
March 1 - 4, 1994

AGENDA

Tuesday, March 1, 1994

8:00 a.m.	Buffet Breakfast Dining Room	
9:00 a.m.	Welcome Address	Matthew Zuniga
	Conference Room 1	
9:30 a.m.	What is TQM?	Jackson Triggs, MBA
	Conference Room 1	
10:00 a.m.	Coffee Break Coffee Shop	
10:30 a.m.	Technology and TQM	Richard Maltz, MBA
	Conference Room 1	
11:15 a.m.	Question & Answer Session	Maltz and Triggs
	Conference Room 1	
12:00 p.m.	Lunch	
1:00 p.m.	Round Table Discussion	Team Management
	Leader: Jackson Triggs Conference Room 2	
2:00 p.m.	Round Table Discussion	Reengineering
	Leader: Richard Maltz Conference Room 2	
3:00 p.m.	Question & Answer Session	Maltz and Triggs
	Conference Room 2	

Tab leaders fill the spaces between left-aligned and right-aligned tab stops, "Modifying Selected Pages," p. 126

Large font size, italics, and boldface make the word "Memo" stand out, "Understanding Character Attributes," p. 98

Bullets are part of the Bullet 1 style, "Selecting Styles," p. 47

Memo

To: *Robin Reisman*
From: *Richard Maltz*
Date: *January 6, 1994*
Re: *TQM Conference*

Rob --

Attached is the agenda for day 1 of the TQM conference in March. Decker faxed it to me this morning. Any comments?

Some issues we may want to address:

- Why does Triggs speak first?
- Will anyone really attend the afternoon round tables?
- Do we need two question and answer sessions?

Let's talk.

By the way, remember to bring your tennis gear.

Line in the left margin adds class, "Adding Borders and Lines," p. 155

This row in the table is a different size than the others, "Changing the Appearance of a Table," p. 231

Landscape mode fits the calendar on the page, "Modifying Selected Pages," p. 126

Create light text on a dark background, "Changing the Appearance of a Table," p. 231

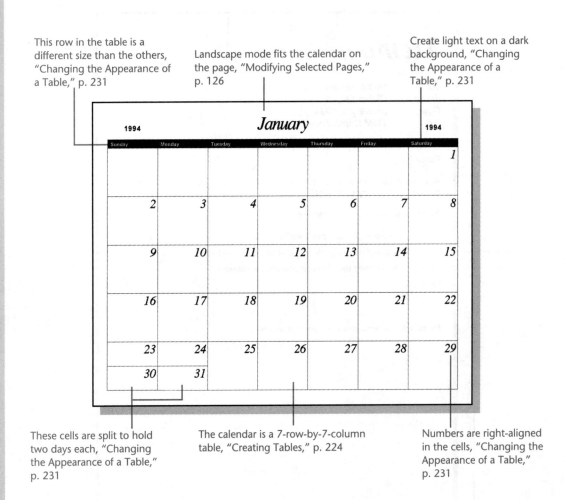

These cells are split to hold two days each, "Changing the Appearance of a Table," p. 231

The calendar is a 7-row-by-7-column table, "Creating Tables," p. 224

Numbers are right-aligned in the cells, "Changing the Appearance of a Table," p. 231

Gridlines are part of the table, "Changing the Appearance of a Table," p. 231

Body Text paragraphs are indented and justified, "Aligning Text," p. 108

Inventory Report

Store 1

Store management has tabulated the results of the January inventory control check and is prepared to make recommendations for purchasing. Table 1.1 shows the results for Store 1.

Table 1.1

	Red	Blue	Black	White
Sweaters	35	32	20	28
Turtleneck Shirts	32	31	29	25
Denim Jeans	38	19	15	35
Lycra Shorts	40	35	28	40
Total	145	117	92	128

Store 2

Store management has tabulated the results of the January inventory control check and is prepared to make recommendations for purchasing. Table 1.2 shows the results for Store 2.

Table 1.2

	Red	Blue	Black	White
Sweaters	34	30	28	27
Turtleneck Shirts	30	31	28	21
Denim Jeans	35	22	29	28
Lycra Shorts	35	35	33	40
Total	134	118	118	116

Subheadings have top borders, "Using Styles," p. 163

Page tables present the information in a readable format, "Understanding Tables," p. 221

Quick Add totals the columns, "Changing the Appearance of a Table," p. 231

The Draw program was used to enhance the charts, "Changing the Appearance of a Chart," p. 248, "Adding Text to a Drawing," p. 216, and "Changing Line Styles and Color," p. 211

Double-line border has a customized look, "Adding Borders and Lines," p. 155

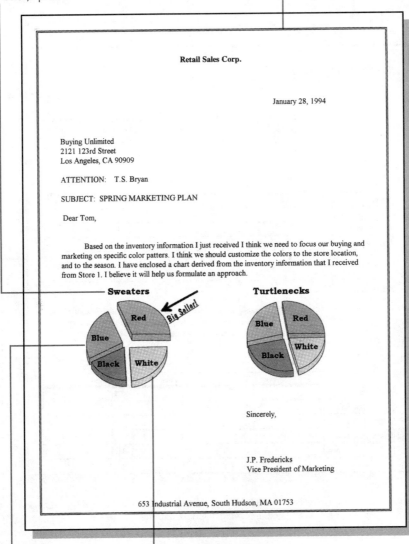

Retail Sales Corp.

January 28, 1994

Buying Unlimited
2121 123rd Street
Los Angeles, CA 90909

ATTENTION: T.S. Bryan

SUBJECT: SPRING MARKETING PLAN

Dear Tom,

Based on the inventory information I just received I think we need to focus our buying and marketing on specific color patters. I think we should customize the colors to the store location, and to the season. I have enclosed a chart derived from the inventory information that I received from Store 1. I believe it will help us formulate an approach.

Sweaters Red *Big Seller!* Blue Black White

Turtlenecks Blue Red White Black

Sincerely,

J.P. Fredericks
Vice President of Marketing

653 Industrial Avenue, South Hudson, MA 01753

Charts illustrate the text using data copied from another document, "Creating a Chart from Existing Data," p. 244

Charts use 3-D effect, as well as expanded pie chart variation, "Changing the Appearance of a Chart," p. 248

Placing text in a frame enhances the text, "Entering Text in a Frame," p. 187

Connected cells provide a place for a title, "Changing the Appearance of a Table," p. 231

To: J.T. Fredericks

From: Erica T. Jones

Date: Friday, January 7, 1994

Subject: Inventory Report Figures

J.T. -

Thought you'd be interested in the inventory figures from store 1 and store 2:

STORE 1			
	Red	Blue	Black	White
Sweaters	35	32	20	28
Turtleneck Shirts	32	31	29	25
Denim Jeans	38	19	15	35
Lycra Shorts	40	35	28	40
Total	145	117	92	128

STORE 2			
	Red	Blue	Black	White
Sweaters	34	30	28	27
Turtleneck Shirts	30	31	28	21
Denim Jeans	35	22	29	28
Lycra Shorts	35	35	33	40
Total	134	118	118	116

Frame tables highlight data imported from another document, "Understanding Tables," p. 221

Simple frames emphasize table data, "Changing the Appearance of Frames," p. 194

Data is linked from a 1-2-3 spreadsheet,
"Linking Data into Ami Pro," p. 304

Retail Sales Corp.

January 26, 1994

Thomas Johnson
Directory of Manufacturing
Johnson Mills Corp.
1111 Old Mill Lane
New Sudbury, MA 01776

Dear Tom:

I've updated the figures based on the new 1-2-3 worksheet you sent over. How do they look?

MANUFACTURING			
Machinist	378	$31.23	$11,805
Assembler	1374	$26.03	$35,765
Direct Mfg Labor			$47,570
Manufacturing O/H	120.00%		$57,084
Total Manufacturing Labor			$104,654

I've also included figures from last years prodcution run for comparison. They are on the next page. Of course I know expenses are greater this year, but the difference is pretty big. Can you justify?

Sincerely,

J.P. Fredericks
Vice President of Marketing

Merge document created for use in
a merge, "Creating the Merge
Document," p. 267

January 26, 1994

<GREETING> <CONTACT_FIRST_NAME> <CONTACT_LAST_NAME>
<TITLE>
<COMPANY_NAME>
<STREET_ADDRESS_1>
<STREET_ADDRESS_2>
<CITY>, <STATE> <ZIP_CODE>

Dear <GREETING> <CONTACT_LAST_NAME>,

I am writing to tell you about a new product I think you will find quite useful.

It is called "Super Sponge" and it will revolutionize cleaning around the world.

Super Sponge is destined to save millions of house cleaning professionals much time and money. Its unique design makes it last four times as long as an ordinary sponge, and its patented Saturation Level 1^{TM} feature makes it hold water and cleaning fluids nearly ten times longer than any other cleaning surface.

I am sure you will be amazed by this product.

To receive additional information about Super Sponge, or to arrange for a demonstration, please contact me.

I look forward to hearing from you.

Sincerely,

Alexandra Nagle
Product Specialist
Super Sponge, Inc.

A personalized form letter created using a merge data file and a merge document, "Performing the Merge," p. 269

January 26, 1994

Ms. Cynthia Brown
Manager of Customer Services
New Day Housecare
62 West Main Street
Westville, MA 02188

Dear Ms. Brown,

I am writing to tell you about a new product I think you will find quite useful.

It is called "Super Sponge" and it will revolutionize cleaning around the world.

Super Sponge is destined to save millions of house cleaning professionals much time and money. Its unique design makes it last four times as long as an ordinary sponge, and its patented Saturation Level 1™ feature makes it hold water and cleaning fluids nearly ten times longer than any other cleaning surface.

I am sure you will be amazed by this product.

To receive additional information about Super Sponge, or to arrange for a demonstration, please contact me.

I look forward to hearing from you.

Sincerely,

Alexandra Nagle
Product Specialist
Super Sponge, Inc.

Revision marking makes it easy to identify changes made to a document, "Using Revision Marking," p. 277

Suzanne Weixel
119 Barnard Road
Marlborough, MA 01752
508-624-7595

29 Words

© Suzanne Weixel

ON 34

by

Suzanne Weixel

As January stretches on and on, one wonders whether it is the short~~ness of the~~ days or the bitter winds that make one long for summer.

December *is a joyous and festive time of year. It overflows*~~,~~ with ~~its~~ holidays and parties, *and*~~its~~ evergreens and colored lights. *It truly heralds a future of hope.*~~, is joyous, festive, and full of hope.~~ But January *is*~~,~~ so dark and cold. It *is*~~, is~~ dreary beyond belief. *In January, there is* ~~n~~Nothing to look forward to but more snow and slush. By the time February rolls around, the promise of spring rings false. Not withstanding *Groundhog Day* ~~Puxatawney Phil~~, by February *everyone realizes*~~the realization~~ that winter lasts longer than any other season.~~ has finally taken hold.~~

Part I
Creating and Editing Basic Documents

Learning the Basics

This lesson introduces you to Ami Pro 3 for Windows. You get an overview of Ami Pro's features and information on how to use them.

Before you begin this lesson, you should have Ami Pro 3 already installed on your computer system. If you need information on installing Ami Pro, see Appendix A.

In this lesson, you learn how to

- Start Ami Pro.

- Identify the different parts of the Ami Pro screen.

- Use menus and SmartIcons.

- Use Help.

- Exit Ami Pro.

Introducing Ami Pro 3

Ami Pro 3 is a word processing program that combines basic editing features, such as text underlining and spell checking, with sophisticated publishing features such as charts, tables, and integrated text and graphics.

The following list describes some of the features available in Ami Pro:

- Ami Pro is a *WYSIWYG* (what-you-see-is-what-you-get) word processor, which means that it displays documents on-screen in the same way it prints them on a page.

- All the tools you need to create and format documents of all types can be displayed on-screen while you work or can be hidden until you need them. You can quickly access commands using your choice of menus, SmartIcons, or the status bar.

- Context-sensitive help is available everywhere in the program.

- You can format characters in different fonts and sizes and dress them up by applying underlining, boldface, or italic type.

- Ami Pro takes advantage of the convenience of the mouse so you can select commands and manipulate text and graphics using simple click-and-drag techniques.

- Ami Pro comes with more than 55 style sheets, so you can lay out and design all types of documents with ease. You can create and change style sheets to meet your requirements.

- Ami Pro comes with a spell checker, a thesaurus, and a grammar checker, so you can make sure your documents meet the highest standards of quality.

- Macros and glossaries enable you to automate repetitive tasks.

- Bookmarks, notes, tables of contents, indexes, and even tables of authorities can be generated by Ami Pro.

- Ami Pro enables you to create professional-looking documents that include newspaper-style columns, tables, charts, pictures, and clip art.

The following section serves as a refresher course to prepare you for using Ami Pro.

Getting Started with Ami Pro

Mouse
A device you use to move the insertion point in text, or a pointer in a Windows program.

Before you start Ami Pro, make sure you're familiar with how to use your *mouse* and the keyboard. (Using the mouse and keyboard is the same in Ami Pro as in Windows and other Windows applications; if you are reasonably familiar with these operations, you can skip to the section "Starting Ami Pro.")

Using a Mouse

The four basic mouse maneuvers used in Windows and in Windows applications such as Ami Pro 3 are described in table 1.1.

Table 1.1. Basic Mouse Maneuvers	
Operation	**Description**
Point	To move the mouse pointer so that it is touching an item on-screen
Click	To press a mouse button (unless otherwise indicated, the left mouse button)
Double-click	To press the left mouse button twice in rapid succession
Drag	To hold down the left mouse button while you move the mouse pointer to a different location

Using the Keyboard

You can operate most Windows and Ami Pro for Windows functions using only the keyboard. (You are likely to find, however, that using both a mouse *and* the keyboard is much easier.)

To choose a menu command using the keyboard, follow these steps:

1. Press Alt to activate the menu bar.

2. To open a menu, perform one of the following operations:

   ■ Press the underlined letter in the menu name.

   ■ Use the arrow keys to highlight the menu name, and then press Enter.

3. To choose a menu command, perform one of the following operations:

   ■ Press the underlined letter in the command name.

   ■ Use the arrow keys to highlight the command, and then press Enter.

   Note: *Throughout this book, the underlined letter you can press on the keyboard to activate a menu or command is shown in* **boldface** *type.*

Starting Ami Pro

Windows provides a consistent operating environment for running applications such as Ami Pro and the other programs in the Lotus Suite. If you want to learn more about using Windows, you might want to read Que's *Using Windows 3.1*, Special Edition.

In the title bar at the top of the window, you see the name of the program that is running. At the bottom of the window are program group icons.

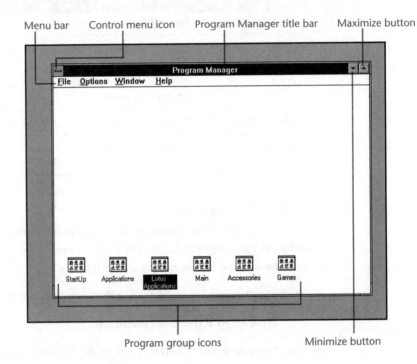

Menu bar   Control menu icon   Program Manager title bar   Maximize button

Program group icons   Minimize button

Ami Pro 3 must run in the Windows operating environment. You can start several ways in Windows. The easiest way is from the Lotus Applications program group window.

Note: *During installation, Ami Pro is installed by default in the Lotus Applications program group.*

To start Ami Pro from the Windows Program Manager, follow these steps:

Icons
Small pictures that represent programs or program groups in Windows or a Windows application.

1. Open the Lotus Applications program group window by double-clicking the Lotus Applications group *icon.*

2. Double-click the Ami Pro 3.0 program item icon. Ami Pro starts, and the initial Ami Pro screen appears.

1

If you have problems...
If nothing happens, you might not be double-clicking fast enough. Try again, making sure that you press the mouse button twice, quickly and firmly.

Menu name

To open a menu using the mouse, point at the menu name and click. To choose a command in that menu, point at the command and click.

Program Manager

File   Options   Window   Help

New...
Open   Enter
Move...   F7
Copy...   F8
Delete   Del
Properties... Alt+Enter
Run...
Exit Windows...

Command name

StartUp   Applications   Lotus Applications   Main   Accessories   Games

Understanding the Ami Pro Screen

Default
A setting that Ami Pro (or any other program) automatically goes to in a given situation.

No matter how you start the program, you see the *default* Ami Pro screen first. A new, blank document is open. The name in the title bar of the new document is [Untitled].

If you have problems...
If you installed the QuickStart Tutorial (see Appendix A), the tutorial's main menu appears on-screen the first time you start Ami Pro. Choose any topic from this menu, or choose Exit Tutorial to leave the tutorial screen. To view the tutorial in the future, choose it from the Ami Pro Help menu.

Ami Pro Control menu icon · SmartIcon bar · Title bar · Menu bar · Minimize button · Restore button

The Ami Pro screen is designed to provide quick and easy access to the features you use

Document Control menu icon

Margin areas

Status bar

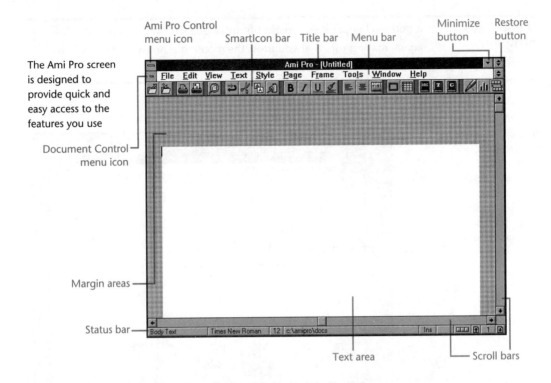

Text area · Scroll bars

The title bar at the top of the screen displays the name of the program and the name of the document in which you are working. The menu bar displays the names of the Ami Pro menus. Choose a menu name to drop down a menu of commands.

The SmartIcon bar displays icons you can choose to execute Ami Pro commands. See Lesson 9, "Customizing Ami Pro," to learn more about customizing the SmartIcons.

The text area is where you enter the document text. See Lesson 2, "Creating a Document," to learn more about entering text. The status bar displays information about the current document. You can choose buttons on the status bar to change the displayed information and to execute commands.

Making Choices

In Ami Pro, you accomplish tasks by choosing options from menus, from the SmartIcon bar, and from dialog boxes. The easiest way to make these choices is by using the mouse. However, you can execute some commands without opening a menu, by using keyboard shortcuts.

Using the Status Bar

The status bar does not just display information about the current document—it also provides quick access to shortcut menus you can use to make choices.

In all, there are eight buttons on the status bar. Table 1.2 describes the button names and their functions.

Table 1.2. Status Bar Buttons	
Button	**Function**
Style status button	Displays the styles list from which you can choose a new style
Face button	Displays a list of fonts
Point size button	Displays a list of font sizes
Document path button	Toggles to show the document path, the date and time, and the current location of the insertion point
Typing mode button	Toggles from insert mode to typeover mode to revision marking mode
SmartIcons button	Displays a list of SmartIcon sets
Page status button	Displays the current document page
Page arrow buttons	Let you move forward and backward in the document

Using Menus

In Windows and all Windows applications, you choose menus and menu commands by pointing and clicking with the mouse or by pressing Alt+ the highlighted letter in the menu or command name. Different menu choices lead to different types of options, as shown in the following figure.

An arrow indicates that another menu follows.

If more keyboard shortcuts are available, they are listed on the menus, to the right of the menu command. Press Ctrl and the letter shown.

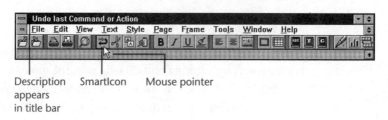

An ellipsis indicates that a dialog box follows.

To close a menu without making a choice, click outside the menu area or press Esc.

Using SmartIcons

SmartIcons—the small pictures that appear on-screen—provide direct access to many of Ami Pro's menu commands. To select one, point to it, and click.

Ami Pro has more than 100 SmartIcons, which you can organize according to the tasks you do most often, and you can choose how you want these icons displayed. In Lesson 9, "Customizing Ami Pro," you learn more about selecting and arranging SmartIcons.

To determine the function of any SmartIcon, point to the icon and click the right mouse button. A description of the SmartIcon's function appears in the title bar.

Description appears in title bar   SmartIcon   Mouse pointer

1

Note: *To take advantage of the SmartIcons, you must use a mouse. You cannot choose a SmartIcon using the keyboard.*

Using Dialog Boxes

Dialog box
A window that appears on-screen whenever Ami Pro needs you to enter more information.

Many Ami Pro commands require you to provide additional information before being carried out. You can enter this information using a *dialog box.*

Dialog boxes may include all the options shown here in the Modify Style dialog box, but most dialog boxes are more simple and less cluttered.

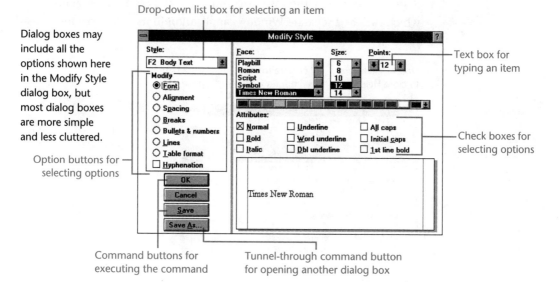

Drop-down list box for selecting an item

Text box for typing an item

Check boxes for selecting options

Option buttons for selecting options

Command buttons for executing the command

Tunnel-through command button for opening another dialog box

You can use the mouse or keyboard to move among and select options in a dialog box, as described in the following list:

■ To move among options in a dialog box, use the mouse or press Tab.

■ To select an option, click it with the mouse, or press Alt and the underlined letter of the option.

■ To execute the command after selecting the option, click the OK button with the mouse or press Enter.

■ To clear a dialog box from the screen without executing the command, click the Cancel button or press Esc.

Getting Help

Ami Pro comes with extensive on-line context-sensitive help—which means you can display help at any time about any topic.

You can get help in Ami Pro in the following ways:

- Use the **H**elp menu

- Use context-sensitive help

Regardless of the method you use, Ami Pro starts the Help program, which runs as a separate Windows application in its own program window.

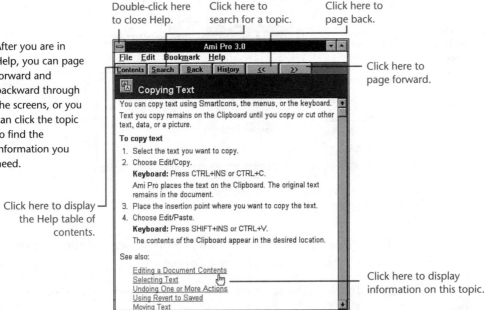

Double-click here to close Help.

Click here to search for a topic.

Click here to page back.

After you are in Help, you can page forward and backward through the screens, or you can click the topic to find the information you need.

Click here to page forward.

Click here to display the Help table of contents.

Click here to display information on this topic.

Note: *In Help, after the pointer changes to the shape of a hand, click the mouse to display information about the topic at which you are pointing.*

Finding the Help You Need

The Help menu provides access to general Help information about Ami Pro itself and about how to use Ami Pro's features. After you choose a **H**elp menu command, the Ami Pro Help program starts.

From the Help menu, you can access specific topics by choosing the Contents or the How Do I? commands, or you can choose one of the general information commands, such as Keyboard.

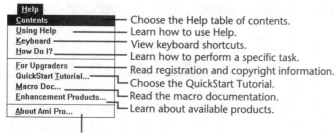

— Choose the Help table of contents.
— Learn how to use Help.
— View keyboard shortcuts.
— Learn how to perform a specific task.
— Read registration and copyright information.
— Choose the QuickStart Tutorial.
— Read the macro documentation.
— Learn about available products.

View information on a new version of Ami Pro.

Once you are in the Help program, you can go quickly to a topic by doing one of the following:

- Choose **S**earch. In the Search dialog box, type the topic name, choose **S**how Topics, then select the topic. Choose Go To to display the help screen.

- Click any underlined topic to display the help screen for that topic.

- Choose **C**ontents to display the Help table of contents.

- Choose His**t**ory to display a list of topics you have already seen. Double-click a topic to display it again.

You can also print the help information. Choose **F**ile, **P**rint to print the information displayed on your screen.

Note: *Depending on how your program was installed, your Help menu may display different commands. If you installed the SwitchKit for WordPerfect Users, for example, a For WordPerfect Users command appears on your Help menu.*

Displaying Help about the Current Action

You can display help about the current action or screen without using the Help menu. Press F1 to start the Help program and display context-sensitive help information.

For example, to display information about the Save As command, highlight it on the **F**ile menu, then press F1. If the Help SmartIcon is displayed, click it for the current action.

If a dialog box is on-
screen, click the
question mark in
the top-right corner
to access context-
sensitive help.

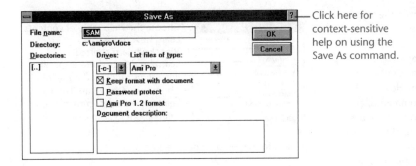

Click here for
context-sensitive
help on using the
Save As command.

Using the Mouse Pointer to Get Help

You can display help about a command before you choose it by turning
the mouse pointer into a *help requester*. With the help requester, you
can point and shoot at any command or screen part to display context-
sensitive help.

To use the help requester, follow these steps:

1. Press Shift+F1. The mouse pointer changes to the help requester—a
question mark with an arrow on its top.

2. Point at the command or at the area of the screen for which you
need help, and click the mouse. The Help program starts, and information about that topic appears.

Here the mouse
pointer has
changed to the help
requester shape.

Help requester pointer

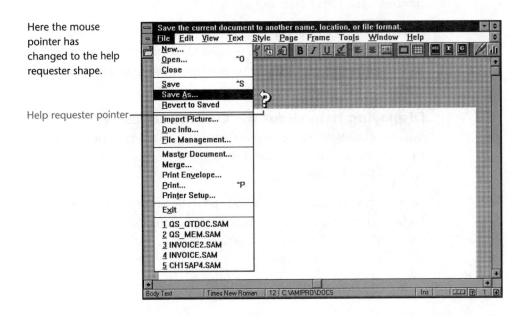

1

After you exit the Help program, the mouse pointer returns to its normal shape.

Exiting Ami Pro

As is true of any other Windows application, you can exit from Ami Pro in any of the following three ways:

■ Choose **F**ile, E**x**it.

■ Choose **C**lose from the Ami Pro Control menu.

■ Double-click the Control menu box.

 If you made changes to a document, a message box appears asking if you want to save the changes. Choose **Y**es to save the changes and exit. Choose **N**o to exit without saving the changes. Choose **C**ancel to continue working in Ami Pro.

Lesson Summary

To	Do This
Start Windows	Type **WIN** at the DOS prompt.
Start Ami Pro from Windows	Open the Lotus Applications group window, and double-click the Ami Pro 3 icon.
Choose an Ami Pro command	Point at the command name and click. Using the keyboard, press the underlined letter in the command name.
Use a SmartIcon	Point at the icon and click.
Get Help in a dialog box	Click the question mark.
Exit Ami Pro	Open the **F**ile menu and choose E**x**it. Or double-click the Ami Pro Control menu box.

On Your Own

Estimated Time: 10 minutes

To get started with Ami Pro, follow these steps:

1. Turn on your computer.

2. From the DOS prompt, start Windows.

3. From Windows, start Ami Pro.

4. Use the **H**elp menu to find out more about a topic—for example, to learn more about using mouse shortcuts.

5. Close the Help window.

6. Use context-sensitive help to display help on the **F**ile, **N**ew command.

7. Use the help requester to get information on using the status bar.

8. Use the **F**ile menu to exit Ami Pro.

Lesson 2

Creating a Document

With Ami Pro 3, you can create different kinds of documents, ranging from business letters and memos to complex reports and presentations.

In this lesson, you learn to create a new document by choosing a style sheet and typing text. You also learn how to save the document for future use, to print it, and to close it. Specifically, you learn how to

- Open a new document.
- Type and format text in the document.
- Save the document.
- Print the document.
- Close the document.

Understanding Style Sheets

Style sheet
An existing file that contains predefined settings for the page layout and for typical paragraphs used to format a particular kind of document.

In Lesson 1, "Learning the Basics," you learned that when you start Ami Pro, a blank document [Untitled] opens on-screen. If you plan to create a simple document with no particular formatting requirements, you can begin typing right away. If you know, however, that you are creating a business letter, a memo, or other kind of document that is clearly defined by page layout, use the **F**ile, **N**ew command to open a new document based on a specific style sheet.

When you select a *style sheet*, Ami Pro automatically applies the pre-defined page layout settings such as margins and tab stops. As you type, you can easily select from the style sheet's built-in paragraph *styles* to

Style
A collection of settings you can apply to a paragraph for quick formatting.

embellish your text with different fonts, font sizes, alignment, and spacing.

Each Ami Pro document is based on a style sheet. When you start Ami Pro, the document [Untitled] is based on the _DEFAULT.STY style sheet.

The _DEFAULT.STY style sheet provides a basic page layout setting and nine paragraph styles that you can use for a variety of simple documents. Here, you see four paragraph styles used.

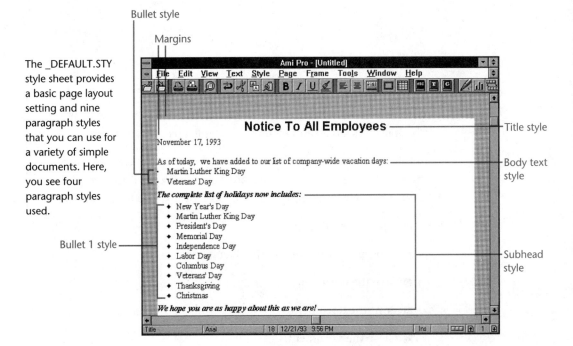

Bullet style

Margins

Title style

Body text style

Bullet 1 style

Subhead style

When you open a new document, you select the style sheet closest to the kind of document you want to create. This selection makes formatting even sophisticated documents easy.

In the following section, you learn to open a new document and select a style sheet. You learn more about using style sheets in Lesson 9, "Customizing Ami Pro."

Opening a New Document

Ami Pro always starts with the document [Untitled] open on-screen. If you want to create a document that uses a style sheet other then _DEFAULT.STY, or if you typed in [Untitled] and want to start a new document, you must use the **F**ile, **N**ew command.

Note: *If you type in [Untitled] and then open a new document without closing or saving the first document, Ami Pro changes the title of the first document to [Untitled:1], and names the new document [Untitled:2]. Each new document is numbered sequentially, up to [Untitled:9].*

To open a new document, follow these steps:

1. Choose **F**ile, **N**ew. The New dialog box appears.

In the New dialog box, choose a style sheet to use for opening a new document.

Select a style sheet.———

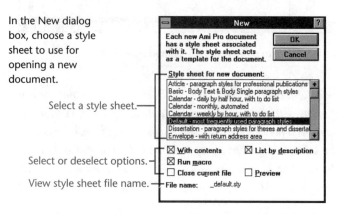

Select or deselect options. —

View style sheet file name. —

2. In the **S**tyle Sheet for New Document list box, highlight the style sheet you want to use. In this case, a style sheet suitable for creating a memo document is highlighted.

3. To see an example of the highlighted style sheet before you open the new document, select the **P**review check box.

With the Preview check box selected, you can preview as many style sheets as you want before selecting one. Here, the _MEMO2.STY style sheet is displayed.

Select to list style sheet descriptions.   Preview of selected style sheet

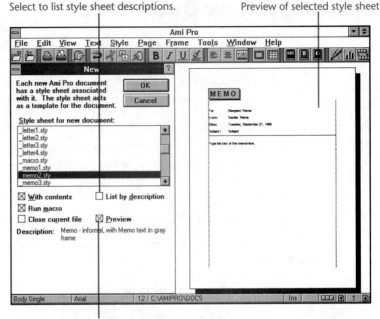

Select to preview the highlighted style sheet.

Note: *The default options in the New dialog box are set so that the new document opens with pertinent information already entered. (You see the information if you preview the style sheet before selecting it.) For now, deselect the **W**ith Contents box to open a blank document. For now, deselect the Run **M**acro option to cancel the style sheet macro. You learn about running a style sheet macro in Lesson 9, "Customizing Ami Pro."*

4. Choose OK to open a new document, based on the highlighted style sheet. The document appears on-screen.

Typing in the Text Area

Now, a new document [Untitled], based on the selected style sheet, is displayed on-screen.

If you have problems...	If a Default Information dialog box appears on-screen, choose Cancel. You learn about running style sheet macros in Lesson 9, "Customizing Ami Pro."

Insertion point
A flashing bar in the document window that indicates where text will appear when you type.

Note: *If you selected the **W**ith Contents check box in the New dialog box, text already may be entered in the document. Use the Backspace key and typeover mode—explained in a following part of this section—to replace the existing text with your text.*

Start typing. The characters you type appear to the left of the flashing bar, called the *insertion point*. By default, the characters are formatted according to the Body Text paragraph style of the selected style sheet.

2

If you have problems...

If characters are uppercase when you want them lowercase, and lowercase when you want uppercase, it means you pressed the Caps Lock key on your keyboard. Press the key again to turn off the Caps Lock indicator and resume typing.

Word wrap
The way text moves down to the beginning of the next line when the current line is filled.

Do not press Enter when you reach the end of a line. Ami Pro has *word wrap*, which means text is automatically moved to the beginning of the next line. Press Enter only when you are ready to start a new paragraph.

If you notice a mistake such as a typo, press Backspace to delete the character to the left of the insertion point. Press Backspace until you delete the mistake, and then type the correct text. (Other ways to correct mistakes are covered in Lesson 3, "Revising a Document.")

Text appears to the left of the insertion point. On the status bar, the names of the current style, font, and font size, are displayed from left to right.

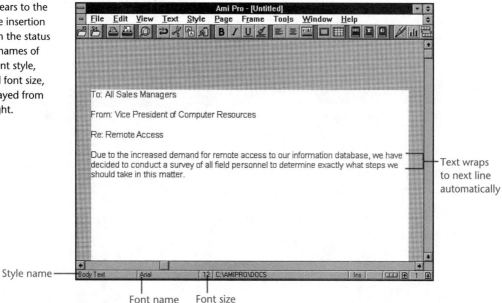

Style name

Font name   Font size

Text wraps to next line automatically

Inserting and Typing Over Text

Insert mode
A setting that tells Ami Pro to insert new text to the left of the insertion point, pushing existing text to the right.

Typeover mode
A setting that tells Ami Pro to replace existing text as you type.

By default, Ami Pro enters text in *insert mode*, which means that text is inserted in the document to the left of the insertion point. If the insertion point is in the middle of a sentence, text is inserted in the middle of the sentence. The existing text moves to the right.

If you change to typeover mode, the text you type replaces text to the right of the insertion point. When you press Enter in typeover mode, the insertion point moves to the next line, and Ami Pro starts a new paragraph. Text to the left of the insertion point remains in its original location.

Insert mode is used when you want to add text in the middle of existing text. Also, when you type in Insert mode, you cannot accidentally type over text you want to keep. Typeover mode is used when you want to replace existing text with new text.

Look at the status bar to see if you are typing in insert mode or typeover mode. To change from one mode to the other, press Ins on your keyboard, or click the Insert button on the status bar.

If you have problems...

If the word REV appears on the status bar, it means you are in revision marking mode. Just click the button again to get to insert mode. You can learn more about revision marking in Lesson 15, "Working with Document Notation."

If the letters Ins appear, you are in insert mode.

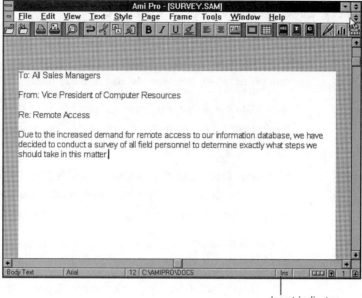

Insert indicator

If the word Type appears, you are in typeover mode.

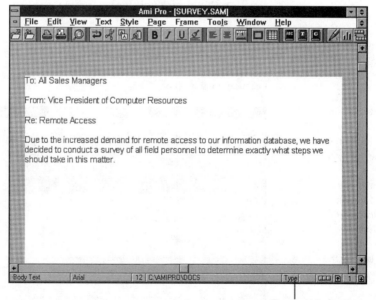

Typeover indicator

Moving the Insertion Point

You can move the insertion point throughout the document by using either the keyboard or the mouse. This way, you can position the insertion point where you want to edit or enter text.

Note: *You cannot move the insertion point into the screen area past the end of the document. The end of the document is either the last line of text, or the last new paragraph started by pressing Enter.*

Moving the Insertion Point with the Mouse

To move the insertion point with the mouse, position the mouse pointer where you want to place the insertion point and click.

To position the insertion point in a part of the document that is not displayed on the current screen, follow these steps:

1. Use the scroll bars, or click the Page Up and Page Down buttons on the status bar until the part of the document you want appears.

2. Position the mouse pointer where you want to place the insertion point.

3. Click to move the insertion point.

Insertion point location

Scroll bar

You must click the mouse button at the new location to move the insertion point. Here, the mouse pointer is at the new location, but the insertion point is not. If you start typing, text appears back at the insertion point.

Ami Pro - [Untitled]

File   Edit   View   Text   Style   Page   Frame   Tools   Window   Help

To: All Sales Managers¶

From: Vice President of Computer Resources¶

Re: Remote Access¶

Due to the increased demand for remote access to our information database, we have decided to conduct a survey of all field personnel to determine exactly what steps we should take in this matter.¶

When we have completed the survey, we will move ahead with the necessary action.¶

Here is the information we are hoping to gather:¶

Mouse pointer location

Page Up button

Body Text   Arial   12   C:\AMIPRO\DOCS   Ins

Page Down button

Moving the Insertion Point with the Keyboard

To move the insertion point with the keyboard, use the direction keys. For example, press the left arrow to move left and the right arrow to move right. To move quickly, use the keystrokes described in table 2.1.

Table 2.1. Common Keystrokes for Moving the Insertion Point	
Key or Key Combination	**Effect**
Ctrl+left arrow	Moves one word to the left
Ctrl+right arrow	Moves one word to the right
Home	Moves to the beginning of the line
End	Moves to the end of the line
Ctrl+up arrow	Moves to the beginning of the paragraph
Ctrl+down arrow	Moves to the end of the paragraph
PgUp	Moves up one screen
PgDn	Moves down one screen
Ctrl+Home	Moves to the beginning of the document
Ctrl+End	Moves to the end of the document

2

Selecting Styles

As you learned earlier in this lesson, each style sheet comes with a preformatted page layout and a few built-in paragraph styles. All the text you typed so far appears in the Body Text style of the style sheet you selected when you opened the document. When you want the paragraph to have a different look, you can select a different style to use for typing new text.

To select a style,
use the Styles list or
the Styles box.

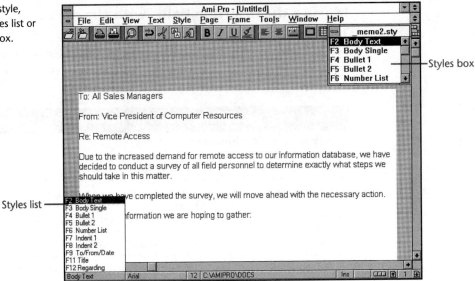

Styles box

Styles list

To display the Styles list, click the name of the current style on the status bar. (This is called the Style button).

To display the Styles box, choose **V**iew, Show Styles **B**ox.

Note: *To close the Styles box, double-click the box's control menu button or choose **V**iew, Hide Styles **B**ox.*

To select a style, follow these steps:

1. Position the insertion point where you want the text in the new style to begin. If necessary, press Enter to begin a new paragraph.

2. Perform one of the following options:

- Click the style name in either the Styles list or the Styles box.

- Press the function key that appears beside the style name.

- Use the arrow keys to highlight the style name and press Enter.

When you type, the characters appear formatted according to the selected style—in this case, the Number List style.

Body Text style ———

Number List style ———

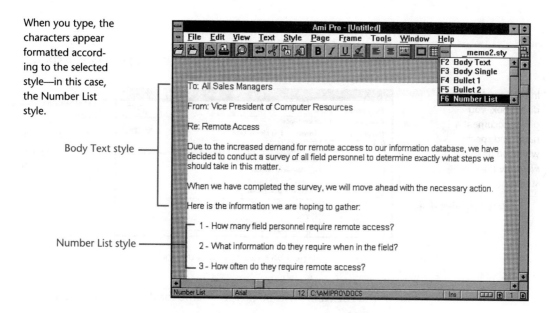

Note: *After you are familiar with a style sheet, you can change styles quickly by pressing the appropriate function key without opening the Styles list or the Styles box.*

Saving the Document

Ami Pro has two commands for saving a document. You use **File**, **S**ave to save any document; you use **File**, Save **A**s to save a document with a new name.

Note: *To save a new document, you can use either **File**, **S**ave or **File**, Save **A**s. If the document was never saved before, both commands display the Save As dialog box.*

Saving a New Document or a Document with a New Name

With the File, Save As command, you not only save the document to disk, you also give the file a name and specify the drive and directory path where you want to store the document. Use **File**, Save **A**s to save a new document or to save a copy of an existing document with a different name or path.

To save a new document, follow these steps:

1. Choose **F**ile, Save **A**s. The Save As dialog box appears on-screen.

In the Save As
dialog box, you
give a document a
name and specify
where on disk you
want the document
stored.

Select a different directory.

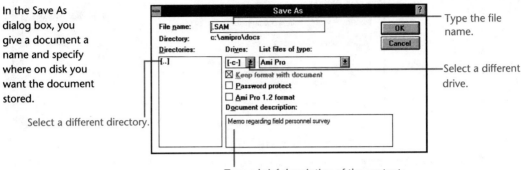

Type the file
name.

Select a different
drive.

Type a brief description of the contents.

2. In the File **N**ame text box, type a name for the document, following DOS naming conventions. The name can be up to eight characters; Ami Pro assigns the extension SAM when the document is
saved.

Note: *If the document already has a name, it appears in the File Name
text box. If the document isn't named, only the SAM extension appears.
To type over the existing text, just type. To insert text to the left of or
within the existing text, position the insertion point before you type.*

3. In the D**o**cument Description text box, you can type a brief description of the contents of the document. The description displays in
the Open dialog box the next time you return to open the
document. (For more information on opening an existing document, see Lesson 3, "Revising a Document.")

4. Make all desired changes to the directory or drive where the file will
be saved. If you make no changes, the file is saved in the current
directory, usually \AMI PRO\DOCS on drive C.

5. Choose OK. Ami Pro saves the file in the specified drive and directory. The document remains displayed on-screen so that you can
continue working. Notice that the document name now appears in
the title bar at the top of the screen.

Caution
If an existing document was saved with the name you entered in the File Name text box, Ami Pro displays a message that warns you of its existence. If you choose **Y**es, the new file is saved over the old file. If you choose **N**o, Ami Pro returns to the document. Choose **F**ile, Save **A**s and type a different name in the File Name text box.

Saving a Document Again

After you save a document once, you can save this document over and over with the same name, directory, format, and other specifications without going through the Save As dialog box each time. To save the file again, if you don't want to change anything in the Save As dialog box, choose **F**ile, **S**ave. The file you save overwrites the old version on the disk and any changes you made since the last time you saved. The document is still displayed on-screen, so you can continue to edit it.

Note: *Save your documents often! Until you save, your work is stored only in memory. If you lose power, you lose all the work done since your last save. Develop the habit of saving at regular intervals, or use Ami Pro's automatic saving option to save files. Auto timed save is covered in Lesson 9, "Customizing Ami Pro."*

Note: *If you use File, Save to save a document you haven't saved before, Ami Pro displays the Save As dialog box.*

If you have problems...

If you just want to save the document with the same name and file specifications, but you accidentally select File, Save As and the Save As dialog box appears, just choose Cancel to close the dialog box, then choose **F**ile, **S**ave.

Printing Your Document

After you create the document, you can print it. Before printing, make sure your printer is connected to the computer, turned on, and loaded with paper.

Viewing the Document before Printing

By default, Ami Pro displays a document on-screen in Layout mode, customized to show the full width of the page. You can change the view to see how a full page of the document looks when printed.

To change the document view, choose **V**iew, **F**ull page.

In Full Page view, Ami Pro displays the page as it will print. You can edit the document in this view, although the small size makes editing difficult.

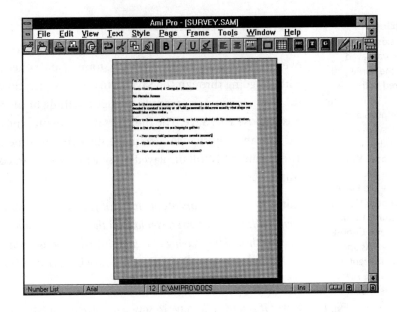

To return to the previous view, choose **View**, **Custom**.

In Lesson 8, "Making Your Pages Pretty," you learn about other ways to view documents using Ami Pro.

Printing the Active Document

To print the document displayed on-screen, follow these steps:

1. Choose **File**, **Print**. The Print dialog box appears on-screen.

In the Print dialog box, you specify print options such as how many copies and which pages you want to print.

Specify the number of copies to print.

Choose to select additional printing options.

Specify a page range.

Select to print even pages, odd pages, or both.

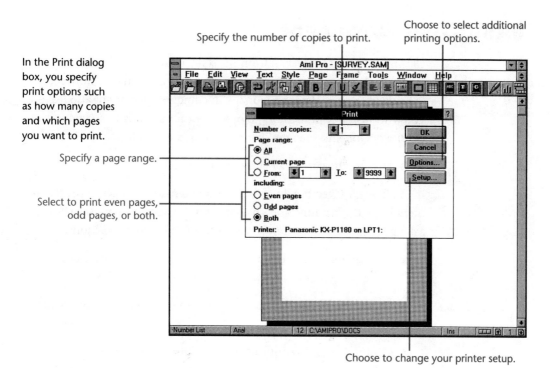

Choose to change your printer setup.

2. Indicate the number of copies to print, what range to print, and which pages to include. Choose the **O**ptions button to select additional printing options, or the **S**etup button to select printer options.

3. Choose OK to print the document. Ami Pro prints the document.

If you have problems... If the document doesn't print, make sure the printer is loaded with paper and correctly connected to the computer. Then try printing again.

Closing Your Document

Closing a document clears it from the screen and the computer's memory. If too many documents are open at once, you may notice Ami Pro slowing down. Having too many documents open might also leave you with insufficient memory to open another document, so saving and closing documents you aren't working on is a good idea.

 ■ To close the current document, choose **F**ile, **C**lose.

If you haven't saved the document, or if you made changes to the document since the last time you saved it, Ami Pro displays a message box asking if you want to save now. Take one of the following actions:

■ Choose **Y**es to save the document and clear it from the screen. If the document is new, the Save As dialog box appears.

■ Choose **N**o to clear the document from the screen without saving the changes.

■ Choose Cancel to continue working with the document.

When Ami Pro closes the current document, it displays another open document. If no other documents are open, Ami Pro displays a blank application screen.

To close all open documents, exit Ami Pro. For each document that you have not yet saved, a message box appears, asking if you want to save the changes.

Lesson Summary

To	Do This
Open a new document	Choose **F**ile, **N**ew. In the New dialog box, choose a style sheet. Choose OK.
Change from insert to typeover mode	Click the Insert indicator on the status bar.
Move the insertion point with the mouse	Position the mouse pointer and click.
Move the insertion point	Press the arrow keys.

To	Do This
Select a style	Open the Styles box or Styles list. Choose the style.
Save a new document	Choose **F**ile, Save **A**s. In the Save As dialog box, enter a document name, then choose OK.
Print your document	Choose **F**ile, **P**rint. In the Print dialog box, choose OK.
Close your document	Choose **F**ile, **C**lose.

2

On Your Own

The following exercises take you through each step of creating, saving, printing, and closing the memo document used to illustrate this lesson.

Creating a New Document
Estimated Time: 5-10 minutes

1. Start Ami Pro if it is not already running.

2. Create a new document, using the _MEMO2.STY style sheet.

3. Type the following memo text, as illustrated in the lesson. Remember to press Enter when it is time to start a new paragraph.

   To: All Sales Managers

   From: Vice President of Computer Resources

   Re: Remote Access

   Due to the increased demand for remote access to our information database, we have decided to conduct a survey of all field personnel to determine exactly what steps we must take in this matter.

   Here is the information we are hoping to gather:

4. Choose the Number List style.

5. Type the following text:

   How many field personnel require remote access?

   What information do they require when in the field?

   How often do they require remote access?

6. Change back to the Body Text style and type the following text:

   When we have completed the survey, we will move ahead with the necessary action.

7. Save the document.

8. Change the view to see how the document will look when printed.

9. Print the document.

10. Close the document.

If you want to do more, try some of the following suggestions as optional exercises:

- Use different styles to complete the memo.

- Save the document with a new name, or in a different directory.

- Create another new document using a different style sheet.

Lesson 3

Revising a Document

One major advantage of creating a document with a word processor rather than a typewriter is that you can make changes without having to retype entire pages, even entire documents. In this lesson, you learn how to use Ami Pro to open and revise a document that you have already created and saved. Specifically, you learn how to

- Open a file.

- Start a new line.

- Insert the time or date.

- Select, move, and copy text within a document and between documents.

- Change the style of existing text.

- Correct mistakes by deleting or undoing.

- Revert to the last saved version of a document.

- Find and replace text in a document.

Opening an Existing Document

To revise a closed document, open it on-screen by using menu commands or the SmartIcon bar.

To open an existing document, follow these steps:

1. Choose **File**, **O**pen. The Open dialog box appears.

Type or verify file name.

In the Open dialog
box, select the
document you want
to display on-screen.

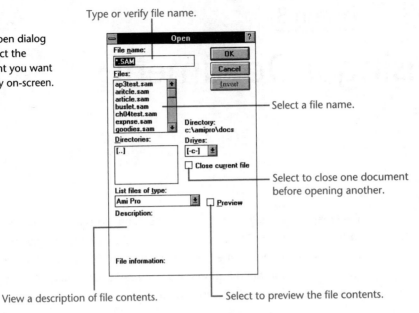

Select a file name.

Select to close one document
before opening another.

View a description of file contents.

Select to preview the file contents.

2. In the File **N**ame text box, type the name of the document you
   want to open.

3. Choose OK.

Note: *After you enter a document name in the File Name text box, the document description you entered for that file in the Save As dialog box appears in
the Description area.*

Note: *Select the document you want to open in the Files list to automatically
enter its name in the File Name text box. Double-click the name to open the
document.*

**If you have
problems...**

If the name of the document you want to open does not appear in the Files
list box, it is probably stored in a different directory or on a different drive.
Use the Dri**v**es and **D**irectories options to display a Files list that includes the
document you want.

Opening a Document from a Different Drive or Directory

To open a file from a different drive or directory, follow these steps:

1. Choose **File**, **O**pen. The Open dialog box appears.

You also use the Open dialog box to open files from other drives or directories.

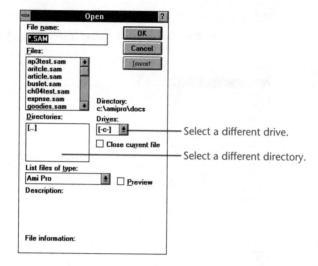

— Select a different drive.

— Select a different directory.

2. From the **Dri**ves drop-down list, select the drive on which your file is stored.

3. In the **D**irectories list box, double-click the name of the displayed directory for a list of other directories.

3. Double-click the name of the directory that contains the file you want to open. The files in that directory appear in the **F**iles list box.

4. In the **F**iles list box, double-click the name of the file you want to open.

If you have problems...

If the document you want to open doesn't appear in the Files list box, you may have opened the correct directory but not the correct subdirectory. Try double-clicking the directory name to display a list of subdirectories. Then select the correct subdirectory's name.

If Ami Pro displays a System Error Message stating that it cannot read from the selected drive, you probably forgot to insert a disk. Insert a disk and choose **R**etry.

Opening a Recently Used File

Ami Pro keeps track of the documents you open and displays them at the bottom of the File menu. You can set Ami Pro to display as many as five of the most recently opened documents. (See Lesson 9, "Customizing Ami Pro," for more information.)

To open a recently used document from the **F**ile menu, choose **F**ile and then choose the document's name from the end of the menu.

Here the five most recently used files are listed at the bottom of the File menu.

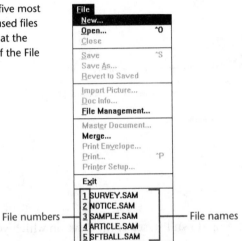

File numbers — File names

Starting a New Line

As described in Lesson 2, "Creating a Document," Ami Pro wraps text from one line to the next as you type. Sometimes, however, you want to start typing text on a new line. You can start a new line in two ways:

Paragraph mark
A symbol that Ami Pro inserts each time you start a new paragraph by pressing Enter. Paragraph marks contain information about the current paragraph style.

■ Start a new paragraph.

■ Insert a line break within a paragraph.

To start a new paragraph, simply press Enter. Ami Pro inserts a *paragraph mark* and moves the insertion point to the beginning of the next line.

Note: *To see the paragraph marks on your screen, choose **V**iew, View **P**references. In the View Preferences dialog box that appears, choose the Tabs & **R**eturns check box, and then choose OK.*

After you press Enter to start a new line, the amount of blank space left between two paragraphs is determined by the current paragraph style.

In the _DEFAULT.STY style sheet, for example, the Body Text style is set to leave no space above or below paragraphs, so no blank space is left after you press Enter. The Title style is set to leave .10 inches above and .05 inches below each paragraph, so .15 inches is left between paragraphs in the Title style.

If you are typing in the Body Text style in a document created by using the _DEFAULT.STY style sheet, you must press Enter twice to leave blank space between paragraphs. If you use the Title style, press Enter only once. To learn more about changing styles, see Lesson 2, "Creating a Document."

The paragraph marks in this section of text indicate that Enter was pressed twice in the Body Text style, but only once in the Title style.

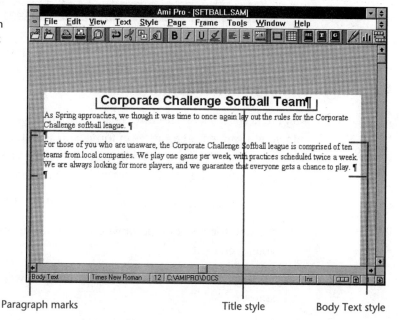

Paragraph marks   Title style   Body Text style

To insert a line break in your text without adding a paragraph mark, follow these steps:

1. Position the insertion point at the end of the previous line.

2. Press Ctrl+Enter.

If you insert a line break, the insertion point jumps to the beginning of the next line, but Ami Pro does not start a new paragraph. No blank space is left between the lines.

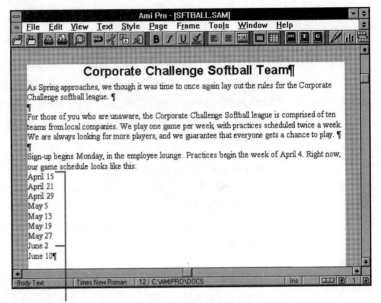

Corporate Challenge Softball Team¶

As Spring approaches, we though it was time to once again lay out the rules for the Corporate Challenge softball league. ¶

¶

For those of you who are unaware, the Corporate Challenge Softball league is comprised of ten teams from local companies. We play one game per week, with practices scheduled twice a week. We are always looking for more players, and we guarantee that everyone gets a chance to play. ¶

¶

Sign-up begins Monday, in the employee lounge. Practices begin the week of April 4. Right now, our game schedule looks like this:

April 15
April 21
April 29
May 5
May 13
May 19
May 27
June 2
June 10¶

Line Breaks; no paragraph marks.

Inserting Today's Date

Ami Pro keeps track of the current date. You can easily insert the date into your document in a variety of formats. This feature is useful for keeping track of the day on which you make certain changes or just to avoid typing the date again and again.

To insert the date into your document, follow these steps:

1. Position the insertion point where you want the date to appear in your document.

2. Choose **Edit, Insert, Date**/Time. The Insert Date/Time dialog box appears.

3. In the Insert area, choose **T**oday's Date.

4. In the **S**tyle list box, select the format you want to use.

5. Choose OK. Ami Pro inserts the date at the insertion point's location.

You can choose
from a variety of
styles for inserting
today's date.

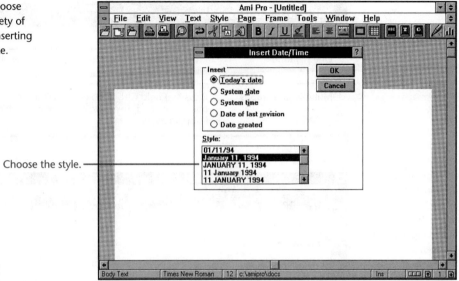

Choose the style.

Selecting Text

Select

To identify the text
you want to change
or manipulate by
using the mouse or
the keyboard to
highlight that text.

In Ami Pro, you must *select* the text you want to change before you can change it. You can select text by using the mouse or the keyboard.

Table 3.1 lists techniques for selecting text by using the mouse. To cancel, or deselect, selected text, click anywhere on-screen with the mouse.

Table 3.1. Select Text by Using the Mouse	
To Select	**Use the Mouse To**
Any block of text	Click and drag from the first character you want to select to the last character you want to select.
One word	Double-click anywhere within the word.
Multiple words	Double-click within the first word, and then drag to the last word.
One sentence	Press and hold Ctrl as you click anywhere within the sentence.
Multiple sentences	With the mouse pointer in the first sentence, press and hold Ctrl, and then click and drag to anywhere within the last sentence you want selected.

(continues)

Table 3.1. Continued	
To Select	**Use the Mouse To**
One paragraph	Press and hold Ctrl as you double-click anywhere within the paragraph.
Multiple paragraphs	Press and hold Ctrl, double-click within the first paragraph, and then drag to anywhere within the last paragraph.

No matter what selection method you use, the selected text appears highlighted on-screen.

Selected text

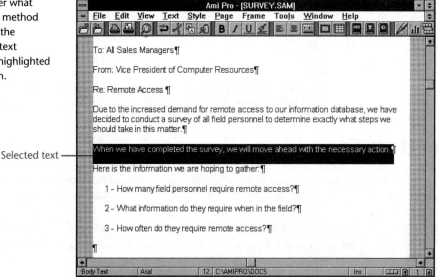

Table 3.2 lists some common key combinations for selecting text by using the keyboard. To cancel, or deselect, selected text, press any arrow key.

Caution

Regardless of whether you use the mouse or the keyboard to select text, if you press *any* letter key after text is selected, Ami Pro deletes the selected text and replaces it with the character you press.

Table 3.2. Selecting Text by Using the Keyboard	
Key Combination	**Effect**
Shift+arrow	Selects characters in the arrow direction.
Ctrl+Shift+Home	Selects text to the beginning of the document.
Ctrl+Shift+End	Selects text to the end of the document.

Moving Text

Clipboard
A temporary storage area provided by Windows.

To move selected text, you *cut* it from its current location, store it in the Windows *Clipboard*, and then *paste* it into its new location. You can move selected text in either of the following two ways:

- By using commands.

- By using drag-and-drop editing.

Cut
To remove selected text from its current location and store it in the Clipboard.

Paste
To copy text from the Clipboard back into a document.

Drag-and-drop editing is a quick and easy way to move or copy text to nearby locations. Commands are useful if you need to move or copy text to another page in the document.

3

Moving Text by Using Commands

To move text by using commands, follow these steps:

1. Select the text you want to move.

2. Choose **E**dit, **C**ut. Ami Pro removes the selected text from the document and places it in the Clipboard. The text disappears from your screen.

3. Position the insertion point where you want the text to appear in your document. (Remember to click the left mouse button to move the insertion point here from its previous location.)

4. Choose **E**dit, **P**aste. Ami Pro inserts the text at the new location.

Moving Text by Using Drag-and-Drop Editing

Caution
The Clipboard can hold only one selection at a time; if you cut or copy a new selection, the old selection is replaced.

Drag-and-drop editing is a useful feature that enables you to manipulate text using a mouse. To move text by using drag-and-drop editing, follow these steps:

1. Select the text you want to move.

2. Position the mouse pointer anywhere within the selected text.

3. Click and hold the left mouse button.

4. Drag the mouse pointer. As you drag the pointer its appearance shifts.

As you drag, the
pointer changes to
include an arrow
with a scissors and a
nonflashing
insertion point.

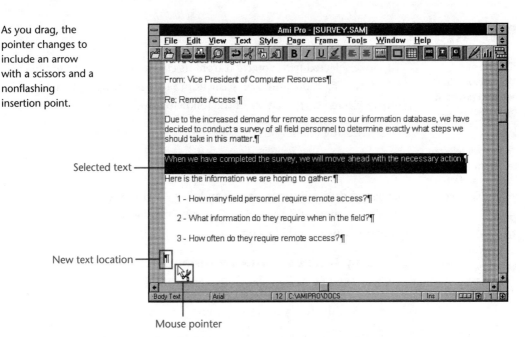

Selected text ——

New text location ——

Mouse pointer

5. After the insertion point is positioned where you want to insert the selected text, release the mouse button. Ami Pro moves the text to the new location.

An alternative method of drag-and-drop editing is to use the right mouse button shortcut. This shortcut is faster and can be more precise. To use this shortcut, follow these steps:

1. Select the text you want to move.

2. Press and hold Ctrl, then position the mouse pointer at the new location. *Do not click* to move the insertion point, and *do not release* Ctrl.

3. Click the right mouse button. Ami Pro moves the text to the new location.

Copying Text

Copy
To duplicate selected text. You copy text to the Clipboard, from which it can be inserted back into a document.

To copy selected text, you *copy* it from its current location into the Clipboard and then paste it into the new added location.

You can copy text in either of the following two ways:

- By using commands.

- By using drag-and-drop editing.

Copying Text by Using Commands

To copy text by using commands, follow these steps:

1. Select the text you want to copy.

2. Choose **E**dit, **C**opy. Ami Pro copies the selected text from the document to the Clipboard.

Note: *After you choose* **E**dit, **C**opy, *the selected text doesn't disappear. It is copied to the Clipboard but also remains in the original location.*

3. Position the insertion point where you want the copied text to appear in your document. (Remember to click the left mouse button to move the insertion point from its previous location.)

Note: *After you move the insertion point, the text you selected to copy is no longer highlighted. Don't worry, however. It remains safe in the Clipboard until you cut or copy another selection.*

4. Choose **E**dit, **P**aste. Ami Pro copies the text in the new location.

After you copy text to the Clipboard, you can copy it into your document as many times as you want. Simply continue to reposition the insertion point, and then paste the text at each new location.

Copying Text by Using Drag-and-Drop Editing

To copy text by using drag-and-drop editing, follow these steps:

1. Select the text you want to copy.

2. Position the mouse pointer anywhere within the selected text.

3

3. Press and hold Ctrl, and then press and hold the left mouse button. After you press the left mouse button, you can release Ctrl.

4. Drag the mouse pointer to the new location in your document where you want to insert the copied text.

As you drag, the pointer changes to an arrow with two identical rectangles and a nonflashing insertion point.

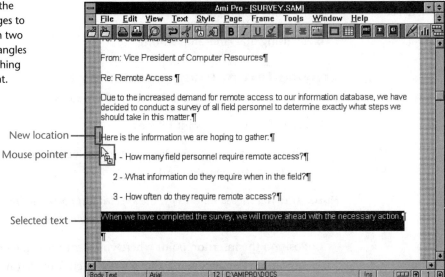

New location

Mouse pointer

Selected text

5. After the insertion point is positioned where you want to copy the selected text, release the mouse button. Ami Pro copies the text to the new location.

If you have problems...   If Ami Pro is moving the text instead of copying it, you did not press Ctrl before you pressed the left mouse button. You must press Ctrl first.

To use the right mouse button shortcut, follow these steps:

1. Select the text you want to copy.

2. Press and hold Ctrl+Shift, and position the mouse pointer at the new location. *Do not click* to move the insertion point.

3. Click the right mouse button. Ami Pro copies the text to the new location.

Changing the Style of Existing Text

In Lesson 2, "Creating a Document," you learned to select a different style before typing text. You also can change the style after the text is typed.

To change the style of a paragraph, simply position the insertion point within the existing paragraph and choose the new style from either the Styles list or the Styles box. To display the Styles list, click on the Styles button on the status bar. To display the Styles box, choose **V**iew, Show Styles **B**ox.

3

After you select a new style, Ami Pro changes the paragraph to the selected style—in this case, to the Regarding style.

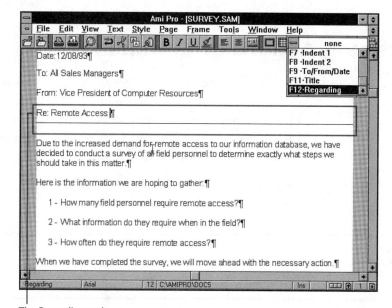

The Regarding style

If you don't want to change a whole paragraph, you can change the style of selected text. You can select as much, or as little, text as you want, including words, sentences, or more than one paragraph. To change the style of selected text, select the text before you choose the style.

Deleting Text

In Lesson 2, "Creating a Document," you learned to press Backspace to erase characters to the left of the insertion point. Ami Pro offers numerous additional ways for deleting unwanted text.

Table 3.3 lists some common ways to delete selected text.

Table 3.3. Deleting Text	
Action	**Effect**
Del	Deletes the selected text or deletes one character to the right of the insertion point.
Shift+Del	Deletes (cuts) the selected text and stores it in the Clipboard.
Edit, Cut	Cuts selected text to the Clipboard.

Undoing Actions or Commands

The Undo command on Ami Pro's Edit menu is a powerful tool that proves most useful on many occasions. Undo enables you to reverse most editing actions or commands, including deletions and the results of the Undo command itself. That means that you can fix almost every mistake you make, simply by choosing **U**ndo.

 To undo an action or command, choose **E**dit, **U**ndo. Ami Pro immediately reverses the last action.

If you have problems...   If Undo appears dimmed on the Edit menu, you cannot undo the last action. See the following section for information on reverting to the last saved version of the document.

You can set Ami Pro to Undo up to four levels. If you set Undo to one level, you can undo only the most recent action. If you set it to four, you can undo the last four editing actions or commands. (See Lesson 9, "Customizing Ami Pro," for more information on setting Undo levels.) If Undo is set to more than one level, Ami Pro undoes the actions in reverse order.

Reverting to the Last Saved Version of a Document

Caution
After you choose Revert to Saved, you lose all changes made to the document since the last time you saved it. If you haven't saved for a while, you could lose a great deal of work.

If you make more mistakes than you can reverse by using Delete or Undo, you can use the **R**evert to Saved command. Revert to Saved reverses all actions since the last time you saved the document, restoring the most recently saved version.

To revert to the most recently saved version of your document, follow these steps:

1. Choose **F**ile, **R**evert to Saved. Ami Pro displays a message warning you that this command causes you to lose all editing changes made since the last time you saved the document.

2. Choose OK to undo all the changes since the last time you saved. Choose Cancel or press Esc to return to the existing version.

If you have problems...

If Revert to Saved appears dimmed on the File menu, you have not made any changes since the last time you saved the document. You do not need to use this command if you have made no changes.

Finding and Replacing Text in a Document

In Ami Pro, you can quickly find and replace incorrect text anywhere in a document. This feature is especially useful if you make the same mistake in more than one location or if you do not know exactly where an error occurs.

You can use Find & Replace to find text, or to find and replace at the same time.

Finding Text

To find text, follow these steps:

1. Position the insertion point at the beginning of the document.

2. Choose **E**dit, Find & **R**eplace. The Find & Replace dialog box appears.

Use the Find &
Replace dialog box
to quickly find text
anywhere in the
document.

Type the text to find.

Click here to find the first occurrence of the text.

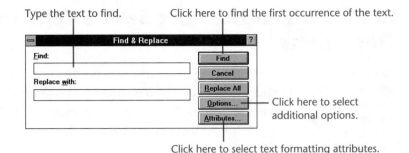

Click here to select
additional options.

Click here to select text formatting attributes.

3. In the **F**ind text box, type the text you want to find.

4. Choose Find. Ami Pro highlights the first occurrence of the text in the document, and displays another Find & Replace text box.

5. Choose Find **N**ext to highlight the next occurrence of the text in the document.

Replacing Text

To find and replace text, follow these steps:

1. Position the insertion point at the beginning of the document.

2. Choose **E**dit, Find and **R**eplace. The Find and Replace dialog box appears.

Use the Find &
Replace dialog box
to quickly replace
one or more
occurrences of
incorrect text with
the correct text.

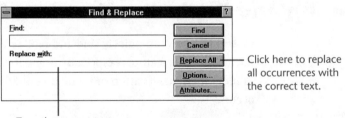

Click here to replace
all occurrences with
the correct text.

Type the correct text.

3. In the **F**ind text box, type the incorrect text that you want to find.

4. In the Replace **w**ith text box, type the correct text you want used in place of the incorrect text.

5. To replace all occurrences of the incorrect text, choose the **R**eplace All button. Ami Pro automatically changes the text.

To verify the text before you replace it, choose **F**ind instead of **R**eplace All. Ami Pro highlights the first occurrence of the text entered in the Find text box and displays a second Find & Replace dialog box. Choose one of the following:

- Replace & **F**ind Next to replace the highlighted text and find the next occurrence of the text entered in the Find box.

- Find **N**ext to skip the highlighted text and find the next occurrence of the text entered in the Find box.

- Replace Remaining to replace the highlighted text as well as all the occurrences in the document.

- Cancel to stop the Find & Replace function and return to editing the document.

After all the incorrect text has been replaced, Ami Pro flashes in the status bar the number of changes made and then returns to the document.

If you have problems...

By default, Ami Pro searches for text to find and replace from the insertion point to the end of the document. If only some of the occurrences of the incorrect text are changed, you may have neglected to move the insertion point to the beginning of the document before choosing Edit, Find & Replace.

Using Find and Replace Options

You can set options to help Ami Pro find exactly the text you're looking for. To set find and replace options, follow these steps:

1. Choose **E**dit, Find & **R**eplace.

2. In the Find & Replace dialog box, choose **O**ptions. Table 3.4 describes the Find and Replace options.

Table 3.4. Find and Replace Options	
Option	**Effect**
Find Whole Word Only	Ami Pro highlights only whole words, not parts of a word that are composed of the letters in the specified Find text.
Exact Case	Ami Pro finds or replaces text that matches the case of the specified text. Use Exact Case to match capitalization.
Exact Attributes	Ami Pro finds or replaces text that matches the attributes of the specified text (for more information, see Lesson 5, "Dressing Up Your Text").
Beginning of Document	Ami Pro searches for the specified text from the beginning of the document.
Include Other Text Streams	Ami Pro searches through all tables, headers, footers, and other parts of the document, in addition to the main body of the document.
Find Backwards	Ami Pro searches up from the insertion point.

Using Multiple Windows

In Ami Pro, you can have up to nine document windows open at one time. Each document window can contain a different document or a copy of the same document.

The following list describes some of the ways you can use multiple document windows:

- You can work with different documents in different full-sized windows.

- You can work with copies of the same document in different full-sized windows.

- You can split one window into smaller parts that can both be displayed on-screen at the same time.

- You can work with different documents in different windows.

- You can work with one document split into different windows.

- You can move or copy text from one window to another.

Opening Multiple Document Windows

To open more than one document window at a time, follow these steps:

1. Choose **F**ile, **O**pen to open the first document.

2. Without closing the first document, choose **F**ile, **O**pen again to open another document, or choose **F**ile, **N**ew to create a new document. Ami Pro opens the second document window *on top* of the first.

3. You can continue opening or creating documents until you run out of memory, or nine windows are open.

Active window
The window in which you are currently working.

You can work in only one document window at a time—the *active window*. By default, the active window is maximized to fill the entire screen—all other open windows are hidden behind it. The insertion point is always in the active window, and the title bar of the active window is always highlighted.

To make a window active, click anywhere in that window *if you can see any part of it on-screen*, or choose Window and then choose from the list at the bottom of the menu the document you want active.

All open documents are listed at the bottom of the Window menu. A check mark appears beside the active window.

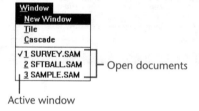

Arranging Open Windows

You also can arrange multiple windows on-screen so that they are not all hidden behind the active window.

You have two options for automatically sizing and arranging windows. The first, called *tiling*, arranges the windows so that all open windows are visible on-screen. The other option is *cascading*. This layers all the open windows so that the active window is on top, with the title bar of each window visible behind it.

To use one of these arrangements, choose **W**indow and then choose either **T**ile or **C**ascade.

Tiled windows split the Ami Pro window into equally sized windows for each document. You can see part of each open document on-screen.

The active window   Click here to maximize the window.

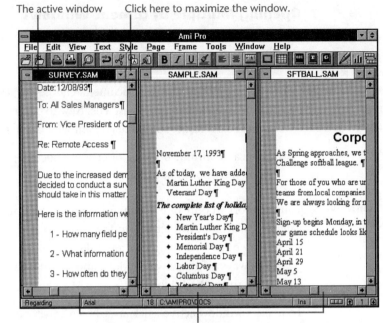

Equally sized windows

Cascaded windows overlap. The editing screen of the active window is fully visible, but only the title bars of the other windows can be seen on-screen.

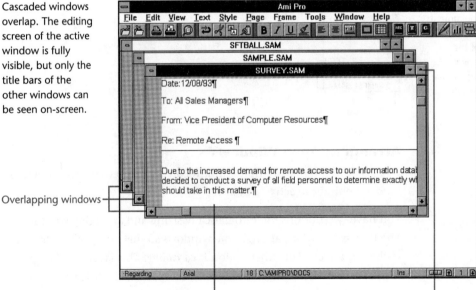

Overlapping windows

The active window   Click here to maximize the window.

Copying or Moving Text Between Document Windows

The procedures for copying and moving text between documents are the same as those for copying and moving text within a document. You use the Edit menu's Cut, Copy, and Paste commands and the Windows Clipboard.

Note: *You cannot use drag-and-drop editing to copy or move text between windows.*

To move or copy text between documents, follow these steps:

1. Choose **F**ile, **O**pen to open the document that contains the text you want to move or copy (the source document).

2. Choose **F**ile, **O**pen, to open the document to which you want to copy or move the text (the destination document).

   Note: *To make it easy to see what you are doing, choose **W**indow, **T**ile to arrange the open documents side by side.*

3. Make the source document the active window.

4. Select the text.

5. Perform one of the following procedures:

   ■ To move the text, choose **E**dit, Cu**t**.

   ■ To copy the text, choose **E**dit, **C**opy.

6. Make the destination document the active window, and position the insertion point where you want the text to appear in the document.

7. Choose **E**dit, **P**aste. Ami Pro inserts the text into the destination document.

Caution
If the documents were created using different style sheets, the text is formatted according to the *destination* document's styles. If the original style does not exist in the destination document's style sheet, Ami Pro uses the Body Text style and highlights the style name in the status bar.

Opening Multiple Copies of One Document

In Ami Pro, you can open more than one copy of a document on-screen at the same time so that you can enter, edit, or format text at one location in the document while simultaneously looking at another location.

Ami Pro adds a number and the words Read Only to the title bar of the copy. No matter how many copies of a document you open, you can save only the changes made to the original. You cannot save any changes made to a copy.

Displaying two copies of a document on-screen at once can be useful if you are working on long documents. You can display in the Read Only window, for example, a table of contents, an outline, or the key points you need to cover while you work on the original document in another window.

To open multiple copies of the same document, follow these steps:

1. Choose **F**ile, **O**pen to open the document, and make it active by clicking in it.

2. Choose **W**indow, **N**ew Window. Ami Pro displays a message telling you that you cannot save changes made to the new copy.

3. Choose OK. Ami Pro opens a copy of the active document.

The Read Only copy, on the left, is used to display important points that must be covered in the article. You can write, edit, or format the original article, on the right.

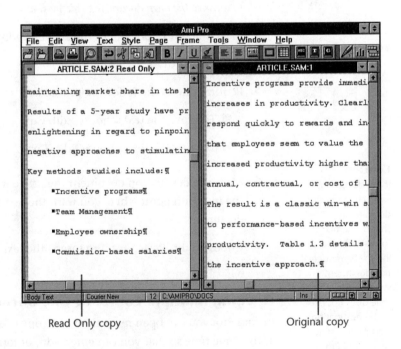

Read Only copy   Original copy

Note: *You also can use the **F**ile, **O**pen command to open multiple copies of the same document.*

If you have problems...	If you choose **W**indow, **N**ew Window, but Ami Pro opens a new [Untitled] document instead of a copy of the original document, you probably are trying to open a copy of a document you have not yet saved. Close the new [Untitled] document, save the original document, and then try **W**indow, **N**ew Window again.

Lesson Summary

To	Do This
Open an existing document	Choose **F**ile, **O**pen. In the Open dialog box, type the document name in the File **N**ame text box, and then choose OK.
Select text	Drag from the first character to the last character.
Move selected text	Choose **E**dit, Cu**t**, reposition the insertion point, and then choose **E**dit, **P**aste.
Copy selected text	Choose **E**dit, **C**opy, reposition the insertion point, and then choose **E**dit, **P**aste.
Change styles	Position the insertion point within the paragraph, or select the specific text. Select the new style from the Styles list or the Styles box.
Undo the last action	Choose **E**dit, **U**ndo.
Find text	Choose **E**dit, Find & **R**eplace. Enter text to find. Choose Find.
Find and replace text	Choose **E**dit, Find & **R**eplace. Enter text to find. Enter text to replace. Choose **R**eplace All.
Open multiple document windows	Choose **F**ile, **O**pen as many times as necessary to open additional documents.
Open multiple copies of the active document	Choose **W**indow, **N**ew Window.

3

On Your Own

The following exercises take you through the steps required to open and edit the memo created in the On Your Own exercises in Lesson 2, "Creating a Document."

Open an Existing Document and Insert Today's Date
Estimated Time: 5 minutes

1. Start Ami Pro if it's not already running.

2. Open the document you saved in Lesson 2.

3. Insert a blank line at the beginning of the document.

4. On the blank line, insert today's date.

Select and Revise Text
Estimated Time: 5 minutes

1. Select the fourth line of the memo ("Re: Remote Access").

2. Change the line from its current style to the Regarding style.

3. Select the last line of the memo ("When we have completed the survey, we will move ahead with the necessary action.")

4. Move that line up so that it becomes the second paragraph of the memo.

5. Change one or more of the numbered items to indented items.

6. Change the item back, without using styles. (Hint: Remember the Undo command.)

Use Multiple Windows
Estimated Time: 5 minutes

1. Create a new document.

2. Arrange the open windows on-screen so that you can see them both.

3. Copy the numbered list from the memo to the new document.

4. Delete the numbered list from the memo.

5. Put the numbered list back into the memo.

6. Close the new document without saving.

The following are some optional exercises you can try for more practice revising a document:

- Revert to the last saved version of the document, and go through the On Your Own exercises again.

- Open an existing document without using the Open dialog box.

- Change all occurrences of "field personnel" in the memo to "sales people."

- Change all these occurrences back to "field personnel"—it sounds more professional.

- See if you can open nine document windows without running out of memory.

- Copy the entire memo into a new document with a different style sheet.

- Use the new document's styles to change the memo's paragraph formatting.

Proofreading Your Document

Ami Pro 3 provides three tools to help you produce a well-written, professional-quality document. With Spell Check, you can check the spelling of one word or of the entire document. With Grammar Check, you can guard against unmatched cases and dangling participles. And with the Thesaurus, you can find the perfect word to suit any occasion.

In this lesson, you learn to

- Use Spell Check to check and correct the spelling in a document.

- Use Grammar Check to check and correct the grammar in a document.

- Use the Thesaurus to choose synonyms and alternative wordings.

Using Spell Check

Spell Check comes with a 115,000-word dictionary that includes legal, business, financial, and insurance terms. If your document has words that are not in the Spell Check dictionary, you can add them to a separate dictionary for future use.

Spell Check locates misspelled words in your document and suggests replacements. You also can choose for Spell Check to locate words that have been typed twice (such as *the the*), words with incorrect capitalization, and words that include numbers, such as *Catch-22*.

Checking an Entire Document

To check a document for incorrect spelling, follow these steps:

You can check the spelling in the document from the insertion point to the end, or you choose to check the entire document.

1. Choose Too**l**s, **S**pell Check. The Spell Check dialog box appears.

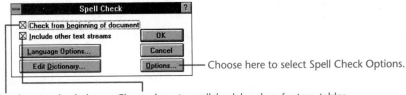

Select here to check the entire document.

Choose here to spellcheck headers, footers, tables, and other areas of text not part of the document.

Choose here to select Spell Check Options.

2. Select the Check from **B**eginning of Document check box to spell check the entire document.

3. Choose the **O**ptions button to display the Spell Check Options dialog box.

Select to check words that include numbers (such as *Catch-22*).

Select to check for repeated words (such as *the the*).

Select more specific Spell Check options from this dialog box.

Select to check words for correct capitalization.

Select to display user dictionary alternatives.

4. Make your selections in the Spell Check Options dialog box, then choose OK to return to the Spell Check dialog box.

5. Choose OK in the Spell Check dialog box to start checking the document's spelling.

If you have problems...

If Ami Pro displays a message stating that it cannot find a dictionary, choose **L**anguage Options in the Spell Check dialog box, and specify the correct path to the dictionary file in the Language **p**ath text box. The default path is `c:\Ami Pro`.

Note: *To check the spelling in selected text only, select the text before beginning the spell check.*

If you have problems...

If only part of the document is checked, you probably forgot to select the Check from **B**eginning of Document check box in the Spell Check dialog box.

Making Corrections

If Spell Check finds a spelling mistake, it highlights the word and displays another Spell Check dialog box.

You can select the correctly spelled word from the Alternatives list, or you can type the correction in the Replace With text box.

Highlighted typo ⸺

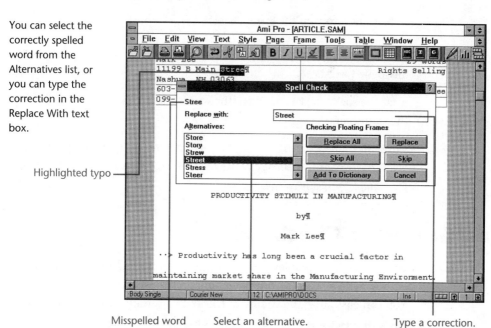

Misspelled word   Select an alternative.   Type a correction.

To continue, choose one of the following command buttons:

■ **R**eplace All to replace all occurrences of the misspelled word with the word entered in the Replace **W**ith text box.

■ **Re**place to replace only the highlighted occurrence of the misspelled word. If the misspelled word appears again in your document, Spell Check highlights it.

■ **S**kip All to move on without replacing the misspelled word. Spell Check does not stop to highlight any other occurrences of the same misspelled word.

■ **S**kip to move on without replacing the highlighted word. If the misspelled word appears again in your text, Spell Check highlights it.

■ **A**dd to Dictionary to add the highlighted word to your User Dictionary. In future checks, Spell Check does not highlight this word, because it is now included in the dictionary.

■ Cancel to stop the Spell Check.

Unless you choose Cancel, Spell Check continues, stopping at the next misspelled word.

After the spell check is finished, the words `Spell Check Complete` flash in the status bar.

Note: *Spell Check doesn't stop if you use a correctly spelled word in the wrong place. It considers the sentence "I like the color read more then the color blew," for example, perfectly correct.*

Using Grammar Check

Grammar Check enables you to monitor your writing for conformance with generally accepted rules of grammar, style, usage, and punctuation. You can customize the Grammar Check to a certain writing style, and you can select specific rules for each check you conduct.

If Grammar Check finds an error, it explains the rule it believes was broken and suggests a remedy.

Checking an Entire Document

To check the grammar in an entire document, follow these steps:

1. Choose Too**l**s, **G**rammar Check. The Grammar Check dialog box appears.

In the Grammar Check dialog box, select the grammar and style set that is appropriate for this document.

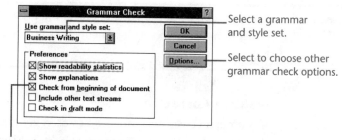

Select a grammar and style set.

Select to choose other grammar check options.

Select to check the entire document.

2. Select the Check from **B**eginning of Document check box to grammar check the entire document.

3. Choose the **O**ptions button to display the Grammar and Style Options dialog box.

Choose the rule options to display.   Choose the rules to use.

In the Grammar and Style Options dialog box, select the rules you want to use for checking the grammar of this document.

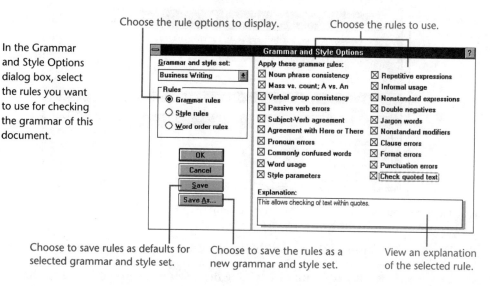

Choose to save rules as defaults for selected grammar and style set.

Choose to save the rules as a new grammar and style set.

View an explanation of the selected rule.

4. Make any choices you want for your grammar check in this dialog box, and then choose OK to return to the Grammar Check dialog box.

5. Choose OK to begin the grammar check.

    Note: *To check grammar within selected text only, select the text before beginning the grammar check.*

If you have problems...   If only part of the document is checked, you probably forgot to mark the Check from **B**eginning of Document check box in the Grammar Check dialog box.

Making Corrections

If Grammar Check encounters an error in grammar or style, it highlights the text and displays the Grammar Checker dialog box.

In the Suggestions text area, Ami Pro identifies the problem it found in the highlighted text and suggests a correction. Sometimes, one passage may have more than one error.

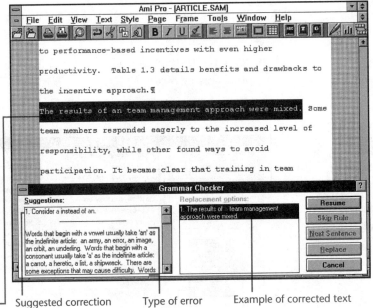

Highlighted text ┘ Suggested correction   Type of error   Example of corrected text

To continue, choose one of the following command buttons:

- **Sk**ip to continue checking the document without changing the highlighted sentence. If another sentence breaks the same rule, Grammar Check highlights it.

- **Ski**p Rule to continue checking the document without changing the highlighted sentence. If another sentence breaks the same rule, Grammar Check won't stop and highlight it.

- **N**ext Sentence to move on and check the next sentence without changing the current sentence.

■ **R**eplace to make the suggested changes to the highlighted sentence.

■ Cancel to stop the Grammar Check.

If you have problems... If the Replace option is dimmed, either Grammar Check has no suggestion for correcting the error, or you clicked inside the document window. If you want, you can change the document text manually while the insertion point is in the document window. Choose another button to continue the check.

Unless you choose Cancel, Grammar Check continues through the document, stopping at the next error.

After the check is finished, the Readability Statistics dialog box appears. Choose Close to conclude the Grammar Check.

You can use the Readability Statistics to gauge the quality of your writing style.

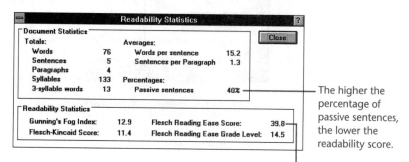

The higher the percentage of passive sentences, the lower the readability score.

The higher the Flesch Reading Ease Score, the easier it is to read the document.

If you have problems... If the Readability Statistics dialog box does not appear, you deselected the Show Readability Statistics check box in the Grammar Check dialog box.

Using the Thesaurus

The Ami Pro 3 Thesaurus contains 1.4 million definitions, variations, and synonyms for 40,000 words. Looking up a word in the Thesaurus is similar to looking for one in a printed thesaurus. In Ami Pro, however, after you find an alternative, you can quickly insert it into a document.

To look up a word in the Thesaurus, follow these steps:

1. Position the insertion point within the word you want to look up.

2. Choose Tools, **T**hesaurus. The Thesaurus dialog box appears.

The Thesaurus offers a list of synonyms for the highlighted word, as well as a definition and a list of words with similar meanings.

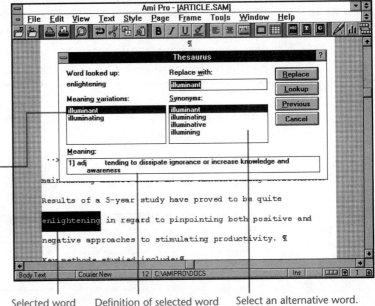

Choose to display synonyms of one of these similar words.

Selected word   Definition of selected word   Select an alternative word.

3. To continue, choose one of the following command buttons:

   ■ **R**eplace to replace the selected word in your document with the word in the Replace **W**ith text box.

   ■ **L**ookup to look up the word highlighted in the **S**ynonyms list. The definition, list of synonyms, and list of words with similar meaning, change for the selected word.

   ■ **P**revious to return to the word previously looked up.

   ■ Cancel to quit the Thesaurus.

To remove the Thesaurus dialog box, choose Cancel.

Lesson Summary

To	Do This
Check Spelling	Choose Tools, **S**pell Check.
Correct Spelling	Choose **Re**place in the Spell Check dialog box.
Check Grammar	Choose Tools, **G**rammar Check.
Correct Grammar	Choose **R**eplace in the Grammar Checker dialog box.
Use the Thesaurus	Choose Tools, **T**hesaurus.

On Your Own

Estimated Time: 10 minutes

4

The following exercises are designed to help you become comfortable using Ami Pro's proofreading tools.

1. Open an existing document, or create a new document.

2. Check the spelling in the document.

3. Use the Spell Check options to check for repeated words and words that begin with capital letters.

4. Check the grammar in the document.

5. Use the Grammar Options to check the grammar using a different grammar and style set.

6. Use the Thesaurus to choose an alternative word or words within the document.

7. Use the Thesaurus to look up definitions of some of displayed synonyms.

The following are some optional exercises you can use to reinforce your knowledge of the proofreading tools:

■ Add your name to the Spell Check user dictionary. (Hint: Choose Edit **D**ictionary from the Spell Check dialog box.)

■ Compare the readability statistics of a document checked by using different grammar and style sets.

Part II
Formatting for a Professional Look

Dressing Up Your Text

You can easily make your Ami Pro documents more attractive by changing the appearance or emphasis of your text. This is called *formatting*.

Ami Pro offers three categories of formatting:

Formatting
The means by which you enhance the appearance of text.

- *Page formatting* refers to the way the pages of a document are arranged.

- *Paragraph formatting* refers to the way paragraphs and other blocks of text are arranged.

- *Character formatting* involves specifying the appearance of the letters, numbers, punctuation marks, and symbols that make up the body of your text.

By learning to use style sheets and styles, you have already learned about page and paragraph formatting. In this lesson, you learn to use character formatting. Specifically, you learn to

- Choose fonts.

- Choose font sizes.

- Choose a text color.

- Apply character attributes, such as boldface, italics, and underlining.

- Copy character formatting.

Understanding Fonts

One of the easiest ways to change the appearance of text in a document is to change the text *font*.

Font
A distinctive type-face available in a variety of sizes. Some common fonts are New Times Roman, Courier, and Helvetica.

With Ami Pro, you can select a font typeface, a font size, and a font color. Text appears on-screen with the selected formatting. Whether the text prints the way it looks on-screen, however, depends on the fonts available in your system. For example, the Adobe Type Manager fonts that can be installed with Ami Pro look the same on-screen as they do on the printed page, but you cannot print these fonts unless your printer supports them.

Note: *For more information about using screen fonts and printer fonts, consult Que's* Using Windows 3.1, *Special Edition. For information on installing Adobe Type Manager fonts, see Appendix A, "Installing Ami Pro 3 for Windows."*

Font sizes are measured in *points*. There are 72 points in an inch, which means that if you use a 12-point font, you get six lines of text in an inch. Most typed documents use 12-point fonts for body text; books and magazines usually use 9- or 10-point fonts. Larger font sizes are good for titles, headings, and other text that you want to make stand out.

You have already used different fonts and font sizes in the styles you used to create documents. In the _DEFAULT.STY style sheet, for example, the Body Text font is 12-point New Times Roman.

You can dress up your text by using different fonts and font sizes. To see which font and font size you are currently using, look at the status bar of your Ami Pro screen.

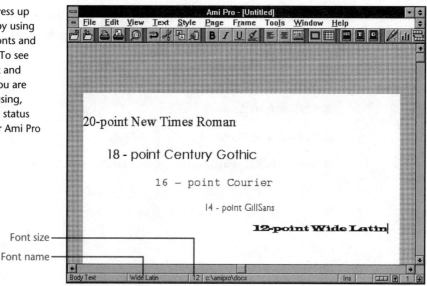

Font size ——
Font name ——

Choosing Fonts

You can choose a font, a font size, and a font color by using menu commands. You also can choose a font and a font size by using the status bar.

To choose a font with menu commands:

1. Choose **Text, Font.**

In the Font dialog box, you can select a font, a font size, and a text color.

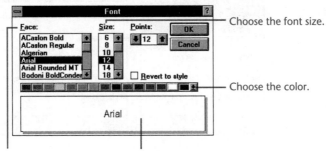

Choose the font size.

Choose the color.

Choose the font.   View a sample of the highlighted font.

2. Choose the font face, size, and color from the appropriate sections of the dialog box, as shown in the figure.

Note: *If the size you want does not appear in the **S**ize list box, type the size you want in the **P**oints text box.*

3. After you make your choices, choose OK.

When you type, text appears in the selected font, size, and color.

You also can use the status bar to change font or font size.

5

Choose the font
and font size from
the lists that
appear. Here, the
selected text font
has been changed
from Arial to
Roman. The font
size remains 12
points until the new
font size is selected.

Selected text   Choose a new font size.

Current style —

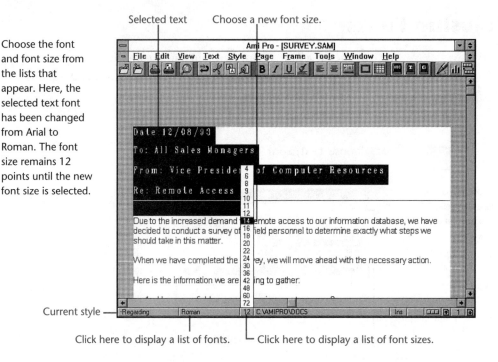

Click here to display a list of fonts.   └ Click here to display a list of font sizes.

To change the font and font size with the status bar:

1. To display a list of fonts, click the font name in the status bar.

2. Choose the font name you want to use.

3. Click the font size in the status bar to display a list of point sizes.

4. Choose the size you want to use.

No matter which method you use, text appears in the chosen font and size until you choose different ones.

Note: *You can use any of these methods to change the font, font size, and font color of existing text. Simply select the text first.*

Understanding Character Attributes

Attributes are the modifications or enhancements you make to characters to give them emphasis or a unique look. The most common attributes applied to characters are boldface, italics, and underlining, but Ami Pro offers many others, including superscript, subscript, strikethrough, and overstrike.

By applying character attributes, you can make your words stand out on the page. Too many attributes on one page, however, can be overwhelming.

Normal text   Bold text   Italics   Word underline   Double underline

Continuous underline
Uppercase
Overstrike with +
Strikethrough
Initial caps
Small caps

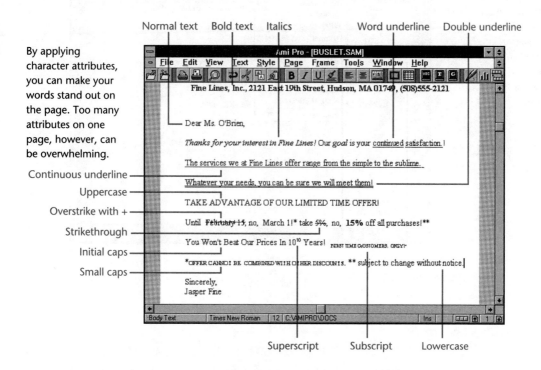

Superscript   Subscript   Lowercase

You can apply more than one attribute to a character. For example, you can apply boldface and italics to a word; for even more emphasis, you can underline it as well.

Applying Character Attributes

You can choose character attributes before you type text, or you can apply them to existing text by selecting the text before you choose the attribute.

To see which attributes are being used at the current insertion point location, choose **T**ext. A check mark appears in the menu next to each chosen attribute.

In the Text menu, a check mark appears next to a chosen attribute. If no check mark appears, text is being entered according to the current style setting.

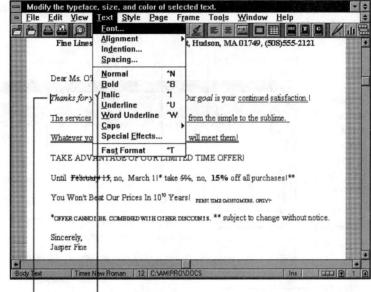

Text appears in the chosen attribute.   Check mark

To apply character-formatting attributes:

1. Choose **T**ext.

> **Note:** *Ami Pro has SmartIcons for many character attributes, although only Bold, Italics, and Underline appear in the default SmartIcon bar. For information on displaying different SmartIcons, see Lesson 9, "Customizing Ami Pro."*

2. Choose any of the following attributes:

- To apply boldface, choose **B**old or press Ctrl+B.

- To apply italics, choose **I**talic or press Ctrl+I.

- To apply a continuous underline, choose **U**nderline or press Ctrl+U.

- To underline words only, choose **W**ord Underline or press Ctrl+W.

- To type in uppercase characters, choose **C**aps, **U**pper Case.

- To type in lowercase characters, choose **C**aps, **L**ower Case.

- To start each word with an uppercase character, choose **C**aps, **I**nitial Caps.

- To type in small uppercase characters, choose **C**aps, **S**mall Caps.

To remove character attributes and revert to the style settings, choose **T**ext, **N**ormal or press Ctrl+N. To remove a single character attribute, choose that attribute again.

If you have problems...

If you are not happy with the character attribute you selected, simply select the SmartIcon again, or select the Normal Text icon. The attribute disappears.

5

Applying Special-Effects Character Attributes

If the simple character attributes described in the previous section do not give your text the look you want, you can use Ami Pro's Special Effects attributes. Using the Special Effects character attributes, you can add superscript or subscript, double underline, strikethrough, or overstrike. You must use the Special Effects dialog box to apply certain character attributes. To apply one of these attributes:

1. Choose **T**ext, Special **E**ffects.

In the Special Effects dialog box, you can choose character attributes that are not available directly from the Text menu.

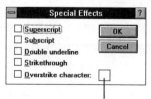

Type the character to use for overstriking here.

2. Choose any of the attributes in the dialog box, as shown in the figure. If you choose **O**verstrike character, you need to type a character in the box after the option name.

3. Choose OK.

If you have problems...

If you try to use a keyboard shortcut and a letter appears in your document at the insertion point, you did not hold down the Ctrl key. Delete the character that appeared—probably *B, N, I, U,* or *W*—and try again, this time holding down the Ctrl key.

Copying Character Formatting

If you use a mouse, you can quickly copy character formatting. Copying is useful if you spend a great deal of time getting exactly the formatting you need for certain text and then decide to duplicate the formatting somewhere else in the document.

To copy character formatting:

1. Apply character formatting to text. You can use SmartIcons, menu commands, or keyboard shortcuts to apply the formatting.

2. Select the formatted text.

3. Choose **T**ext, Fas**t** Format. The mouse pointer becomes an I-beam with a paintbrush attached. If an entire paragraph is selected, the Fast Format dialog box appears on-screen, asking what formats to extract. You can choose text font and attribute or paragraph style.

4. Select the text to which you want to apply the formatting. Ami Pro copies the character formatting to the selected text.

With Fast Format, you can copy the formatting attributes of selected text.

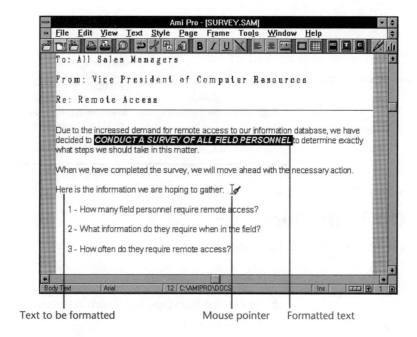

Ami Pro - [SURVEY.SAM]

File Edit View Text Style Page Frame Tools Window Help

To: All Sales Managers

From: Vice President of Computer Resources

Re: Remote Access

Due to the increased demand for remote access to our information database, we have decided to *CONDUCT A SURVEY OF ALL FIELD PERSONNEL* to determine exactly what steps we should take in this matter.

When we have completed the survey, we will move ahead with the necessary action.

Here is the information we are hoping to gather:

    1 - How many field personnel require remote access?

    2 - What information do they require when in the field?

    3 - How often do they require remote access?

Body Text   Arial   12 C:\AMIPRO\DOCS   Ins

Text to be formatted   Mouse pointer   Formatted text

You can continue applying the selected format to other text. To turn off Fast Format and return the mouse pointer to normal, choose **T**ext, Fas**t** Format again.

Note: *You can copy more than one character format at a time, as long as all the formats have been applied to the text you copy.*

Lesson Summary

To	Do This
Choose a font, font size, or color	Choose **T**ext, **F**ont.
Apply boldface, italics, or underlining to text	Choose **T**ext; then choose **B**old, **I**talic, **U**nderline, or **W**ord Underline.
Change capitalization	Choose **T**ext, **C**aps; then choose **U**pper Case, **L**ower Case, **I**nitial Caps, or **S**mall Caps.

(continues)

To	Do This
Add special effects to text	Choose **T**ext, Special **E**ffects, and then choose the check box next to the effect you want. For **O**verstrike, type an overstrike character in the text box.
Copy character formatting	Select formatted text; choose **T**ext, Fas**t** Format; select text to be formatted.
Turn off Fast Format	Choose **T**ext, Fas**t** Forma**t**.

On Your Own

Estimated Time: 15 minutes

1. Create a business letter.

2. In the first line, type a company name and address, using the Company name style.

3. Change the company name to a different font.

4. Make the company name appear in a larger point size.

5. Change the company address to a different color.

6. Type a recipient's address, using the Body Text style.

7. Type the salutation in boldface.

8. Type the first paragraph of the letter in italics.

9. Apply a continuous underline to the first sentence of the letter.

10. Finish typing the letter, using as many different character attributes as you want.

11. Type the closing for the letter.

12. Copy the formatting from the company name to the letter closing.

Here are some optional exercises you can use to practice character formatting:

- ■ Type a letter in which each paragraph appears in a different font.

- ■ Type a letter in which each paragraph appears in a different font size.

- ■ Type a letter in which each paragraph appears in a different color.

- ■ See how many character attributes you can include in one page.

5

Lining Up Your Paragraphs

In Ami Pro, a *paragraph* is any amount of text or graphics followed by a paragraph mark. So far, you have formatted paragraphs using the styles built into Ami Pro's style sheets. In this lesson, you learn how to override the style settings to adjust paragraph formatting. This process is useful for changing the way one or two paragraphs are positioned.

In this lesson, you learn how to

- Display paragraph marks on-screen.

- Align text.

- Indent text.

- Set line spacing.

Viewing Paragraph Marks

In Lesson 3, "Revising a Document," you learned that Ami Pro uses paragraph marks to keep track of paragraph-formatting information. Ami Pro inserts a paragraph mark whenever you press Enter. Paragraph marks are nonprinting characters, which means that they do not print along with the rest of your document.

When you edit in Ami Pro, keeping paragraph marks visible is useful. That way, you know exactly where each paragraph begins and ends. Also, if you delete a paragraph mark, you also delete the paragraph-formatting information. When you can see paragraph marks on-screen, you are less likely to delete them accidentally.

To view paragraph marks on-screen:

1. Choose **V**iew, View **P**references.

In the View
Preferences dialog
box, you can
choose to display
paragraph marks
on-screen.

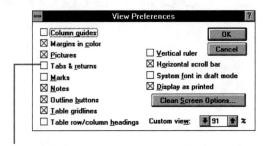

Select to display paragraph marks on-screen.

2. Click the Tabs & **R**eturns checkbox.

3. Choose OK.

Aligning Text

Alignment
The way text is
positioned in rela-
tion to the margins.

One way to change the appearance of paragraphs on-screen is to change the text *alignment*.

Ami Pro provides four text-alignment settings:

- *Flush left*, which means that all lines are flush against the left margin and the right margin is left uneven.

- *Centered*, which means that text is evenly positioned around the center of the page, leaving both the left and right margins uneven.

- *Flush right*, which means that all lines are flush against the right margin, leaving the left margin uneven.

- *Justified*, which means that text is spaced across each line so that both the left and right margins are even.

By changing text alignment, you can single out paragraphs for attention or customize the format of a document. Titles, for example, look good when they are centered on a page. In formal business letters, the return address is often placed flush right. Justified text has a neat, orderly appearance.

You can choose an alignment before you type the paragraph text, or you can change the alignment of an existing paragraph.

To change the alignment of one existing paragraph, position the insertion point anywhere within the paragraph. (You do not need to select the whole paragraph.) To change the alignment of two or more existing paragraphs, select the paragraphs first.

To align text:

1. Position the insertion point where you want to begin the paragraph, or position it within the existing paragraph.

2. Choose **T**ext, **A**lignment. The Alignment menu appears.

3. Choose one of the following options:

 ■ To align flush left, choose **L**eft or press Ctrl+L.

 ■ To center, choose **C**enter or press Ctrl+E.

 ■ To align flush right, choose **R**ight or press Ctrl+R.

 ■ To justify, choose **J**ustify or press Ctrl+J.

> **Note:** *Only the Flush Left and Center Text SmartIcons appear in the default SmartIcon bar. To learn how to change the SmartIcon bar, see Lesson 9, "Customizing Ami Pro."*

6

In this document, different alignments are used to format the paragraphs.

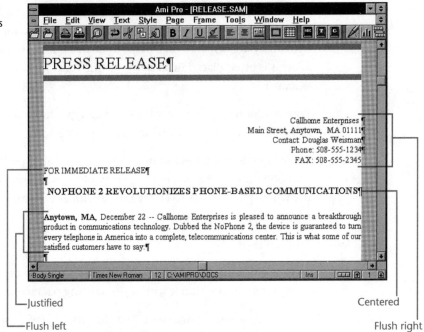

Justified

Flush left

Centered

Flush right

If you have problems... If you do not like the alignment you selected, you can remove it easily by selecting it again or by choosing **T**ext, **N**ormal.

Note: *A check mark appears beside the Alignment option in the Text menu if any alignment has been selected from the menu.*

Indenting Text

Indention
The starting or ending position of a line or lines in relation to the normal text margins.

In Ami Pro, you can use different *indention* settings to create customized effects. Indention differs from alignment because you can customize the size of the indent.

Ami Pro provides the following four indention settings:

 ■ *All*, meaning that all lines in the paragraph are indented from the left margin.

■ *From right*, meaning that all lines in the paragraph are indented from the right margin.

 ■ *First*, meaning that the first line in the paragraph is indented from the left margin. The other lines in the paragraph remain positioned according to the paragraph-alignment setting.

■ *Rest*, meaning that all lines in the paragraph except the first line are indented from the left margin. This kind of indent is often called a *hanging indent*.

Note: *The SmartIcons for indenting text do not appear in the default SmartIcon bar. To learn how to change the SmartIcon bar, see Lesson 9, "Customizing Ami Pro."*

When you choose an indention setting from the text menu, you enter the precise distance you want Ami Pro to indent the text from the margin. When you use SmartIcons, Ami Pro automatically indents .5 inches.

To choose an indention setting:

1. Position the insertion point where you want the paragraph to begin, or position it within the paragraph you want to change.

2. Choose **T**ext, In**d**ention.

6

You customize the indentions by entering the distance to indent from the margin.

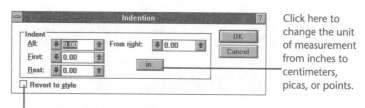

Click here to change the unit of measurement from inches to centimeters, picas, or points.

Click here to return to the indention setting of the current paragraph style.

3. Beside the indention type, enter the distance you want Ami Pro to indent from the margin.

4. Choose OK. Ami Pro indents the paragraph.

A check mark appears beside the **I**ndention option in the **T**ext menu, indicating that an indention setting has been entered.

Note: *You can use more than one indention setting for one paragraph. For example, you can indent a paragraph from both the left and right margins, or you can indent all lines 0.5 inch and the first line 0.5 inch (Ami Pro adds the two measurements and indents the first line 1 inch).*

If you have problems... If you don't like the indentions you set, remove them by choosing the Revert to Style checkbox in the indention dialog box.

You can combine alignment and indention options to achieve an interesting-looking document.

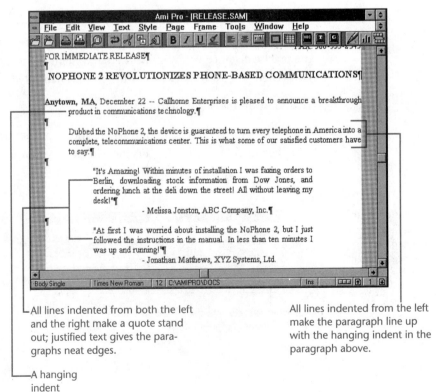

All lines indented from both the left and the right make a quote stand out; justified text gives the paragraphs neat edges.

A hanging indent

All lines indented from the left make the paragraph line up with the hanging indent in the paragraph above.

Setting Line Spacing

The amount of blank space left between lines in a document is called *line spacing*. Single-spaced text leaves no blank space; double-spaced text leaves one blank line between each line of text. With Ami Pro, you can select single spacing, double spacing, 1.5-line spacing, or customized spacing.

You can set line spacing before you type the text, or you can change the spacing of existing text.

To set line spacing:

1. Position the insertion point where you want to begin the paragraph, or position it within the paragraph you want to change.

2. Choose **Text**, **S**pacing.

In the Spacing dialog box, select the line-spacing setting you want. For customized spacing, enter the measurement in the Custom text box.

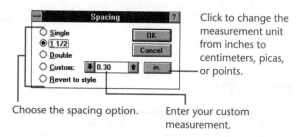

Click to change the measurement unit from inches to centimeters, picas, or points.

Choose the spacing option.   Enter your custom measurement.

3. Choose the spacing option you want.

4. Choose OK.

A check mark beside the Spacing option in the Text menu indicates that a spacing setting other than the paragraph style setting has been selected.

6

Spacing lines closer together makes room for more text on a page; spacing lines farther apart leaves less room but makes the text easier to read.

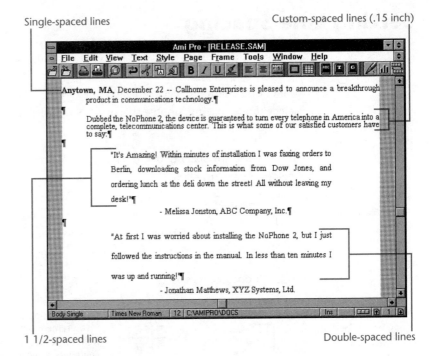

Single-spaced lines

Custom-spaced lines (.15 inch)

1 1/2-spaced lines

Double-spaced lines

Lesson Summary

To	Do This
Display paragraph marks	Choose **V**iew, View **P**references; choose Tabs & **R**eturns.
Set text alignment	Choose **T**ext, **A**lignment; choose **L**eft, **C**enter, **R**ight, or **J**ustify.
Set text indention	Choose **T**ext, In**d**ention. Then type the size of the indent beside the indent option you want: **A**ll, **F**irst, **R**est, or From Right.
Set line spacing	Choose **T**ext, **S**pacing. Choose **S**ingle, **1** 1/2, **D**ouble, or **C**ustom. If you choose Custom, enter the measurement size in the Custom text box.

On Your Own

These exercises are designed to reinforce your knowledge of paragraph and character formatting. In following these exercises, you create a report-type document that contains titles, subheads, body text, and a numbered list. You can use the document in the exercises for Lesson 7 as well.

You can use your own text or enter the text supplied with these steps.

Aligning Text
Estimated Time: 10 minutes

1. Create a new document, using the _BASIC.STY style sheet.

2. Display paragraph marks on-screen.

3. Set line spacing at 1.5 inches.

4. Type a centered title in the top line. You can use any font in any size (for example, 22-point Arial). Type the following text:

December Sales Projections

Changing Line Spacing
Estimated Time: 5 minutes

1. Change to single-spaced lines. Type a centered explanation of the report. Type the following text, using 14-point Times New Roman in italics:

Based on Information (press Return)

Filed As of January 15, 1994.

2. Change back to 1.5-inch line spacing.

3. Type a centered subhead, using 18-point Times New Roman in italics. Type the following text:

Preliminary Figures Look Positive.

6

Indenting Paragraphs
Estimated Time: 10 minutes

1. Start a new paragraph. Set alignment to flush left. Indent all lines 0.10 inch from the left margin. Indent the first line of each paragraph an additional .20 inches. In Times New Roman, type:

   Despite a slow start, early returns indicate that December sales are up from last year. How much of an increase will be realized, however, remains to be seen.

   As you all know, after the disastrous results of the past few seasons, we have finally learned to keep our forecasts conservative.

2. Type a centered subhead, using 16-point New Times Roman in italics. Start a new paragraph. Change indention back to the default style settings, and change alignment to centered. Type the following text:

   Gross Estimates Up

3. Change alignment to flush left, and type:

   While most stores throughout the region are submitting estimates of gross profits up modestly from last year, at least two locations are claiming sales that rival the boom years of the eighties.

   This wonderful news is certainly cause to celebrate. However, due to the cost-containment measures implemented during the lean years, no parties, lunches, or other events will occur without the written consent of the director of the board and the chief operating officer.

Changing Alignment, Indentations, and Line Spacing
Estimated Time: 10 minutes

Type a centered subhead, using 16-point Times New Roman in italics.

1. Center-align the following text:

   Points to Note

2. Use a hanging indent to create a single-spaced numbered list. Use the following indention settings: first line, 1.5 inches; other lines, 1.75 inches; from the right, 2 inches.

   Type the following text:

   1. Crowds were larger than last year. 2. Fewer items were returned. 3. New pricing strategies were implemented.

3. Revert to the default style indentations to create another centered subhead. Type the following text:

   Larger Crowds

4. Left-align a body-text paragraph. Type the following text:

   Unofficial audits had traffic up more than 30% in three of our top five outlets.

5. Center the following text:

   Fewer Returns

6. Left-align a body-text paragraph. Type the following text:

   Training classes for our sales help has also proved to be a good investment. Already, stores are reporting fewer returned items. We believe that this has a lot to do with the fact that our sales help was well-informed about the merchandise.

6

7. Center the following text:

   New Pricing Strategies

8. Left-align a body-text paragraph. Type the following text:

   Finally, learning from our mistakes, we managed to keep prices competitive, yet profitable. By marketing our merchandise at reasonable prices from the outset instead of resorting to drastic markdowns, we built customer trust and loyalty. This is why we believe our success will continue into 1994.

9. Center the following text:

   Conclusion

10. Left-align a body-text paragraph. Type the following text:

    In conclusion, it is important to remember that the figures are still only preliminary. However, if they hold, it looks like our lean years may finally be over.

11. Save the document. You can use it to practice page formatting in the next lesson.

Here are some additional exercises you can try:

■ Change the alignment of a paragraph or two. See how the text looks right-aligned and justified.

■ Change the line spacing for part of the document or for the whole document. Customize the spacing to see whether you can fit all the text on one page.

Setting Up Pages

Page formatting
The method you use to set up a consistent layout for pages in a document.

In Lesson 5, "Dressing Up Your Text," you learned about character formatting; in Lesson 6, "Lining Up Your Paragraphs," you learned about paragraph formatting. In this lesson, you learn about basic *page formatting*.

Specifically, in this lesson you learn how to

- Understand page layouts.
- Use rulers.
- Insert or modify a page layout.
- Choose a page size and orientation.
- Set margins and tabs.
- Divide the page into columns.

Understanding Page Layouts

The overall look of a document depends in large part on the way you arrange text and graphics on each page. With Ami Pro's page formatting features, you can customize page layout to suit a particular document.

Components of a page layout include margins, tabs, headers, footers, columns, lines, and borders. You also can choose a page size and orientation, number pages, and divide a document into sections.

In Ami Pro, each style sheet defines page-formatting settings for one page layout. When you choose a style sheet, you try to pick a style that provides the page settings you want for the new document. If the settings are not exactly what you want—for example, if the margins are not the size you want or if you want to add a border—you can modify the page layout.

If some pages in your document require a different look, you can insert a new page layout.

 Note: *You must be in Layout mode to modify or insert a page layout. To change to Layout mode, choose* **V***iew,* **L***ayout Mode. For more information about Ami Pro's display modes, see Lesson 8, "Making Your Pages Pretty."*

Using Rulers

In Ami Pro, you can use rulers to set margins, tabs and indents, as well as column widths. Rulers are useful because they let you see on-screen the selected settings as you work.

Vertical ruler
Measures the height of the page along the left margin. The vertical ruler includes markers for the top and bottom margins.

Current ruler
The ruler that was inserted into the paragraph that currently contains the insertion point.

Page layout ruler
The horizontal ruler in the Modify Page Layout dialog box.

Ami Pro has the following three kinds of rulers that you can use to set or modify the page layout:

- The *vertical ruler* can set top and bottom margins.

- You can insert a *current ruler* to set tabs, margins, indentions, and column widths for sections or paragraphs.

- In the Modify Page Layout dialog box, you can use the *page layout ruler* to set default tabs, left and right margins, and column widths for the entire document. (The Modify Page Layout dialog box is discussed in the later section "Modifying Selected Pages.")

Using the Vertical Ruler

You use the vertical ruler to quickly set top and bottom margins, and to position objects, such as frames, charts, or drawings, accurately on the page.

To display the vertical ruler, follow these steps:

1. Choose **V**iew, View **P**references. The View Preferences dialog box appears.

2. Choose the **V**ertical Ruler option.

3. Choose OK. The vertical ruler appears along the left side of the document area.

On the vertical ruler, drag the margin markers up or down to set top and bottom margins.

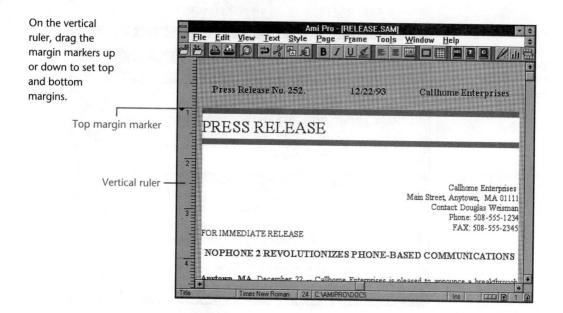

Top margin marker

Vertical ruler

Inserting a Ruler

You can insert a ruler into a paragraph for setting tabs, margins, or indentions for the paragraph that currently contains the insertion point. By using a current ruler, you can modify the page layout settings for a paragraph or two without modifying the page layout for the entire document, or inserting a new page layout.

To insert a ruler into a paragraph, follow these steps:

1. Choose **V**iew, Show **R**uler to display the page layout ruler.

2. Position the insertion point at the beginning of the paragraph, or select more than one paragraph.

3. Choose **P**age, **R**uler, **I**nsert.

Ami Pro inserts a ruler that has the same settings as the page layout ruler, or as the previous ruler.

7

To see where in a document rulers were inserted, choose **V**iew, View **P**references. In the View Preferences dialog box, choose **M**arks, and then choose OK.

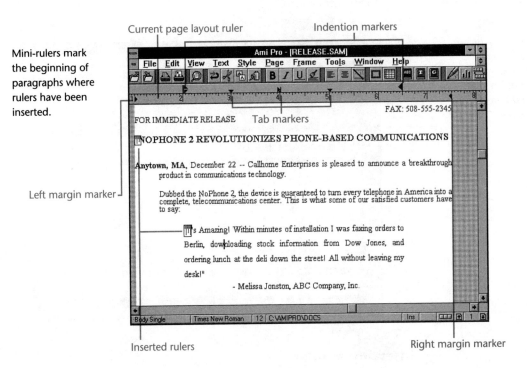

Current page layout ruler · Indention markers

Mini-rulers mark the beginning of paragraphs where rulers have been inserted.

Tab markers

Left margin marker

Inserted rulers · Right margin marker

If you don't want the ruler displayed on-screen, choose **V**iew, Hide **R**uler.

Removing a Ruler

To remove an inserted ruler, follow these steps:

1. Position the insertion point within the text that contains the inserted ruler.

2. Choose **P**age, **R**uler, **R**emove.

Ami Pro removes the ruler. The tabs, margins, and indentions for the paragraph revert to the original page layout settings.

Changing Indentions with a Ruler

In Lesson 6, "Lining Up Your Paragraphs," you learned how to set indents. You can use the current ruler to set indents for the paragraph that contains the insertion point.

To set indents using the ruler, follow these steps:

1. Position the insertion point within the paragraph you want to modify.

2. Choose **V**iew, Show **R**uler. The current ruler is displayed.

3. Take one of the following steps:

   - To indent all lines in a paragraph, drag the entire left indention arrow to the new location.

   - To indent only the first line, drag only the upper half of the left indention arrow to the new location.

   - To indent all but the first line, which creates a hanging indent, drag only the bottom half of the left indention arrow to the new location.

   - To indent from the right, drag the indention arrow that appears at the far right margin on the ruler.

Left indention arrow

Right indention arrow

Indention markers for the paragraph that contains the insertion point appear in the upper half of the current ruler. In this example, all lines are indented one inch from both the right and the left margins.

Ami Pro - [RELEASE.SAM]

File   Edit   View   Text   Style   Page   Frame   Tools   Window   Help

B I U

FAX: 508-555-2345

FOR IMMEDIATE RELEASE

Current Ruler

NOPHONE 2 REVOLUTIONIZES PHONE-BASED COMMUNICATIONS

Anytown, MA, December 22 -- Callhome Enterprises is pleased to announce a breakthrough product in communications technology.

Dubbed the NoPhone 2, the device is guaranteed to turn every telephone in America into a complete, telecommunications center. This is what some of our satisfied customers have to say:

Current paragraph

"It's Amazing! Within minutes of installation I was faxing orders to Berlin, downloading stock information from Dow Jones, and ordering lunch at the deli down the street! All without leaving my desk!"

- Melissa Jonston, ABC Company, Inc.

Body Single   Times New Roman   12   C:\AMIPRO\DOCS   Ins

7

Modifying a Page Layout

If the page settings associated with the style sheet you used to create a document are not quite right, you can modify the page layout for the entire document.

Note: *Unlike paragraph styles or character attributes, page-layout settings affect the entire document. When you modify the page layout, you change the appearance of every page in the document.*

 Choose **P**age, **M**odify Page Layout to change margins, tabs, and column sizes and to change page size and orientation, add lines, and set headers and footers.

With Ami Pro, you can create page layouts to suit all kinds of documents. This newsletter was created with the _NEWSLET5 style sheet, and then modified for a customized look.

Top margin   Header

Left margin

Line between columns

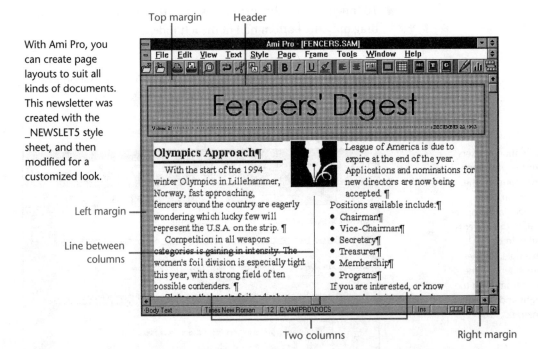

Two columns   Right margin

Note: *To quickly display the Modify Page Layout dialog box, point anywhere in the margin area of the document and click the right mouse button.*

Changes you make to the page layout affect the current document only and do not change the style sheet used to create the document. If you think you will use the modified page layout settings again, you can save these settings as a new style sheet. To learn how to save these changes as a new style sheet, turn to Lesson 9, "Customizing Ami Pro."

Inserting a Page Layout

Occasionally, a few pages in a document may require a different page layout. To change a few pages without changing the entire document, you can insert a new page layout. To insert a new page layout, follow these steps:

1. Position the insertion point at the end of the last paragraph on the page preceding the page where you want the new page layout to begin, unless this point in your document begins at the top of a new page. Ami Pro inserts a page break before the new page layout.

2. Choose **P**age, **I**nsert Page Layout. The Insert Page Layout menu appears.

3. Choose **I**nsert. The Modify Page Layout dialog box appears.

4. Change the settings as described in the previous sections.

5. After you make all the needed changes, choose OK.

In Facing Pages view, you can see the difference between the two page layouts. The inserted layout remains in effect until you revert back to the original page layout settings.

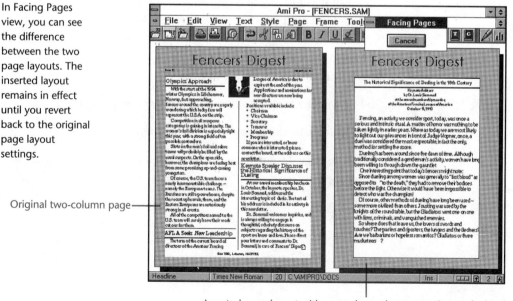

Original two-column page

Inserted page layout with one column, larger margins, and a border

To revert to the original page layout settings, follow these steps:

1. Position the insertion point at the beginning of the inserted layout.

2. Choose **P**age, **I**nsert Page Layout, **R**evert.

To remove an inserted page layout, follow these steps:

1. Position the insertion point within the inserted layout.

2. Choose **P**age, **I**nsert Page Layout, **R**emove.

Modifying Selected Pages

Even when you modify the page layout for an entire document, or insert a page layout for a particular section, you can select the pages you want the changes to affect. You can select any of the following page combinations:

- All pages

- Right-hand pages only (odd pages)

- Left-hand pages only (even pages)

You also can select to **M**irror pages. Mirrored pages use the same layout on both left and right, but the image is reversed. If the left page has a wider margin on the right side, for example, the right page will have the wider margin on the left side. If the left page has a flush left header, the right page will have a flush right header.

Note: *You can use the Mirror option only if you first select Right or Left.*

To select which pages to affect, follow these steps:

1. Choose **P**age, **M**odify Page Layout. The Modify Page Layout dialog box appears.

The Pages options always appear in the lower left of the Modify Page Layout dialog box. Click the option button for the pages that you want to change.

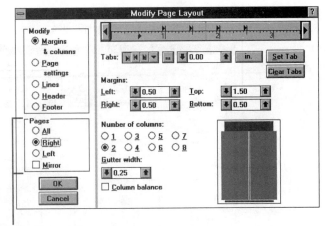

Choose Pages options.

2. Select **A**ll, **R**ight, or **l**eft.

3. If you choose **R**ight or **L**eft and want to mirror-image your pages, select **M**irror.

If you have problems...   If the Mirror image option is dimmed, you selected neither Right nor Left.

---

4. Choose OK.

Choosing a Page Size and Orientation

Orientation

Refers to the way text is printed across a page— either vertically or horizontally.

Perhaps the most basic page layout setting is the page size. In Ami Pro, the default page size is a standard business letter—8-1/2 by 11 inches. The default page *orientation* is Portrait. You can use the Modify Page Layout dialog box to change the page size and orientation.

To change the page size or orientation, follow these steps:

1. Choose **P**age, **M**odify Page Layout. The Modify Page Layout dialog box appears.

2. In the Modify area, choose **P**age Settings. The Page Settings options appear on the right side of the dialog box.

7

As you choose the page settings, you can preview the way the changes affect the page layout.

Click here to display Page Settings options.

Choose a page size.

Enter custom page measurements.

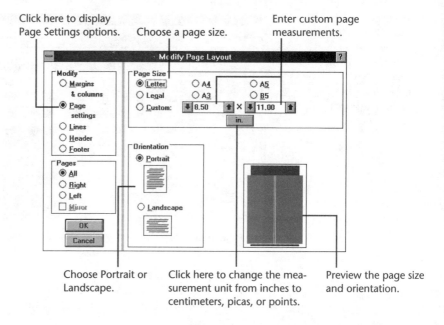

Choose Portrait or Landscape.

Click here to change the measurement unit from inches to centimeters, picas, or points.

Preview the page size and orientation.

3. In the Page Size area, select the page size you want. The actual page dimensions appear in the measurement text boxes, and a sample page appears in the preview area. If you choose Custom, type the measurements in the text boxes.

Landscape
In this mode, text and graphics print vertically on the page.

4. Choose the page orientation you want—either **L**andscape or **P**ortrait.

5. Choose OK.

Portrait
In this mode, text and graphics print horizontally on the page.

Note: Make sure your printer can print the page settings you select. Some printers require special fonts for Landscape printing.

Setting Margins

Margin
The space between the edge of the paper and the edge of the text.

Every page in an Ami Pro document has four *margins*: top, bottom, left and right. By default, margins are shown on-screen in a color different from the document area of the page.

If you have problems...

If the margins on-screen are not shown in a different color, choose **V**iew, View **P**references, then choose Margins in **C**olor, and then choose OK.

Margins are part of the style sheet's page settings. You can change these by modifying the page layout. By changing margin widths, you can change the amount of text that fits on a page. Using smaller margins causes more text to fit on a page, which results in a shorter document. Using larger margins results in a longer document and also leaves room for margin notes or comments, or for binding. Each of the four margins is sized independently.

To change the margin settings, follow these steps:

 1. Choose **P**age, **M**odify Page Layout.

If you have problems...

 If Modify Page Layout is dimmed on the Page menu, you aren't in Layout Mode. Choose **V**iew, **L**ayout Mode and try again.

In the Modify area of the dialog box, choose Margins & Columns to display the margins, columns, and tab settings options in the right side of the dialog box.

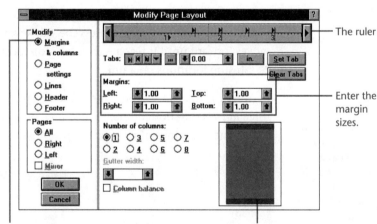

The ruler

Enter the margin sizes.

Click here to display Margins & Columns settings.   View a sample page layout.

2. In the Margins area, enter the size of each margin in the appropriate text box. Notice that the preview of the page layout changes to display the new margin settings.

Note: *By default, margins are measured in inches. Click the measurement button below the ruler to change to centimeters, picas, or points.*

3. Choose OK.

You also can change the left- and right-margin settings by using the ruler in the Modify Page Layout dialog box or on the current ruler. Simply drag the margin markers on the bottom half of the ruler to the desired location.

Left scroll arrow   Right scroll arrow

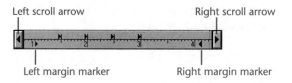

Margin markers appear on the bottom half of the ruler. To change the left- and right-margin settings, drag these markers left or right. If you cannot see the margin markers, click the ruler's scroll arrows.

Left margin marker   Right margin marker

Setting Tabs

In Lesson 6, "Lining Up Your Paragraphs," you learned to change the position of text using alignment and indention. You also can change the position of text on a line by using tabs.

With tabs, you can align text at different tab stop locations across the width of the page. When you press the Tab key, the insertion point moves forward until it reaches a set tab-stop location. You can set up to 22 tab-stop locations on a line.

Tab leader

A series of characters that lead from the location of the insertion point when you press the Tab key to the location of the next tab stop.

In Ami Pro, you can set four kinds of tab stops. You also can select from three *tab leaders*—dotted line, dashed line, or solid line. Table 7.1 describes the four kinds of tab stops.

Table 7.1 Different Tab Types		
Tab Type	**Tab Marker**	**Effect**
Left tab		Left-aligns text at the tab-stop location
Right tab		Right-aligns text at the tab-stop location
Center tab		Centers text evenly around the tab-stop location
Decimal tab		Aligns the decimal point in numbers on the tab-stop location

Tabs and tab leaders are inserted in the document when you press the Tab key. For this example, the horizontal page layout ruler is used to show the tab-stop locations. For more information on using rulers, see the section called "Using Rulers," earlier in this lesson.

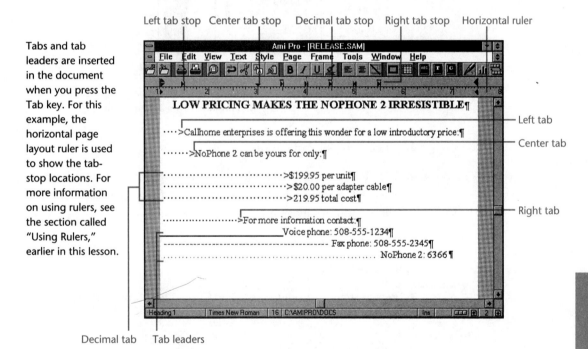

Default tab stops are built into the page-layout settings of style sheets. You change tab settings by using the Modify Page Layout dialog box.

To change tab settings, follow these steps:

1. Choose **P**age, **M**odify Page Layout. The Modify Page Layout dialog box appears.

2. In the Modify area, choose **M**argins & Columns. The margins, columns, and tab settings appear in the right side of the dialog box.

The tab markers appear on the top half of the ruler. The symbols on the tab buttons are the same symbols used to indicate the four tab markers.

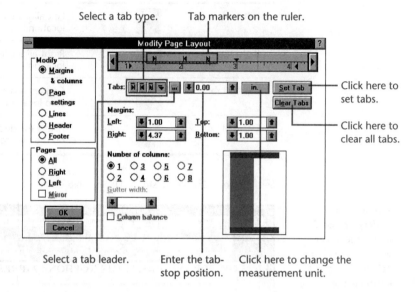

Select a tab type.   Tab markers on the ruler.

Click here to set tabs.

Click here to clear all tabs.

Select a tab leader.   Enter the tab-stop position.   Click here to change the measurement unit.

3. Choose the kind of tab-stop to set.

4. If desired, choose a tab leader type. Click the Tab Leader button to select a solid line, a dotted line, or a dashed line. The leader you choose appears above the tab-stop marker.

5. Type the tab-stop location in the Tabs text box.

6. Choose **S**et Tab.

7. Repeat steps 3 through 6 to set additional tab stops, and then choose OK.

To remove all tabs, choose **C**lear Tabs.

You also can use the mouse to set and clear tabs on the ruler in the Modify Page Layout dialog box, or on the current ruler you can display on-screen. You can follow the following methods:

- To set tabs, select the type of tab and tab leader, then click the top half of the ruler at the tab-stop location. On the current ruler, click any tab marker to display the tab option buttons.

- To move an existing tab, drag the tab marker on the ruler to the new location.

- To remove tabs, drag the tab-stop markers up or down, off the ruler.

    Note: *You cannot place a tab on the ruler in the same location as an existing tab, even if the tab type differs. First, remove the existing tab.*

If you have problems...   If you click on the ruler and Ami Pro doesn't insert a tab stop, you probably are clicking on the bottom half of the ruler. You must set tabs on the top half of the ruler. Try again.

    Note: *If you choose Tabs &* **R***eturns in the View Preferences dialog box, a dotted line followed by an arrow head indicates on-screen where you inserted a tab. If you use a tab leader, the selected leader appears.*

Using Columns

Newspaper-style column
Text flows from the bottom of one column to the top of the next column.

Some documents look best and are easiest to read when divided into columns. With Ami Pro, you can split a page into up to eight *newspaper-style columns*. (If you don't want newspaper-style columns, create a table or chart, not columns. To learn about creating tables, see Lesson 12, "Working with Tables." To learn about creating charts, see Lesson 13, "Working with Charts.")

The style sheet you select when you create a document determines the number of columns on a page. Some style sheets, such as the five newsletter sheets, are formatted with multiple columns. You can use the Modify Page Layout dialog box to change the number of columns in your document, or you can insert a page layout for a section with a different number of columns.

To modify a page layout to include columns, follow these steps:

    1. Choose **P**age, **M**odify Page Layout. The Modify Page Layout dialog box appears.

2. In the Modify area, choose **M**argins & Columns. The margin, tab, and column settings options appear in the right side of the dialog box.

7

Choose the margin and
column settings.

Column margin markers

In the preview area,
you can see how
the page will look
with the column
and gutter width
settings you select.

Choose the number
of columns.

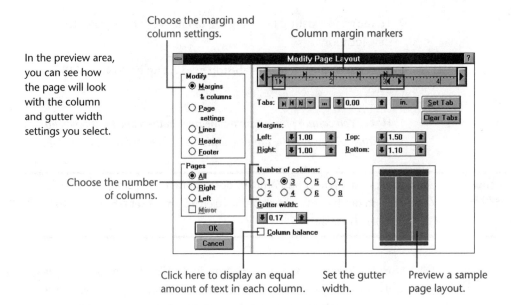

Click here to display an equal
amount of text in each column.

Set the gutter
width.

Preview a sample
page layout.

3. Make your choices, and then choose OK.

Gutter

The space between
columns or be-
tween cells in a
table.

When you divide the page into columns, Ami Pro displays left- and right-margin indicators for each column on the bottom half of the ruler. On the Page Layout ruler, or the current ruler displayed on-screen, you can drag the margin indicators to adjust column and *gutter* widths. You can use the following methods:

- To adjust column width without changing gutter width, position the mouse pointer between the left margin indicator for one column and the right margin indicator for the next column, and drag left or right.

- To adjust both the width of a gutter and a column, drag a margin indicator left or right.

- To adjust gutter width without changing column width, position the mouse pointer between the column's left and right margin markers, and drag until the gutter is the correct width.

Here is the document divided into three columns.

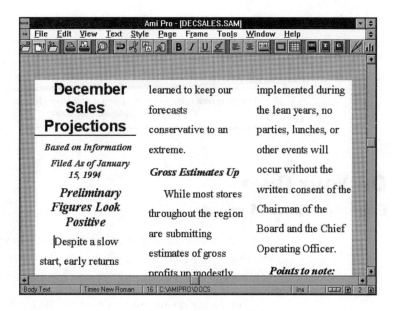

Lesson Summary

To	Do This
Insert a Page Layout	Choose **P**age, **I**nsert Page Layout. Choose **I**nsert. Choose options in the Modify Page Layout dialog box.
Choose a page size and orientation	Choose **P**age, **M**odify Page Layout. Choose **P**age Settings. Choose the Page Size and the Orientation.
Modify margins	Choose **P**age, **M**odify Page Layout. Choose **M**argins & Columns. Enter the margin sizes in each Margins text box.
Modify tabs	Choose **P**age, **M**odify Page Layout. Choose **M**argins & Columns. Choose the type of tab. Choose the type of tab leader. Enter the tab stop location in the Tab text box. Choose Set Tab.
Modify columns	Choose **P**age, **M**odify Page Layout. Choose **M**argins & Columns. Select the number of columns, the gutter width, and whether to balance the columns.
Display the vertical ruler	Choose **V**iew, View **P**references. Choose **V**ertical Ruler.

7

(continues)

To	Do This
Insert a current ruler	Choose **P**age, **R**uler, **I**nsert.
Display a current ruler	Choose **V**iew, Show **R**uler.
Use a current ruler	Drag the margin, tab, or indention markers to the desired location.

On Your Own

Estimated Time: 15 minutes

The exercises in this lesson are designed to help you learn more about creating a page layout. You can use the document created in Lesson 6, "Lining Up Your Paragraphs," or you can create a new document.

1. Open the document you used for the On Your Own exercises in Lesson 6, or use any other document.

2. Check the page size and orientation.

3. At the top of the second page, insert a new page layout. Use the following settings: Left and right margins: 1.5 inches; top and bottom margins, 1.25 inches; three columns.

4. Before the conclusion, revert to the original page layout.

5. At the end of the document, add a paragraph that lists sales figures. Use tab stops to position the text. Use tab leaders for the decimal tabs. Type the following text:

   First line, center text: **Table 12.1 presents sales information.**

   Second line, left aligned: **Table 12.1**; right-aligned: **1/15/94**

   Third, fourth and fifth lines: two columns of decimally aligned dollar values of any amount.

6. On the three-column page, modify the layout to balance the columns.

7. Use the vertical ruler to make the top and bottom margins wider.

8. Insert a current ruler into a body text paragraph on the first page.

9. Use the current ruler to change the margins for that paragraph.

10. Insert a current ruler on the three-column page. Adjust the column and gutter widths.

You can try the following additional exercises:

■ Use the current ruler to adjust the decimal tab settings on the last three lines in the document.

■ Print the document in Landscape mode.

■ Change the three-column page to a two-column page.

7

Making Your Pages Pretty

After you format the basic page layout, you can dress up your pages for a unique and professional look. With Ami Pro, you can easily place headers and footers on your pages, add borders and lines, and add automatic page numbers. In this lesson, you learn how to

- Change the way your document is displayed on-screen.

- Add headers and footers.

- Number pages.

- Insert page and column breaks.

- Add borders and lines.

Changing the Document Display

Using Ami Pro's different views and modes, you can choose the best display for viewing, modifying, or creating a page layout.

In Lesson 2, "Creating a Document," you learned to change from a custom view to a full-page view to prepare for printing. In Ami Pro, you can choose from five views and three display modes to change the way a document is displayed on-screen.

Changing the View

Views determine the size of the characters displayed on-screen by adjusting the amount of magnification. You can select a different view to see how a page will look when printed or to make editing a particular section easier.

Ami Pro offers five views, all accessed from the **V**iew menu.

■ Full Page view is used in Layout mode to display a complete page of the document at one time. This view is useful for checking how text and graphics fit on a page before printing.

Editing in Full Page view is difficult because the text usually is too small. To use Full Page view, choose View, Full Page.

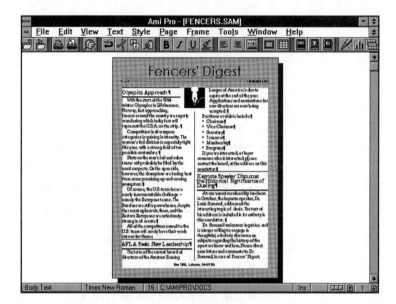

■ Custom view enables you to set a percentage by which the text is magnified for display. By default in Custom view, Ami Pro adjusts the size of the document on-screen so that you can see the full width of the page and read the characters easily. To change the percent of magnification, choose **V**iew, View **P**references, enter the percentage in the Custom **V**iew text box, then choose OK.

Because you can control the size of the characters, Custom view is the easiest view to use for editing. To change to Custom view, choose View, Custom.

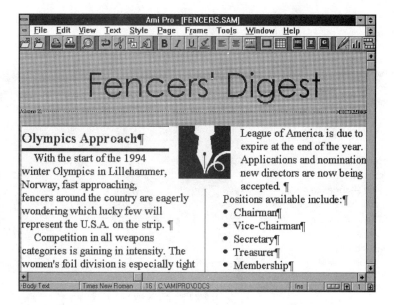

■ Standard view adjusts the document to the size of other Windows documents and files. Usually, the left and right margins are hidden (off the edges of the screen).

Use the scroll bars in Standard view to display the sides of the document. To change to Standard view, choose View, Standard.

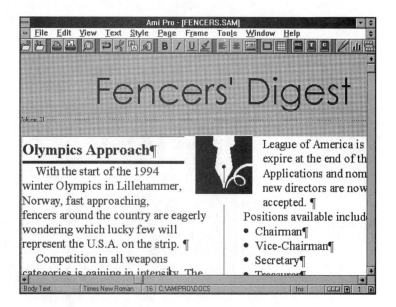

8

■ Enlarged view magnifies the document to 200 times the Standard view.

You can use Enlarged view to look closely at a section of a document, such as when you need to position a frame, edit small text, or make changes to a drawing. To change to Enlarged view, choose View, Enlarged.

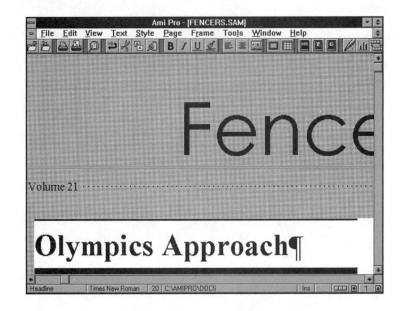

■ Facing Pages view displays two full pages on-screen at the same time in Layout mode. You cannot edit in Facing Pages view.

You can use Facing Pages view to look at the way a page layout or formatting change affects two consecutive pages. To change to Facing Pages view, choose View, Facing Pages. To change back to the previous view, choose Cancel.

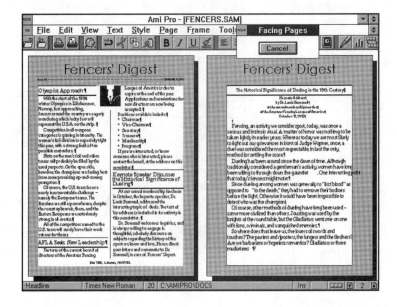

Changing the Mode

In Ami Pro, display modes determine which components of a document appear on-screen, how the components appear, and the options you have for working with the document.

You can change modes at any time while editing, depending on what you are trying to accomplish. Ami Pro provides three modes:

- Layout mode displays a WYSIWYG (what-you-see-is-what-you-get) view of the document. Layout mode is slower than the other modes, because Ami Pro takes time to place all the formatting commands. In Layout mode, you can use any of the five views.

In Layout mode, you can see exactly the way the document prints, including all page, paragraph, and character formatting settings. To change to Layout mode, choose View, Layout Mode.

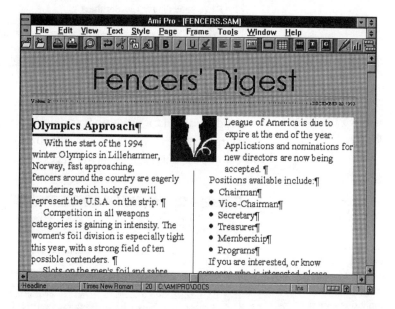

Note: *You must be in Layout mode to modify or insert a page layout.*

- Outline mode displays *only* specified paragraph styles or text. This mode shows no page formatting settings. In Outline mode, you cannot use Full Page or Facing Pages views. In Lesson 17, "Managing Your Files and Documents," you learn how to use Outline mode to outline a document.

8

Outline mode is used for organizing or reorganizing a document. To change to Outline mode, choose View, Outline Mode.

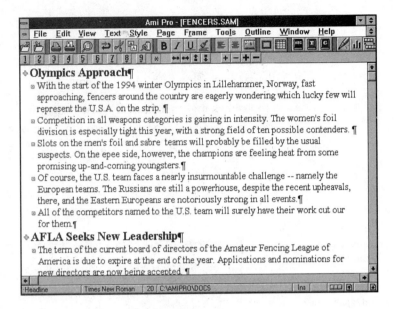

 ■ Draft mode displays a semi-formatted view of the document. Draft mode is useful for entering text quickly when you are not concerned with the way the pages will appear. In Draft mode, you cannot use Full Page or Facing Pages views.

In Draft mode, text attributes and enhancements are displayed, but page formatting settings, such as page breaks, headers, and footers are not. To change to Draft mode, choose View, Draft Mode.

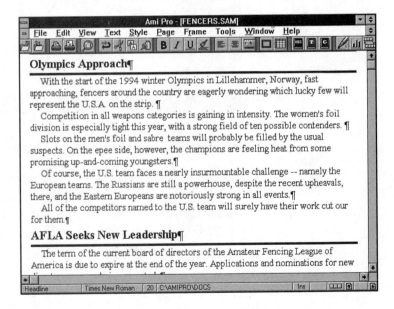

Understanding Headers and Footers

Header
Information that appears in the top margin of a page.

Footer
Information that appears in the bottom margin of a page.

Headers and *footers* are used for displaying information about the document at the top and bottom of each page. Typical header or footer information might include a date, a logo, a company name, an author name, a page number, or a revision number.

With Ami Pro, you can select from three kinds of headers and footers:

- A *fixed* header or footer displays the same information on each page where it appears.

- *Alternating* headers and footers display certain information on all left-hand pages and certain information on all right-hand pages.

- *Floating* headers and footers display different information in different sections of the document.

You can format and edit headers and footers by using the same tools you use in the main document text. You can format, for example, characters with different fonts and attributes, you can use text alignment and indention settings, and you can use the proofreading tools to check the spelling and grammar in headers and footers.

Using Fixed Headers and Footers

You use fixed headers and footers when you want the same header or footer on the same pages throughout the document. Fixed headers and footers can appear on every page, on all pages except the first page, on all right-hand pages, or on all left-hand pages.

To create a fixed header or footer, follow these steps:

1. Choose **View**, **L**ayout Mode to change to Layout mode.

2. Choose **P**age, **M**odify Page Layout.

3. In the Pages area of the Modify Page Layout dialog box, choose the pages on which you want to display the header or footer.

4. In the Modify section, choose either **H**eader or **F**ooter. The header or footer settings options appear in the right side of the dialog box.

8

5. In the **T**op and **B**ottom Margins text boxes, adjust the size of the header or footer, keeping the following points in mind:

   ■ For headers, the Top margin setting measures the distance from the top edge of the page to the top of the header. The Bottom margin setting measures the distance from the bottom edge of the header to the top edge of the document text.

   ■ For footers, the Top margin setting measures the distance from the top edge of the footer to the bottom edge of the document text. The Bottom margin setting measures the distance from the bottom edge of the footer to the bottom of the page.

   ■ The measurements you enter for the header or footer must fit within the size of the current page layout's top or bottom margins.

6. Use the tab and column setting options to set tabs and columns for the header or footer.

7. Use the **L**eft and **R**ight margin settings to adjust the header or footer left and right margins. For example, you can set a header margin to extend beyond the regular text margin.

8. Choose OK.

9. In the document, position the insertion point in the top margin (for headers) or the bottom margin (for footers).

10. Type and format the header or footer text. Ami Pro places the header or footer on the specified pages throughout the document.

If you have problems...

Ami Pro doesn't let you set header or footer sizes that do not fit within the set top and bottom margins. Either adjust the header or footer size to fit in the allotted space, or choose Modify **M**argins & Columns and change the size of your margins.

When you choose
Header or Footer,
the Top and
Bottom margin
settings indicate the
placement of the
header or footer,
not the page's top
and bottom
margins.

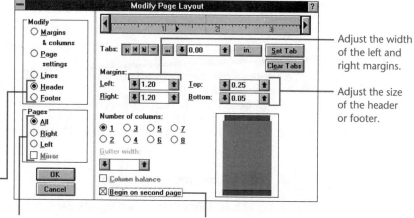

Adjust the width
of the left and
right margins.

Adjust the size
of the header
or footer.

Choose **H**eader
or **F**ooter.

Choose on which pages to place
the header or footer.

Choose to begin the header or footer
on the second page.

You can format the
text in the header
or footer by
applying character
or paragraph
formatting.

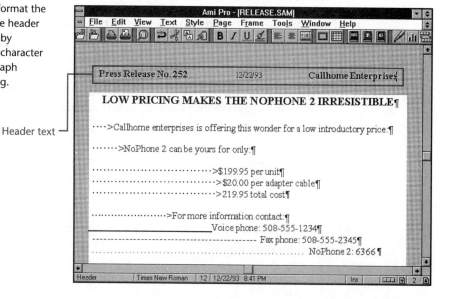

Header text

**If you have
problems...**

If Ami Pro displays a message telling you to go to the second page of the
layout to edit, it means you selected to start the header or footer on the
second page of the document, but you are trying to type the header or
footer in the margin of the first page. Choose OK to get rid of the message
box, then scroll to the next page and type the header or footer there.

8

Using Alternating Headers and Footers

Alternating headers and footers display one set of information on right-hand pages and a different set of information on left-hand pages.

To create an alternating header or footer, follow these steps:

1. Choose **V**iew, **L**ayout Mode to change to Layout mode.

2. Choose **P**age, **M**odify Page Layout. The Modify Page Layout dialog box appears.

3. In the Pages area, choose **R**ight.

4. In the Modify section, choose either **H**eader or **F**ooter. The header or footer settings options appear in the right side of the dialog box.

5. In the **T**op and **B**ottom Margins text boxes, adjust the size of the header or footer.

6. Use the tab and column setting options to set tabs and columns for the header or footer.

7. Use the **L**eft and **R**ight margin settings to adjust the header or footer left and right margins. For example, you can set a header margin to extend beyond the regular text margin.

8. Choose OK.

9. In the document, position the insertion point in the top margin (for headers) or the bottom margin (for footers) of a right-hand page.

10. Type and format the header or footer text that you want displayed on right-hand pages.

11. Repeat steps 9 and 10 on a left-hand page.

In Facing Pages view, you can see that the right and left pages have different headers.

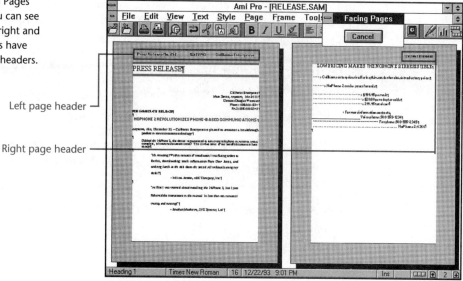

Left page header —

Right page header —

Note: *When you select Right in the Pages area, Ami Pro automatically assumes you will also enter a left-hand header or footer. You only need to go back to the Modify Page Layout dialog box if you want the left-hand page header or footer to have different tab, margin, or column settings. To omit a left-hand header or footer, do not enter text in the left-hand top or bottom margins.*

Using Floating Headers and Footers

Use floating headers and footers if you want different headers or footers to appear in different sections of your document. For example, in a book, you can display a different header and footer in each chapter.

When you create a floating header or footer, Ami Pro inserts a non-printing header or footer mark into the document text at the insertion point location. If the mark is on the first line of a page, the header or footer begins on that page. Otherwise, the header or footer appears on pages following the page with the header or footer mark.

 Note: *To display header or footer marks, choose **V**iew, View **P**references, then choose **M**arks in the View Preferences dialog box.*

8

Ami Pro displays the floating header or footer until it comes to another header or footer mark. You can create a new floating header or footer as often as you want, even on every page.

Note: *Use the Modify Page Layout dialog box to choose header or footer settings before creating a floating header or footer.*

To create a floating header or footer, follow these steps:

1. Position the insertion point in the document text where you want the floating header or footer to start. Ami Pro inserts a header or footer mark at this location.

2. Choose **P**age, **H**eader/Footer. The Headers & Footers dialog box appears.

3. Choose **F**loating Header/Footer. The Floating Header/Footer dialog box appears.

4. From the dialog box, choose among the following options:

    ■ **I**nsert, to add either a floating header or a floating footer.

    ■ **A**ll Pages, to enter a floating header or footer to appear on all pages.

    ■ **R**ight Pages, to enter the right-page header or footer for an alternating floating header or footer.

    ■ **L**eft Pages, to enter the left-page header or footer for an alternating floating header or footer.

5. Choose OK. Ami Pro inserts the header or footer mark.

6. In the margin, type and format the header or footer text.

In the Floating Header/Footer dialog box, you choose to insert or remove a floating header or footer.

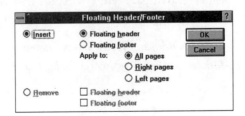

Because the floating header was inserted on the first line of this page, the header is displayed on this page. The footer begins on the next page. Choose Marks in the View Preferences dialog box to see the header and footer marks.

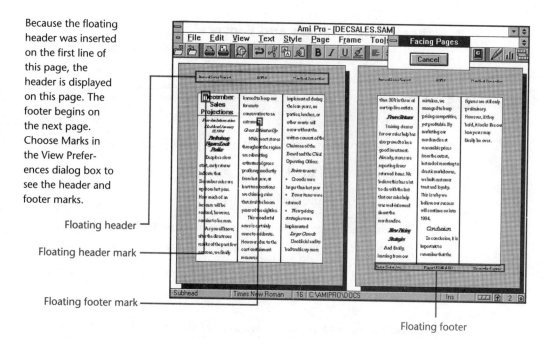

Floating header

Floating header mark

Floating footer mark

Floating footer

If you have problems...

If a floating header or footer appears on a different page than the one you originally placed it on, it means you edited the document after creating the headers or footers. The added or deleted text caused the floating header to move forward or backward in the document, thereby appearing on a different page. To avoid this, do not create floating headers or footers until you have completed editing or formatting the document.

If you have problems...

If you try to create a floating header or footer, but Ami Pro displays the message "Cannot display the header/footer requested," you inserted a floating header or footer mark on the last page of the document. Ami Pro cannot display the header or footer on the page following the header or footer mark, because there are no more pages. Either write more or put the floating header or footer on an earlier page. This message may also appear if you have placed more than one header/footer on the same page.

8

Removing Headers and Footers

You can easily remove all kinds of headers and footers. To delete a floating header or footer, follow these steps:

1. Choose **M**arks in the View Preferences dialog box to show the header and footer marks on-screen.

2. Position the insertion point on the mark you want to remove.

3. Choose **P**age, **H**eader/Footer.

4. Choose **F**loating Header/Footer.

5. Choose **R**emove, then choose the Floating **H**eader or Floating **F**ooter check box, depending on the mark you are going to delete.

6. Choose OK. Ami Pro deletes the mark from the text and the floating header or footer text from the margin.

Note: *You can remove floating headers and footers by cutting the text that contains the header or footer mark. Ami Pro displays a warning box telling you that you are about to delete a header or footer. Choose OK to cut the header or footer along with the text.*

To delete a fixed or alternating header or footer, simply position the insertion point in the header or footer margin and delete the text.

Numbering Pages

If a document is more than one page in length, you should probably number the pages. With Ami Pro, you can start numbering on any page, you can start numbering with any number, and you can precede the number with text, such as the word "Page." In addition, Ami Pro lets you choose from a variety of numbering schemes.

With Ami Pro you can automatically insert page numbers into the top or bottom margins or into headers or footers.

To insert page numbers, follow these steps:

1. Choose **V**iew, **L**ayout Mode.

2. Position the insertion point in the top or bottom margin or the header or footer of any page.

3. Choose **P**age, **P**age Numbering.

Ami Pro auto-
matically numbers
the pages in
your document
according to
the options you
choose in the
Page Numbering
dialog box.

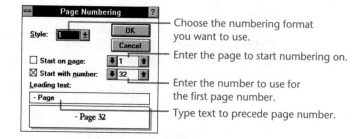

Choose the numbering format
you want to use.

Enter the page to start numbering on.

Enter the number to use for
the first page number.

Type text to precede page number.

4. If you don't want the page numbers to start on the first page of the document, select Start on **P**age and enter the number of the page to start on in the text box beside it.

5. If your first page isn't page one (for example, if the document is chapter two in a book, the first page of the document may not be page one), select Start with **N**umber and enter the number to use in the text box beside it.

6. If you want text to precede the page number, type the text in the **L**eading Text box. Include all necessary spaces.

7. If you want a numbering scheme other than numbers (such as Roman Numerals or letters of the alphabet), select a different scheme from the **S**tyle drop-down list.

8. Choose OK.

Adding Breaks

Ami Pro automatically breaks pages and columns according to the page size, column width, and other page and paragraph formatting settings. Sometimes, however, the automatic breaks come at awkward points in the text. For example, sometimes a break leaves a section heading at the bottom of a page, or a single word alone on a line at the top of a column.

To overcome these awkward breaks, you can insert page and column breaks into your document wherever you think they should be.

8

When Ami Pro inserts a break, it inserts a nonprinting break mark into the text. To display the break marks on-screen, choose **M**arks in the View Preferences dialog box.

Note: *Column break marks appear at the beginning of the paragraph into which the break was inserted.*

To insert a page or column break, follow these steps:

1. Position the insertion point in your document where you want to begin the new page or column.

2. Choose **P**age, **B**reaks.

In the Breaks dialog box, choose the type of break you want to insert or remove.

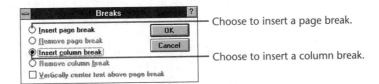

Choose to insert a page break.

Choose to insert a column break.

3. To insert a page break, choose **I**nsert Page Break.

4. To insert a column break, choose Insert **C**olumn Break.

5. Choose OK. Ami Pro breaks the page or the column at the insertion point location by moving the following paragraph to the next page or column.

Note: *If the page preceding the new break looks top-heavy, choose the* **V**ertically Center Text Above Page Break *check box in the Breaks dialog box. Ami Pro centers the text on the preceding page equally between the top and bottom margins.*

If you have problems...

If the page or column breaks in the wrong place, you probably positioned the insertion point one line too low or one line too high in the document text. Remove the break and try again, adjusting the position of the insertion point first.

Here, a column
break moves a
subheading to the
top of the next
column.

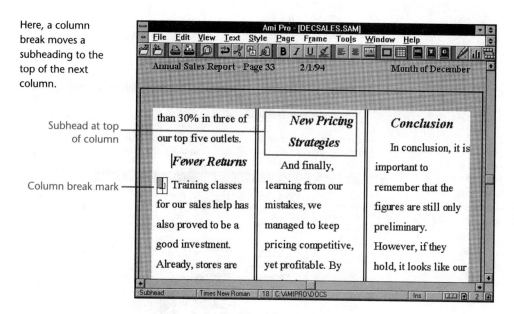

Subhead at top
of column

Column break mark

To remove a break, follow these steps:

1. Position the insertion point on the break mark or in the paragraph that contains the break mark.

2. Choose **P**age, **B**reaks.

3. Choose either **R**emove Page Break or Remove Column **B**reak.

4. Choose OK.

Adding Borders and Lines

For a special look, you can use Ami Pro to add borders and lines to a page. Using lines to box a page or set off a side or two gives your document the appearance of a professional publication.

Ami Pro places lines within the margins, according to the location you select.

8

To add lines to your page layout, follow these steps:

1. Choose **P**age, **M**odify Page Layout.

2. In the Modify area, choose **L**ines. The Lines settings appear in the right side of the dialog box.

You can place lines around the entire page, on any side, or between columns, and you can select a line style and a color.

Choose in which margins to place lines.

Choose where in the margin to place the lines.

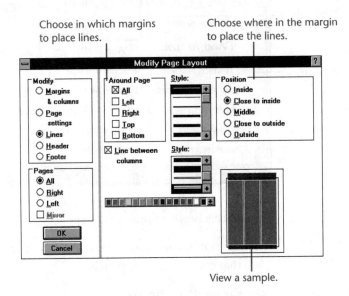

View a sample.

3. Choose:

   ■ In which margins you want to place the lines.

   ■ The line style.

   ■ Where in the margin you want to place the line.

   ■ The line color.

   ■ To put a line between columns.

   ■ The width of the line between columns.

4. Choose OK.

Ami Pro adds the
lines to your
document.

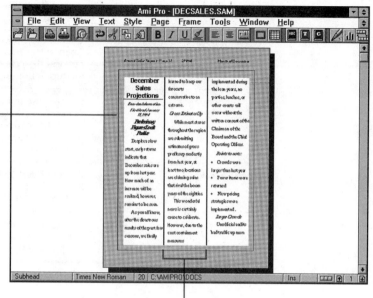

Border around page, close
to the inside of the margin

Double lines between columns

To remove borders or lines, follow these steps:

1. Choose **P**age, **M**odify Page Layout.

2. In the Modify area of the dialog box, choose **L**ines.

3. Deselect all options in the Around Page area.

4. Deselect the **L**ine Between Columns check box.

5. Choose OK.

Lesson Summary

To	Do This
Change the document display	Choose **V**iew, then choose the view or mode.
Add a fixed header or footer	Choose **P**age, **M**odify Page Layout. Choose **H**eader or **F**ooter. Set top and bottom margin measurements. Choose OK. Type text in top or bottom margins.

8

(continues)

To	Do This
Add a floating header or footer	Choose **P**age, **H**eader/Footer. Choose **F**loating Header/Footer. Select the page options, then choose OK. Type the text in the top or bottom margin.
Number pages	Position insertion point in the header or footer. Choose **P**age, **P**age Numbering. Select the numbering style, starting page, starting number, and type leading text. Choose OK.
Add breaks	Position insertion point. Choose **P**age, **B**reaks. Select page break or column break and choose OK.
Add lines	Choose **P**age, **M**odify Page Layout. Choose **L**ines. Select the location, the line style, and the position within the margin. Choose OK.

On Your Own

These exercises are designed to help you learn to use page layout and formatting features. You can use the document created in the exercises in Lessons 6 and 7, or you can use your own document.

Add Headers and Footers
Estimated Time: 5 minutes

1. Open the document you want to format.

2. Add a header.

3. Add a footer.

Add Page Numbers
Estimated Time: 5 minutes

1. Add page numbers to the footer.

2. Include the word *Page* before the page number.

Insert Breaks
Estimated Time: 5 minutes

1. Modify the layout into three columns.

2. Insert a column break.

Add Lines and Borders
Estimated Time: 5 minutes

1. Add lines between the columns.

2. Add a border around the page.

Change the View
Estimated Time: 5 minutes

1. Change to Full Page view to see the pages as they will print.

2. Change to Facing Pages view to see the header and footer in place.

Try these other exercises to further enhance your skills:

- Insert a different layout.

- Add a floating header to the inserted layout pages.

8

Part III
Customizing and Adding Nontext Elements to Documents

Lesson 9

Customizing Ami Pro

Ami Pro is a flexible program. You can easily adjust many settings and options to suit your own work habits. In this lesson, you learn to customize Ami Pro to make the time you spend at your computer more efficient and productive.

Specifically, you learn how to

- Create and modify styles.

- Create and modify style sheets.

- Customize SmartIcons.

- Change program defaults.

- Set startup options.

- Choose the options you want displayed on-screen.

Using Styles

Style sheet
A collection of paragraph styles and page layout commands used to create a particular type of document.

In Ami Pro, every document is based on a *style sheet*, and every style sheet comes with built-in paragraph *styles*.

Sometimes, however, the styles that are built into the style sheet you are using may not be exactly right for the document you are creating.

Style
A collection of character and paragraph formatting commands you can apply all at once to a paragraph or series of paragraphs.

In Lesson 5, "Dressing Up Your Text," and Lesson 6, "Lining Up Your Paragraphs," you learned that you can go through the entire document and change the formatting of selected text, but that takes a lot of time. With Ami Pro, you can change an existing style or create a new style to add to the style sheet.

Modifying Styles

Changing the format of a document you've already created is simple. As long as you used styles to format the text, all you have to do is change the styles.

To modify an existing style, follow these steps:

1. Choose **S**tyle, **M**odify Style. Alternatively, press Ctrl+A.

Choose the style to modify.　　　　Choose the options to change.

Use the Modify Style dialog box, to change the formatting characteristics of any style associated with the current style sheet.

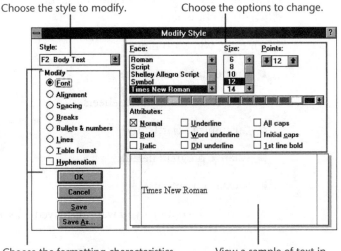

Choose the formatting characteristics you want to change.

View a sample of text in the modified style.

2. From the Style list, select the style you want to modify.

3. In the Modify area, select the formatting characteristics you want to change. The formatting options appear in the right side of the dialog box. Table 9.1 describes the Modify options.

4. Make the changes you want.

5. Choose OK.

Every paragraph in the document that was formatted with the modified style is changed.

Table 9.1. Modify Options

Choose	To
Font	Change the font, font size, font color, or character attributes.
Ali**g**nment	Change tabs, indents, and alignments.
S**p**acing	Change the amount of space left between lines, paragraphs, or characters.
Breaks	Assign page and column break locations.
Bull**e**ts & Numbers	Add bullets or numbers; change the appearance of bullets or numbers; set spacing and attributes for bullets or numbers.
Lines	Add lines above or below paragraphs; change position of lines, length of lines, or color of lines.
Table Format	Set formats for table cells; select symbols for currency, decimals, and thousands separator; change position of minus signs and decimal points.
Hyphenation	Automatically hyphenate words within the paragraph.

Note: *You can modify a style before you begin typing the document so that the document looks the way you want it right from the start. However, styles can be changed at any time.*

If you have problems...   If you modify a style, but some paragraphs do not reflect the changes, you probably modified the character formatting by using the Text menu. Use the Text menu commands again to change the formatting back to Normal.

9

Creating a Style

If the style sheet you're using does not include a style you need, you can create one. By creating a style, you can make sure your document is exactly the way you want it.

Note: *You can save time by selecting text that contains the formatting settings you want to include in the new style before you create the style.*

To create a style, follow these steps:

1. Choose **S**tyle, **C**reate Style.

Type a style name.

Base your new style
on an existing style
with similar
characteristics.

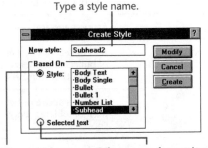

Select to use formatting settings
from an existing style.

Select to use formatting settings
from selected text.

2. In the **N**ew Style text box, type a name for the new style.

3. In the Based On area, choose whether to base the new style on an existing style or on selected text.

▪ Choose **S**tyle if an existing style has similar formatting settings to the style you are creating.

▪ Choose Selected **T**ext if you've selected text with the formatting settings you want in the new style.

4. Depending on the choice you made in step 3, do one of the following:

▪ If you based the style on selected text, choose **C**reate. Ami Pro creates a new style using the formatting settings in the selected text and adds it to the style sheet's Styles list and Styles box. You can apply it to text throughout the document.

■ If you based the style on an existing style, choose Modify. Ami Pro creates a new style with the same formatting settings as the existing style and adds it to the style sheet's Styles list and Styles box. Modify the settings to create the customized style you want. (For information on modifying a style, see the previous section.)

 To quickly modify the current style, use the Define a Paragraph Style SmartIcon. Select the text that has the attributes you want to include in the modified style, then choose the Define a Paragraph Style SmartIcon. Ami Pro warns you that it is about to change the current style. Choose **Y**es.

Creating or Modifying Style Sheets

When you create or modify a style, the style is stored with the current document, but not with the current style sheet. If you create a new document with the same style sheet, the new or modified style is not included.

To save a style with a style sheet in order to use it again in another document, you must either create a new style sheet or modify the existing one.

Note: *Be careful when you modify one of Ami Pro's style sheets! The changes affect all future documents you created with that style sheet. Unless you're sure you want the changes to be permanent, you should create a new style sheet instead of modifying an existing one.*

To create or modify a style sheet, follow these steps:

1. Modify the styles and the page layout so they reflect the settings you want to include in the new or modified style sheet. For information on modifying the page layout, see Lesson 7, "Setting Up Pages," and Lesson 8, "Making Your Pages Pretty."

2. Choose **S**tyle, Sa**v**e as a Style Sheet.

9

Enter a new style sheet name.

Use the Save as a
Style Sheet dialog
box when you want
to create a new
style sheet or make
permanent changes
to an existing one.

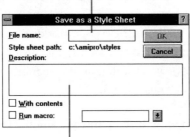

Enter a description.

3. Do one of the following:

■ To modify the current style sheet, choose OK. Ami Pro displays a message warning you that you are about to overwrite
an existing style sheet. Choose **Y**es. Changes you have made
to styles and the page layout become a permanent part of the
current style sheet.

■ To create a new style sheet, enter a new style sheet name in
the **F**ile Name text box, then choose OK. When you create a
new document, you can choose the new style sheet from the
Style Sheet for New Document list in the New dialog box.

Customizing SmartIcons

As you have learned, Ami Pro comes with many SmartIcons that make
using Ami Pro as simple as clicking a mouse. The SmartIcons come pre-
arranged into groups, or sets, which you can display depending on the
type of work you are doing. For example, Ami Pro comes with SmartIcons
already grouped for editing, creating graphics, proofing documents, and
creating tables.

To choose a set of SmartIcons to display, click the SmartIcon button on
the right end of the status bar.

Choose a set of
SmartIcons to
display on the
SmartIcon bar.

Choose a set to display on the SmartIcon bar. ──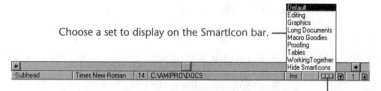

Click here to display a list of SmartIcon sets.

Most of the choices you make regarding SmartIcons take place in the
SmartIcon dialog box. To display the SmartIcon dialog box, choose
Tools, SmartIcons.

Select an icon set.

You can use the
SmartIcons dialog
box to change the
way Ami Pro groups
and displays
SmartIcons.

All available icons
are listed.

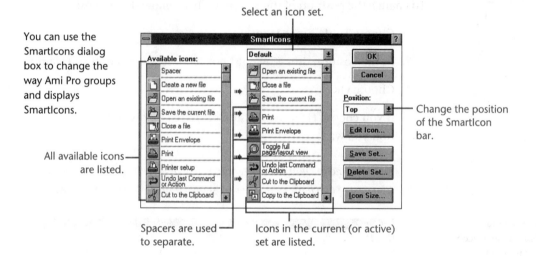

Change the position
of the SmartIcon
bar.

Spacers are used
to separate.

Icons in the current (or active)
set are listed.

You can create your own SmartIcon sets, change the existing groups, or
switch between different groups so the SmartIcons you use most often
display when you need them. You can also change the way SmartIcons
display on your screen, change their order on the SmartIcon bar, or
choose not to display them at all.

To remove the SmartIcon bar from the screen, choose **View**, Hide
SmartIcons. To display it again, choose **View**, Show SmartIcons. The
advantage of hiding the SmartIcon bar is that more of the document
displays on the screen.

Note: *To quickly switch back and forth between showing and hiding the
SmartIcon bar, press Ctrl+Q.*

9

Moving the SmartIcon Bar

You can choose to display the SmartIcon bar in one of five ways:

- Across the top of your screen (the default position)

- Along the left side of your screen

- Along the right side of your screen

- Across the bottom of your screen

- Floating anywhere you want, horizontally on the screen.

To change the position of the SmartIcon bar, follow these steps:

1. Choose Tools, SmartIcons.

2. In the Position drop-down list box, choose the location you want.

3. Choose OK.

4. If you choose Floating, size and drag the SmartIcon bar to the location you want.

   Note: *You can change the size and shape of a floating SmartIcon bar the same way you change the size and shape of any Windows window.*

You can drag a floating SmartIcon bar to position it anywhere on the screen.

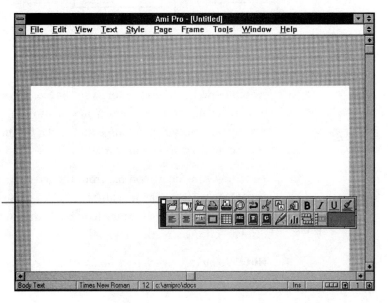

Click here to hide the SmartIcon bar.

Changing the Order of Icons in a Set

SmartIcons display in the dialog box active set list in the same order they display on the SmartIcon bar. Sometimes, a set of SmartIcons is so large that not all icons fit on the screen at once. If an icon you often use doesn't fit on the screen, you can change its location on the SmartIcon bar.

To change the order of SmartIcons, follow these steps:

1. Choose Tools, SmartIcons.

2. In the SmartIcon Set list box, select the set you want to reorder.

3. Drag the icon you're moving until it covers the icon you want it to come before. Ami Pro rearranges the SmartIcons in the dialog box.

4. Choose OK.

Ami Pro rearranges the SmartIcons on the SmartIcon bar.

Adding or Removing SmartIcons from a Set

To add or remove SmartIcons from the current set, follow these steps:

1. Choose Tools, SmartIcons.

2. In the SmartIcon Set list box, select the set you want to change.

3. To add an icon, drag it from the Available Icons list to the current icon set list.

4. To remove an icon, drag it from the current icon set list.

5. Choose OK.

Spacers
Small rectangles that are used to separate and group associated icons.

You can add and remove *spacers* to SmartIcon sets the same way you add and remove SmartIcons.

Note: *You can include the same SmartIcons in as many sets as you want. The list of available SmartIcons always remains the same.*

Creating a SmartIcon Set

To create your own SmartIcon set, follow these step:

1. Choose Tools, SmartIcons.

9

2. Select a SmartIcon set similar to the one you want to create.

3. Add and remove SmartIcons and spacers until you have the set you want.

4. Choose **S**ave Set. The Save SmartIcon Set dialog box appears. A set name may appear in the **N**ame of SmartIcon Set text box.

In the Save SmartIcon Set dialog box, give a name and a file name to the set of SmartIcons you have arranged.

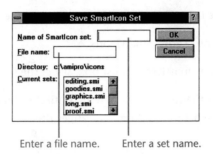

Enter a file name.   Enter a set name.

5. Choose OK after you enter a set name. You can enter a file name, or Ami Pro automatically assigns one by adding an SMI extension to the set name.

6. In the SmartIcons dialog box, choose OK.

The new set is added to the list of SmartIcon sets.

Deleting a SmartIcon Set

To delete a SmartIcon set, follow these steps:

1. Choose Too**l**s, Smart**I**cons.

2. Choose **D**elete Set. The Delete Sets dialog box appears.

3. Choose the set you want to delete.

4. Choose OK.

Ami Pro deletes the set.

Note: *Ami Pro does not warn you before deleting the selected set. Be sure you selected the right set before you choose OK.*

Changing the Size of SmartIcons

You can display SmartIcons in one of three sizes: Small, Medium, or Large.

To change the SmartIcon size, follow these steps:

1. Choose Tools, SmartIcons.

2. Choose Icon Size. The Icon Size dialog box appears.

3. Choose Small, Medium, or Large. You see a sample of the icon as it will be displayed in the bottom right corner of the dialog box.

4. Choose OK.

Setting Program Defaults

Ami Pro is set up to run using common program options. As you become familiar with Ami Pro, you may find that the common options are not the best for your needs. You can change the program default settings to customize Ami Pro to your work environment.

To change the program defaults, choose Tools, User Setup. Table 9.2 describes the options in the User Setup dialog box.

Choose File Saving options.

In the User Setup dialog box, you can customize Ami Pro to work the way you want.

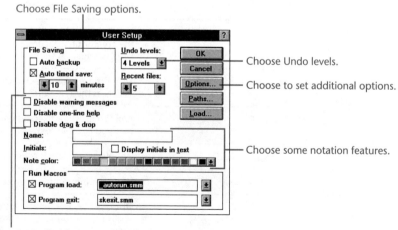

Choose Undo levels.

Choose to set additional options.

Choose some notation features.

Choose to disable some options.

9

Table 9.2. User Setup Options

Option	Effect
Auto **B**ackup	When you save the document, Ami Pro saves a duplicate copy on disk in the specified backup directory.
Auto Timed Save	Ami Pro automatically saves the active document at the specified time interval, releasing you from the burden of remembering to save. The file must be manually saved before Auto Timed Save works.
Undo Levels	Specifies the number of successive actions or commands you can undo using the Edit, Undo command.
Recent Files	Specifies the number of file names displayed at the bottom of the File menu.
Disable Warning Messages	Prevents Ami Pro from displaying messages on-screen to warn you when you are about to perform an action that may result in data loss.
Disable One-Line **H**elp	Prevents Ami Pro from displaying descriptions of commands in the title bar.
Disable **D**rag-and-Drop	Prevents you from copying and moving selected text by using drag-and-drop editing.
Name	Ami Pro uses the name entered here to prevent unauthorized users from editing documents. Ami Pro automatically enters the name you entered during installation.
Initials	Ami Pro uses the initials entered here to identify the creator of a document or a note, if the Display initials in the text check box is selected.
Display Initials in **T**ext	Select this option to automatically include your initials in the text when you add a note.
Note **C**olor	Ami Pro uses the selected color to identify notes that you enter in text.
Pro**g**ram Load	Upon startup, Ami Pro runs the selected macro.
Program **E**xit	Upon exiting, Ami Pro runs the selected macro.
Options	Displays the User Setup Options dialog box for setting typographic and speed defaults.

Option	Effect
Paths	Displays the Default Paths dialog box for specifying default directories for storing documents, style sheets, macros, SmartIcons, and automatic backups.
Load	Displays the Load Defaults dialog box for selecting the view, mode, and style sheet list settings to be displayed upon startup.

Choose the default mode.

Use the Load
Defaults dialog box
to specify startup
display options.
Choose Tools, User
Setup, Load to
display the Load
Defaults dialog box.

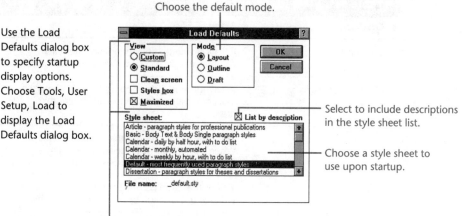

Select to include descriptions
in the style sheet list.

Choose a style sheet to
use upon startup.

Choose the default view.

Setting View Preferences

Throughout this book, you have used the View Preferences dialog box to
change the appearance of Ami Pro on your screen. In the View Preferences dialog box, you can choose which options you want to appear on
your screen, and which options you want to hide.

To display the View Preferences dialog box, choose **V**iew, View **P**references. When you have finished selecting or deselecting options, choose
OK. Table 9.3 describes the options in the View Preferences dialog box.

Use the View
Preferences dialog
box to select the
items you want to
display on your
screen.

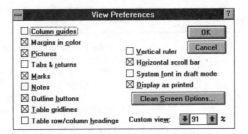

Table 9.3. View Preferences Options	
Option	**Effect**
Column **G**uides	In Layout mode, this option indicates each column margin by using a faint dotted line.
Margins in **C**olor	In Layout mode, this option displays all margins in a color different from the document text area.
Pictures	This option displays graphics in documents. When this option is not selected, Ami Pro displays an X where graphics would be.
Tabs & **R**eturns	This option displays nonprinting symbols to indicate the location of paragraphs and tabs.
Marks	This option displays nonprinting symbols to indicate the location of column and page breaks, inserted rulers, inserted page layouts, and floating headers and footers.
Notes	This option displays notes in the document as small, colored rectangles.
Outline **B**uttons	In Outline view, this option displays the buttons indicating that text contains additional subheadings.
Table Gridlines	This option displays faint dotted lines between rows and columns in tables.
Table Row/Column **H**eadings	This option displays numbers and letters to identify rows and columns in a table.
Vertical Ruler	This option displays the vertical ruler on the left side of the screen.
H**o**rizontal Scroll Bar	This option displays the horizontal scroll bar at the bottom of the window.

Option	Effect
System **F**ont in Draft Mode	In draft mode, this option displays text in the Windows system font instead of the selected style font.
Display as Printed	This option displays the document on-screen as it will print, including fonts, line breaks, and pagination.
Custom Vie**w**	This option sets the magnification percentage for displaying the document in custom view.
Clean **S**creen Options	This option displays the Clean Screen Options dialog box, where you can set the screen elements that you want to display on a Clean Screen. To display a Clean Screen, choose **V**iew, Show Clean Scree**n**.

In the Clean Screen Options dialog box, select the screen elements you want to display when you use a Clean Screen. To use a Clean Screen, choose View, Show Clean Screen.

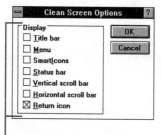

Choose the screen elements to display.

Lesson Summary

To	Do This
Modify a style	Choose **S**tyle, **M**odify Style. Select the formatting characteristics to change. Make the changes.
Create a style based on selected text	Select the text. Choose **S**tyle, **C**reate Style. Enter a **N**ew style name. Choose Based on Selected **t**ext. Choose **C**reate.
Create a style based on a style	Choose **S**tyle, **C**reate Style. Enter a **N**ew style name. Choose Based on **S**tyle. Select the style. Choose Modify. Modify the style settings.

(continues)

9

To	Do This
Create a style sheet	Modify the styles and page layout. Choose **S**tyle, Sa**v**e as a Style Sheet. Enter a new style sheet name.
Add or remove SmartIcons	Choose Too**l**s, Smart**I**cons. Select the set. To add icons, drag them from the Available icons list to the current icon set list. To remove icons, drag them off of the current icon set list.
Create a SmartIcon set	Choose Too**l**s, Smart**I**cons. Add and remove SmartIcons and spacers to the current set list. Choose **S**ave Set. Enter a SmartIcon set name.
Change program defaults	Choose Too**l**s, **U**ser Setup.
Set View Preferences	Choose **V**iew, View **P**references.

On Your Own

These exercises are designed to help you become familiar with the topics covered in this lesson.

Modify a Style
Estimated Time: 10 minutes

1. Create a new document or open an existing document. For example, open a document you created in a previous lesson.

2. If the document is new, type text using different styles. Create a title, a subheading, and some body text paragraphs.

3. Change the body text style so that the font is in a larger font size and the first line of each paragraph is indented from the left margin.

4. Change the subhead style so that all subheads are centered on the page and underlined.

Create a Style
Estimated Time: 10 minutes

1. Create a new style to use for entering quotes. Indent the text from both the left and right margins. Use justified alignment and single line spacing.

2. Enter a quote using the new style.

Create a Style Sheet
Estimated Time: 10 minutes

1. Change the page layout of the document by increasing the left and right margins and adding lines along the margins.

2. Save the modified page layout and the modified styles as a new style sheet.

3. Open a new document using the new style sheet.

Customize SmartIcons
Estimated Time: 5 minutes

1. Create a new SmartIcon set to use with the new style sheet.

2. Display the new SmartIcon set along the left margin.

Set Program Defaults
Estimated Time: 5 minutes

1. Adjust your user setup so that you can undo up to four levels of actions or commands.

2. Set Ami Pro to automatically save the current file every five minutes.

9

3. Set Ami Pro to display the five most recently opened files at the bottom of the File menu.

Set Startup Options
Estimated Time: 5 minutes

1. Set Ami Pro to display only style sheet names in the New file dialog box.

2. Set Ami Pro to start in Custom mode with the Styles box displayed on the screen.

Set View Preferences
Estimated Time: 5 minutes

1. Set Ami Pro to display marks, tabs & returns, and notes.

2. Change the custom view magnification so the document appears larger.

3. Set Clean Screen Options so that when Clean Screen is selected, only the SmartIcon bar and the status bar display.

Lesson 10

Working with Frames

You use frames in Ami Pro to position special objects within a document and to help organize text on a page. Frames can hold many kinds of objects, including graphics, tables, charts, headers, footers, and text.

You can place a frame anywhere on a page, with text above, below, or flowing around it. In addition, you can move, resize, delete, and layer a frame.

In this lesson, you learn to

- Create a frame.

- Enter text and graphics in a frame.

- Size and position a frame.

- Copy and move a frame.

- Delete a frame.

- Layer frames.

Creating Frames

Frame
A box that contains a picture or text within a document. Use frames to emphasize or position objects on a page.

In Ami Pro, you use a *frame* to define an area on a page that you can manipulate independent from the rest of the document's contents. A frame can contain text or graphics you can format separately from the document around it.

You can create a frame in two ways:

■ By manually drawing the frame on your screen.

■ By specifying the dimensions and letting Ami Pro draw it.

Creating a Frame Automatically

If you know the exact dimensions you want to use for the frame, or if the frame must be placed at an exact location on a page, you can create the frame automatically.

Creating a frame automatically is more precise than creating a frame by hand. It is useful when you need to create a frame for an existing object, such as a photograph you've scanned, or when you need to position an object in an exact location, such as a barcode on a postcard.

To create a frame automatically:

1. Choose **F**rame, **C**reate Frame.

Ami Pro will create a frame to your specifications.

Enter the position of the upper left corner from the top margin.

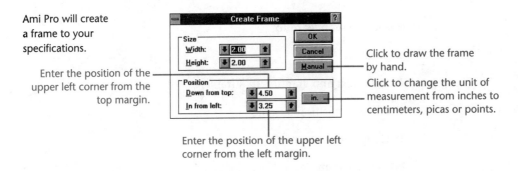

Click to draw the frame by hand.

Click to change the unit of measurement from inches to centimeters, picas or points.

Enter the position of the upper left corner from the left margin.

2. In the Create Frame dialog box, specify the size and position of the frame

3. Choose OK.

Ami Pro creates and
selects the frame.

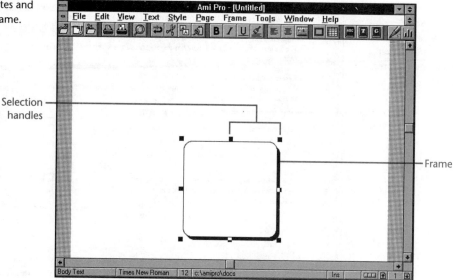

Selection
handles

Frame

Creating a Frame by Hand

You can create a frame easily by using the mouse to draw it on-screen.
Drawing the frame gives you more flexibility in sizing and positioning,
but it's not as exact as creating a frame automatically.

To create a frame by hand, follow these steps:

1. Choose F**r**ame, **C**reate Frame.

2. Choose **M**anual. The dialog box disappears, and the mouse pointer
   changes to the Add a Frame pointer.

3. Position the pointer where you want to locate the top left corner of
   the frame.

4. Press and hold the mouse button, and drag the pointer to where
   you want to locate the bottom right corner of the frame.

5. When the frame is the size you want, release the mouse button.

As you drag, a box bordered by dashed lines appears on-screen, indicating the area of the frame.

Top left corner of frame

Frame border

Mouse pointer

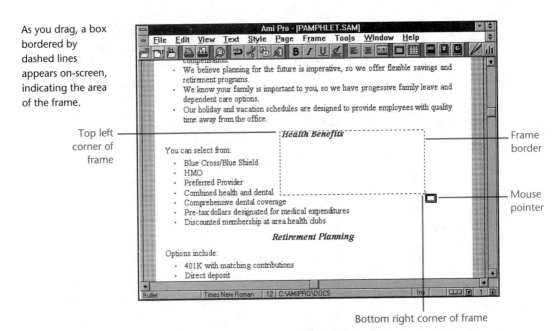

Bottom right corner of frame

When the frame is the size you want, release the mouse button. Ami Pro inserts the frame. Existing text shifts to accommodate the frame, based on the frame settings.

Text flows around the frame.

Handles indicate the frame is selected.

Frame

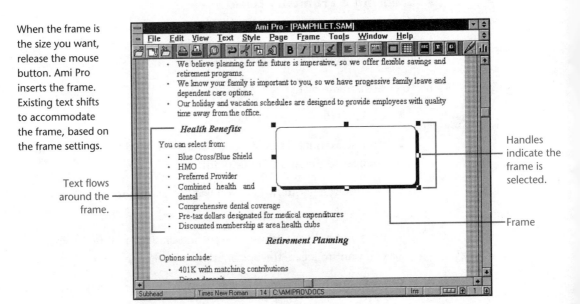

Manipulating Frames

When the frame is positioned in your document, you can change its size, shape, and location on the page.

10

Handles

Small boxes that appear around the edges of a frame or an object, indicating that the frame or object is selected. You use handles to change the size and shape of the frame or object.

Like text, to manipulate a frame you must first select it. If *handles* (eight small boxes) appear around the edge of the frame, the frame is selected.

■ To select a frame, click within its borders. Handles appear.

■ To deselect a frame, click outside of its borders. The handles disappear.

Sizing and Shaping the Frame

To change the size or shape of a frame, drag a handle in the direction you want to go:

■ Drag a top or bottom handle to change the frame's height.

■ Drag a left or right handle to change the frame's width.

■ Drag a corner handle to change both the height and width at the same time.

As you drag the frame, the handles disappear. Dashed lines indicate the frame's new size.

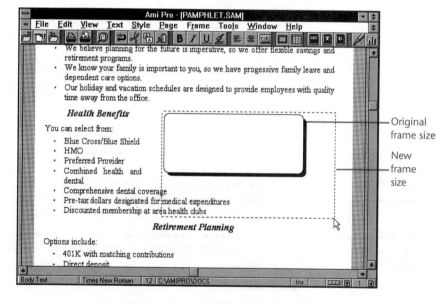

Original frame size

New frame size

If you want more precise control over the size of a frame than you can get with the mouse, you can use menu commands to change the size.

To precisely size a frame:

1. Select the frame.

2. Choose F**r**ame, **M**odify Frame Layout or click the right mouse button inside the frame.

If you have problems... If a dialog box other than the Modify Frame Layout dialog box appears when you click the right mouse button, the frame was not selected. Close the dialog box that appears, select the frame, then click the right mouse button.

3. In the Frame section of the dialog box, choose **S**ize & Position. The right part of the dialog box changes to show size and position options.

4. Make changes to the options in the Size section of the dialog box as needed.

5. Choose OK.

Moving and Copying the Frame

To move a frame, follow these steps:

1. Select the frame.

2. Position the mouse pointer within the frame. Do not point at any of the frame's handles—instead of moving it, you'll change its size.

3. Drag the frame to the new location.

If you have problems... Ami Pro does not let you drag a frame to a new page. Choose **E**dit Cu**t** and **E**dit **P**aste, or SmartIcons, to move a frame from one page to another.

If you have problems... If Ami Pro doesn't let you drag a frame to a new position on the same page, you somehow changed the Placement option in the Modify Frame Layout dialog box. Choose F**r**ame, **M**odify Frame Layout, then choose **W**here Placed in the Placement area and choose OK.

Note: *To position a frame precisely on the page, use the Modify Frame Layout dialog box.*

10

To copy a frame, follow these steps:

1. Select the frame.

2. Choose **E**dit, **C**opy.

3. Choose **E**dit, **P**aste. A copy of the frame appears on the page where the insertion point is located. The copy is selected, and positioned slightly down and to the right of the original frame. Use the methods described above to move it to the new location.

   Note: *When you paste a frame, the copy appears on the same page as the current insertion point location, in the same location as the original frame. You must move the copy to the location you want.*

Deleting the Frame

To delete a frame, follow these steps:

1. Select the frame.

2. Choose **E**dit, **Cut**, or press Del.

   Note: *Ami Pro does not warn you before it deletes the frame. If you delete a frame, then decide you want it back, choose **E**dit, **U**ndo.*

Entering Text in a Frame

Frames are useful for holding text that you want formatted differently from the rest of the document. For example, a frame can hold a single-column title across a three-column newsletter, a sidebar to an article, or a sentence or quote you want to stand out.

To enter text in a frame, follow these steps:

1. Create the frame.

2. Position the mouse pointer within the frame.

3. Double-click, or press Enter. The frame's handles turn gray, and an insertion point appears at the top left corner within the frame.

4. Type and format the text.

5. When you are done, click outside the frame, or press Esc.

If you have problems...

If the selection handles around the frame do not turn gray, and the insertion point does not appear within the frame, you are not double-clicking fast enough. When you single click, you select the frame. Try double-clicking again, this time as quickly as you can.

If you have problems...

If you double-click within the frame, and the handles turn gray but the insertion point does not appear, you may have started the Draw program. You cannot enter text in a frame that already contains a graphic image, but some such frames can be edited with Draw. See Lesson 11, "Using Draw," for more information.

Use Ami Pro's formatting options to change the appearance of text in a frame. Here, a larger font size, italics, and customized spacing help emphasize the text. Text is centered within the borders of the frame.

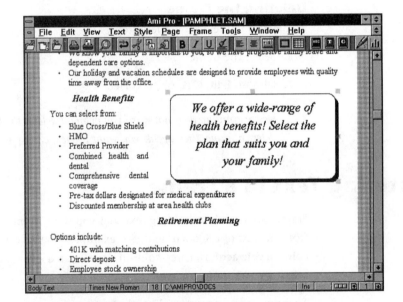

Entering Graphics in a Frame

Graphic images
Pictures such as clip art, charts, or drawings that are stored in graphic file formats.

Ami Pro frames can be used to hold *graphic images* from many different programs. Graphics in a frame can be easily sized and positioned, simply by sizing and moving the frame.

Ami Pro comes with more than 90 clip art files. To place a clip art image in a frame, follow these steps:

1. Create and select a frame.

2. Choose **F**ile, **I**mport Picture. The Import Picture dialog box appears. (For more information on importing files into Ami Pro, see Lesson 16, "Working with Other Windows Applications.")

3. In the File **T**ype list box, choose the type of file you are going to import.

4. In the Files list box, select the file you want to import.

5. To include a copy of the graphic file as part of the Ami Pro document, select the **C**opy Image checkbox. If you do not select the Copy Image checkbox, Ami Pro must access the original graphic file each time you print or display the document.

6. Choose OK. Ami Pro displays the selected image in the frame.

Ami Pro imports the image, maintaining the ratio of height to width. That means that no matter how large the frame, the image is not distorted.

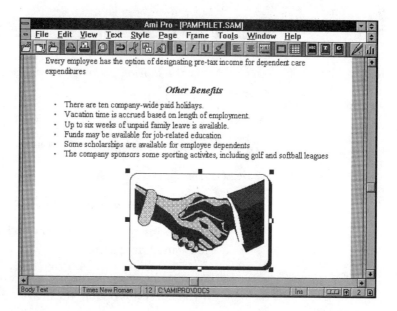

When you import a graphic, Ami Pro adjusts its size proportionately to fit within the selected frame, without distorting the image. If the frame does not have the same height-to-width ratio as the graphic, part of the frame may be left empty. Likewise, when you change the size of the frame, if the height-to-width ratio is not maintained, part of the frame is left empty.

Here, the frame has been elongated. To keep the image from becoming distorted, Ami Pro fits the image in the left half of the frame, leaving the right half empty.

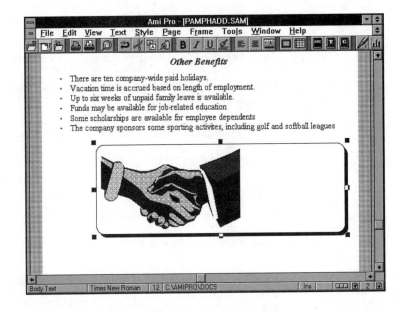

Scale

To change the size of a graphic image.

You can change the *scale* of the image to change the way it fits within the frame.

To change the scale of a graphic image, follow these steps:

1. Select the frame containing the graphic.

2. Choose Frame, Graphics Scaling.

3. Choose one of the following scaling options:

   ■ **O**riginal Size to scale the graphic back to the size it was when you started this session.

   ■ **F**it in Frame to adjust the size to fit within the existing frame. If you select this option, the image may appear distorted.

   ■ **P**ercentage to specify a size in comparison to the original size.

   ■ **C**ustom to specify exact dimensions.

4. Choose **M**aintain Aspect Ratio to ensure that the ratio of height to width is maintained.

5. Choose OK.

You can scale a
graphic image to fit
within a frame.

Choose the
scaling
option.

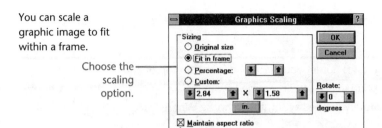

Choose to maintain the height-to-width ratio.

10

Note: *You can rotate the image within the frame by entering the number of degrees in the Rotate text box.*

Note: *You can edit imported graphics using the Draw program. For more information, see Lessons 11, "Using Draw," and 16, "Working with Other Windows Applications."*

Layering Frames

Layering
Positioning frames
in front or in back
of one another to
create different
effects.

In Ami Pro, most frames can hold text or imported graphics, but not both at the same time. You can create the effect of combined text and graphics by *layering* frames.

Note: *Frames containing graphics that can be edited using Draw can also contain text. For more information on using Draw, see Lesson 11, "Using Draw." For more information on importing graphics, see Lesson 16, "Working with Other Windows Applications."*

When you layer frames, you move one frame on top, or in front, of another. You can resize the frames, change the position of the layered frames, or modify the frame layouts to create different effects.

To layer frames, follow these steps:

1. Create both frames.

2. Use the methods described earlier in this lesson to move one frame on top of the other:

   ■ If the frames are on the same page, simply drag the one you want to move.

   ■ If the frames are on different pages, use the **E**dit, Cu**t** and **E**dit, **P**aste commands to move the frame.

3. Move and resize the frames until they are correctly positioned.

If you have problems... If Ami Pro does not let you place one frame on top of another, the Where Placed option in the Modify Frame Layout dialog box is not selected. Choose **F**rame, **M**odify Frame Layout, then choose **W**here Placed in the Placement area and choose OK.

By default, text in a layered frame flows around the frame placed on top of it.

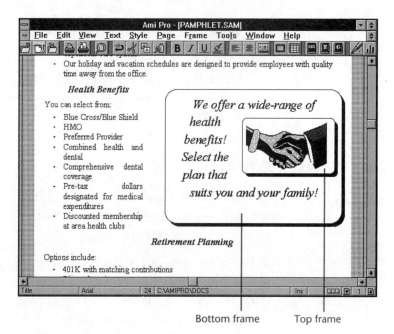

Bottom frame   Top frame

To see the contents of a frame that is layered in back of another frame, the frame in front must be transparent. To make a frame transparent, follow these steps:

1. Select the frame.

If you have problems... If you have trouble selecting layered frames, press and hold Ctrl as you click to select. Each frame is selected in turn. When the frame you want is selected, release Ctrl.

2. Choose **F**rame, **M**odify Frame Layout.

3. In the Display area, choose **T**ransparent.

4. Choose OK. Ami Pro makes the selected frame transparent so you can see the frame in back of it.

To rearrange the layered frames, follow these steps:

1. Select the frame you want to move.

2. Choose F**r**ame, then choose one of the following:

- Bring to **F**ront, to move the selected frame to the front, or top, of all the layered frames.

- Send to **B**ack, to move the selected frame to the back, or bottom, of all the layered frames.

If you have problems...

If you cannot see the contents of a back frame even though the frame in front is transparent, the back frame may not be large enough to show its own contents as well as the contents of the front frame. You can try different ways to make it all fit: enlarge the back frame, shrink the front frame, or change the font size of text in the back frame.

Grouping Frames

Group
More than one frame, joined so you can manipulate them as one.

Sometimes you manipulate more than one frame at a time. With Ami Pro, you can move or copy a *group* of frames.

To create a group of frames, follow these steps:

1. Select one of the frames.

2. Press and hold Shift.

3. Select the other frames you want in the group.

4. Release Shift.

5. Choose F**r**ame, **G**roup.

To move or copy the group, use the commands described earlier in this lesson.

To cancel the grouping, select it, then choose Frame, Group again.

Changing the Appearance of Frames

With Ami Pro, you can change the appearance of frames, or change the default frame settings. For example, you can make exact changes to the frame's size and position on the page, change the way text flows around a frame, create different effects with shadows and lines, make a frame opaque or transparent, or add columns and tabs within a frame.

In this section, you learn to change the flow of text around a frame and to remove lines and shadows. For information on how to use other frame settings, see Que's *Using Ami Pro 3*, Special Edition.

To modify the frame:

1. Select the frame.

2. Choose Frame, Modify Frame Layout or click the right mouse button inside the frame.

Use the Modify Frame Layout dialog box to change the appearance of an existing frame. Settings for changing the frame type are displayed.

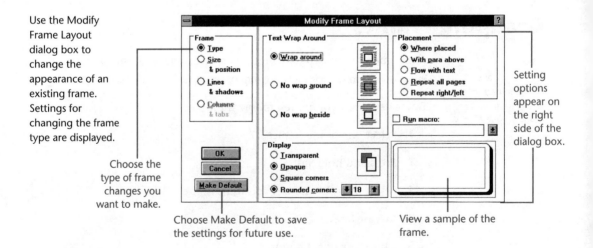

Choose the type of frame changes you want to make.

Choose Make Default to save the settings for future use.

Setting options appear on the right side of the dialog box.

View a sample of the frame.

10

With the dialog box displayed, you are ready to make changes as described in the next two sections.

Changing Text Flow

To change the way text flows around a frame, follow these steps:

1. In the Frame area of the Modify Frame Layout dialog box, choose **T**ype.

2. In the Text Wrap Around area, choose one of the following:

■ Choose **W**rap Around to have text automatically flow around the frame.

■ Choose No Wrap **A**round to have text remain in its original position, with the frame on top of it.

■ Choose No Wrap **B**eside to have text move above and below the frame, but not on either side.

3. Choose OK.

Here the Text Wrap Around option for the larger frame has been set to No wrap beside. The frames were moved as a group to the center of the page.

Text flows above and below the larger frame, but not beside.

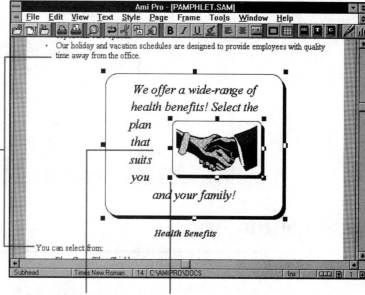

Text within the larger frame still flows around the smaller frame.

Both frames are selected.

Changing Lines and Shadows

By default, a frame appears with a line around its border, and a shadow on the right and bottom sides. You can change the line and shadow positions and colors.

To remove the lines and shadows, follow these steps:

1. In the Frame area of the Modify Frame Layout dialog box, choose **L**ines & Shadows.

2. In the Lines area, deselect the **A**ll box.

3. In the Shadow area, choose **N**one.

4. Choose OK.

Here, the lines and shadows have been removed from the smaller frame, and the shadow for the larger frame has been moved to the left side.

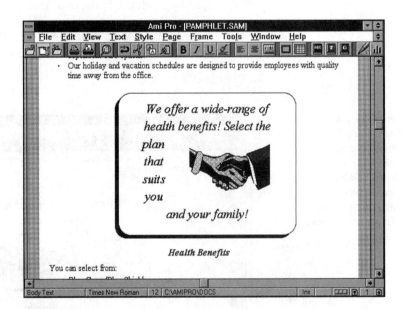

Lesson Summary

To	Do This
Create a frame automatically	Choose F**r**ame, **C**reate Frame. Enter the size and position of the frame.
Create a frame by hand	Choose F**r**ame, **C**reate Frame. Choose **M**anual. Click the pointer at the top left corner of the frame and drag to the bottom right corner.

To	Do This
Select a frame	Click within its borders.
Change the size of a frame	Drag a handle in the direction you want to go.
Move a frame	Point within the frame. Drag the frame to the new location.
Copy a frame	Choose **E**dit, **C**opy. Choose **E**dit, **P**aste. Drag the copy to the new location.
Delete a frame	Choose **E**dit, **Cut**, or press Del.
Enter text in a frame	Point within the frame. Double-click, or press Enter. Type and format the text.
Layer frames	Drag one frame on top of the other. Move and resize the frames until they are correctly positioned.
Group frames	Select one frame. Press and hold Shift. Select the other frames. Release Shift. Choose F**r**ame, **G**roup.

On Your Own

These exercises are designed to help you become comfortable using frames. You can practice by inserting frames into an existing document or into a new, blank document.

Manipulating Frames
Estimated Time: 5 minutes

1. In a document, create a square frame.

2. Select the frame and move it to the top of the page.

3. Copy the frame, and move the copy to the bottom of the page.

4. Change the copy to a rectangle.

Entering Text and Graphics in Frames
Estimated Time: 10 minutes

1. Enter text in one of the frames.

2. Change the font and font size.

3. Center Align the text within the frame.

4. In the other frame, insert a clip-art graphic image.

5. Change the size of the frame.

6. Rescale the image to fit within the frame.

Layering Frames
Estimated Time: 10 minutes

1. Layer the two frames.

2. Modify the frames so you can see both the text and the clip art.

3. Change the order of the layered frames.

4. Change the flow of text in the text frame.

5. Remove the lines and shadow from the graphics frame.

6. Group the two frames and move them to another location in the document.

Using Draw

Ami Pro comes with drawing capabilities similar to those found in drawing software packages. You can use Draw to create shapes and drawings and to incorporate text and drawings.

In this lesson, you learn how to

- Start Draw.
- Select objects.
- Move and copy objects.
- Delete objects.
- Rotate objects.
- Create text objects.

Starting Draw

All drawings created with Draw must be placed in a frame. You can create the frame before you start Draw, or you can let Ami Pro create a frame. For information on creating frames, see Lesson 10, "Working with Frames."

Note: *You cannot create a drawing in a frame that already contains text or an imported graphic.*

To start Draw, choose Tools, **D**rawing.

If a frame is selected in the document, Ami Pro uses the frame. If no frame is selected, Ami Pro creates a frame based on the default settings in the Create Frame dialog box.

When Draw starts, the Ami Pro screen changes: a frame where you can create a drawing is displayed; the Drawing toolbar appears across the top of the screen; and the Draw command is added to the Ami Pro menu bar.

The Draw command added to the Ami Pro menu bar

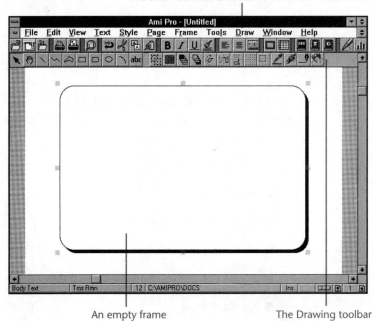

An empty frame   The Drawing toolbar

If you have problems...

If the Drawing toolbar and the frame handles disappear, you clicked outside the frame. Clicking outside the frame turns Draw off. To start Draw again, choose Tools, **D**rawing, or double-click anywhere in the frame.

Creating a Drawing

Object
An image or shape used in the Draw feature to create a drawing.

To create a drawing, you select a Drawing icon, then use the mouse pointer to draw shapes within the frame. The shapes are called *objects*. You can make up a drawing of one object, or many objects.

Drawing Ellipses and Circles

To create a round object, follow these steps:

1. Choose the Ellipse icon.

2. Position the mouse pointer within the frame at the location where you want to place one end of the object. The mouse pointer now is a cross-hair shape.

11

3. Drag the mouse pointer to create the object. To create a perfect circle, press and hold Shift as you drag.

The Ellipse icon

When the object looks the way you want it, release the mouse button.

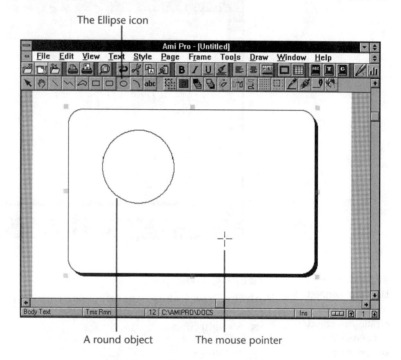

A round object   The mouse pointer

Drawing Rectangles

To create a rectangular object, follow these steps:

1. Choose the Rectangle icon or the Rounded Rectangle icon.

2. Position the mouse pointer within the frame, at the location where you want the top left corner of the rectangle.

3. Drag the mouse pointer to the location where you want the bottom right corner of the rectangle. To create a perfect square, press and hold Shift as you drag.

4. When the object looks the way you want it, release the mouse button.

The Rectangle icon ⎯⎯⎯   ⎯⎯ The Rounded Rectangle icon

Here a rectangle has been added to the drawing.

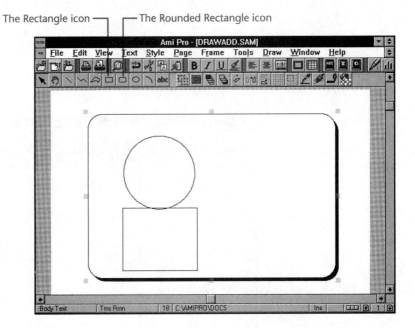

Drawing Lines

With the Draw feature, you can create three kinds of lines:

■ Straight lines

■ Polylines

■ Arcs

Polylines
Lines that connect multiple points, creating an object out of multiple straight lines.

Arcs
Lines that curve in a parabolic arc.

To draw straight lines, follow these steps:

1. Choose the Line icon.

2. Position the mouse pointer where you want the line to begin.

3. Click and drag the mouse pointer to where you want the line to end.

You can use the Line icon to draw a line at a perfect 45-degree angle. Press and hold Shift as you drag the mouse pointer. The line appears in increments of 45 degrees until you release the mouse button to draw the line.

To create an object using polylines, follow these steps:

1. Choose the Polyline icon.

2. Position the insertion point where you want the line to begin and click.

3. Position the insertion point where you want the line to end and click. Ami Pro connects the two points with a straight line.

4. If you want to draw another connected line, position the insertion point at the place where you want the line to end and click. Ami Pro connects the second point and the third point with a straight line. Until you select another icon, Ami Pro continues connecting each place you click with the previous place using a straight line.

You can also use the Polyline icon to draw free-form lines. Press and hold Shift as you drag the mouse to draw.

To draw arcs, follow these steps:

1. Choose the Arc icon.

2. Position the insertion point where you want the arc to begin.

3. Click and drag the mouse pointer to the location where you want the arc to end.

The Polyline icon   The Arc icon   An object created with polylines

Lines of all kinds
have been added
to this drawing.

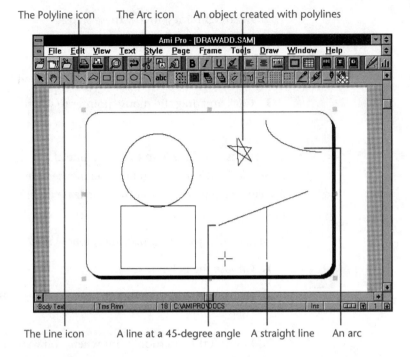

The Line icon   A line at a 45-degree angle   A straight line   An arc

Drawing Polygons

To draw a polygon object, follow these steps:

1. Choose the Polygon icon.

2. Position the insertion point where you want to locate one corner of
   the polygon and click.

3. Move the insertion point to the next corner of the polygon and
   click. Ami Pro connects the corners with a straight line, creating
   the first side of the object.

4. Position the insertion point at the next corner and click. Ami Pro
   draws another side.

5. At the last corner, double-click.

Polygon icon   Polygon shape

You can create
multisided shapes
using the Polygon
icon.

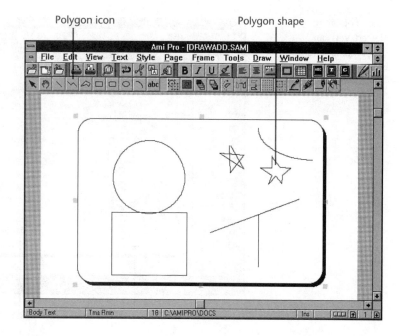

Selecting Objects

To edit or manipulate objects in a drawing, you first must select the
objects.

To select an object, follow these steps:

1. Choose the Selection Arrow icon.

2. Point within the object you want to select and click. Handles
   appear around the selected object.

**If you have
problems...**   To select a straight line, try pointing at the middle of the line, rather than at
the end. To select an object that overlaps or touches another object, press
and hold Ctrl as you select.

After an object is selected, you can edit or manipulate the object.

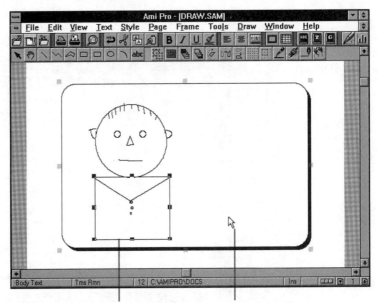

The selected object has handles around it.   The selection arrow

To select more than one object, follow these steps:

1. Choose the Selection Arrow icon.

2. Select the first object.

3. Press and hold the Shift key.

4. Select additional objects.

If you have problems...

If a selected object becomes deselected when you select another object, you are not holding down the Shift key. Press and hold Shift until you finish selecting objects.

You can select
more than one
object at a time.

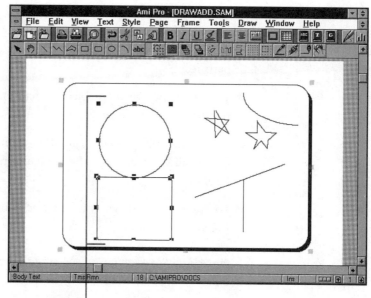

Both the circle and the rectangle are selected.

You can select adjacent objects by dragging the selection arrow. As you drag, a box appears around all the selected objects. When you release the mouse button, the box disappears and the objects' handles appear.

 To select all objects in a drawing, choose **D**raw, **S**elect All.

Manipulating Objects

After an object is selected, you can perform some functions, including the following:

- To move an object, select and then drag the object to the new location.

 - To move all objects in the drawing, use the Hand icon. Select the Hand icon, and then drag it within the frame. Release the mouse button when the dashed box is positioned where you want to place the drawing.

- To crop part of the drawing, use the Hand icon to move the part you want to crop beyond the edge of the frame. You can use the Hand icon to move the drawing back until the hidden parts reappear.

- To change the size of an object, select it, then drag the object's handles in the direction you want to go.

- To copy an object, select it, and then choose **E**dit, **C**opy. The copy appears directly on top of the original. Drag the object to the new location.

- To delete an object, select it and then choose **E**dit, Cu**t**, or press the Del key.

Note: *Ami Pro doesn't warn you before deleting the object. Make sure that you have selected the object you want to delete. If you make a mistake, choose **E**dit, **U**ndo immediately.*

Rotating and Flipping Objects

To rotate an object, select it and then double-click within the object. Rotation arrows appear around the object, and a center-of-rotation mark appears within it.

Rotation arrows and a center-of-rotation mark appear when you double-click within an object.

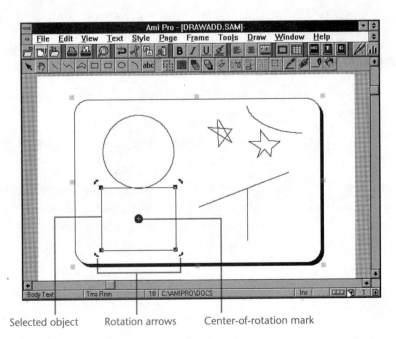

Selected object   Rotation arrows   Center-of-rotation mark

Drag one of the rotation arrows in the direction you want to rotate the object. Drag the center-of-rotation mark to shift the object's center point.

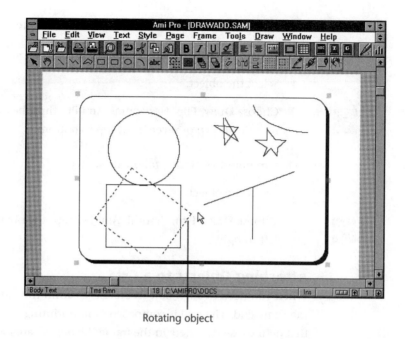

Rotating object

If you have problems...   If the object is moving to a new location rather than rotating, you are not pointing correctly at the rotation mark. Be sure that you point between the arrows.

To rotate an object by a precise measurement, follow these steps:

1. Choose **D**raw, **R**otate.

2. In the **R**otate text box, enter the number of degrees to rotate the object.

3. In the Direction area, select to rotate the object **C**lockwise or C**o**unterclockwise.

4. Choose OK.

If you need to rotate an object using precise measurements, you can use the **R**otate command from the **D**raw menu.

 To quickly rotate an object, use the Rotate an Object SmartIcon. Each time you click the SmartIcon, Ami Pro rotates the selected object according to the settings specified in the Rotate dialog box.

You can flip an object either horizontally or vertically.

To flip an object horizontally, follow these steps:

1. Select the object.

2. Choose **D**raw, **F**lip, Horizontal. Ami Pro flips the object by turning it upside down or reversing it top to bottom.

To flip an object vertically, follow these steps:

1. Select the object.

2. Choose **D**raw, **F**lip, Vertical. Ami Pro flips the object by reversing it left to right.

Attaching Objects to a Grid

When you need to align objects precisely within the frame, you can use the Draw grid. The grid is comprised of nonprinting dots or a dotted line that define exactly where in the frame the objects are located.

To display the grid, choose **D**raw, **Sh**ow Grid. To hide the grid, choose **D**raw, **H**ide Grid.

You can customize the grid using the Grid Settings command. Choose **D**raw, Grid Settings, then specify whether you want to use dots or dotted lines to indicate the grid and how far apart you want the grid spaced.

With the grid displayed, you can manually align objects as you draw them or you can move them to a precise location. However, Ami Pro has a Snap To feature that automatically aligns objects on the grid whether the grid is displayed or not.

To align objects on the grid automatically as you draw them, choose **D**raw, **S**nap To. To turn off the Snap To feature, choose **D**raw, **S**nap To again.

Here the grid is set
to appear as dotted
lines.

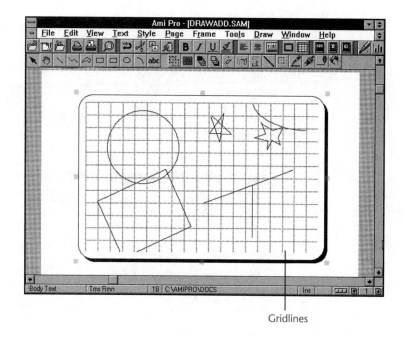

Gridlines

**If you have
problems...**

If objects are not moving where you want them in the frame, it could be
because Snap To is turned on. Ami Pro uses Snap To even if the grid is not
displayed. If a checkmark appears beside the Snap To command on the
Draw menu, Snap To is turned on. Choose it to turn it off.

Changing Lines Styles and Colors

In Ami Pro, you can use different lines styles and colors to create objects.
You can select a line width, a dashed line, or a transparent line. You can
also select the type of endings you want at each end of the line.

You can select a line style and color to use to create an object or you can
change the line style and color of an existing object. To change the line
style or color of an existing object, select the object first.

To choose a line style and color, follow these steps:

1. Choose **D**raw, **L**ine Style.

2. In the Line Style area, choose the line style you want.

3. In the Endings area, choose the ending you want on the left end of the line and the ending you want on the right end of the line.

4. From the **C**olor bar, select the color you want. Click the down arrow to display all the colors available.

5. Choose OK.

You can change the line style of a selected object, or you can change the line style before you draw an object.

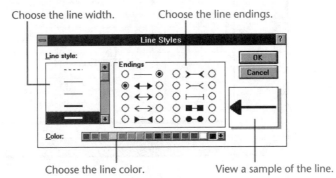

Choose the line width.　　　Choose the line endings.

Choose the line color.　　　View a sample of the line.

Changing the line style and line endings can change the whole look of a drawing.

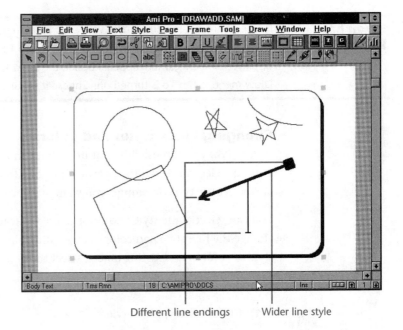

Different line endings　　　Wider line style

Note: *You can use the Extract Line & Fill icon to change the current line style and fill pattern to the style of the selected object. To apply the current line style and fill pattern to a selected object, use the Apply Line & Fill icon.*

Changing the Fill Color and Pattern

Closed objects
In Ami Pro, closed
objects are created
using the Ellipse
icon, the Rectangle
icon, or the
Rounded Rectangle
icon.

In Ami Pro, you can fill *closed objects* with color or patterns.

As with line styles, you can change the color or fill pattern of an existing object, or you can select the color or fill pattern before you create an object.

To select a color or fill pattern, follow these steps:

1. Choose **D**raw, Fill **P**attern.

2. In the Color area, choose the color.

3. In the Pattern area, choose the fill pattern.

4. Choose OK.

You can change the
fill pattern of a
selected object, or
you can change it
before you create
the object.

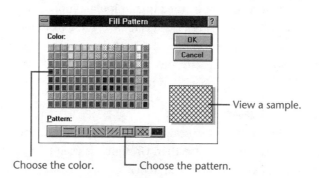

Choose the color.　Choose the pattern.

View a sample.

You can use colors
and fill patterns to
add depth and
texture to your
drawings.

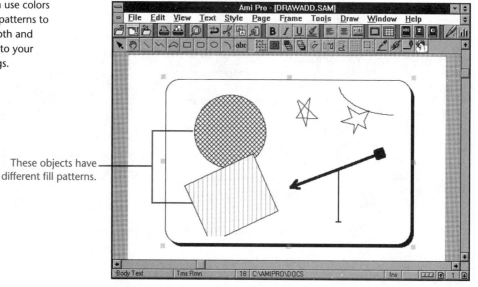

These objects have
different fill patterns.

Modifying the Shape of an Object

You can change the shape of an object by selecting it and using the following methods:

- To change the width of an object, drag one of its side handles.

- To change the height of an object, drag one of its top or bottom handles.

- To change the width and height proportionately, drag one of its corner handles.

Working with Multiple Objects

So far, you have learned to manipulate individual objects within a drawing. Most drawings, however, are created from many objects. With Ami Pro, you can save time and create better drawings by working with multiple objects. Specifically, you can group multiple objects together and you can layer objects on top of or behind one another.

Grouping Objects

With Ami Pro, you can group multiple objects together so that they can be manipulated together. Grouping is useful for duplicating a series of objects or for moving a drawing comprised of multiple objects.

Earlier in this lesson, you learned to select more than one object. You can group selected objects together and then manipulate them as one. Once objects are grouped, any action you perform on one of the objects in the group affects all the objects in the group. To manipulate just one of the objects, you must ungroup them.

To group objects, follow these steps:

1. Select the objects you want to group.

2. Choose **D**raw, **G**roup. Selection handles appear around the grouped objects and a checkmark appears beside the Group command on the Draw menu.

To ungroup the objects, choose **D**raw, **G**roup again.

Here the circle and
the rectangle are
grouped together.

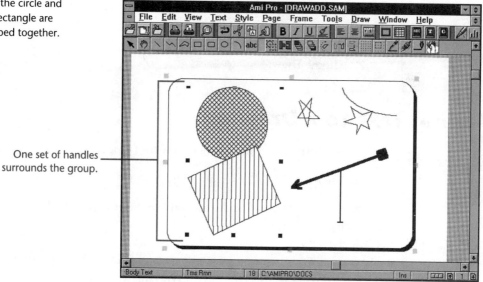

One set of handles
surrounds the group.

**If you have
problems...**

If the Group command is dimmed on the Draw menu, it means you have not
selected multiple objects. Go back to the drawing and select all the objects
you want to group together, and then try the Group command again.

Layering Objects

When you use Draw, the most recently created object appears on the top
of the drawing, which means that sometimes objects overlap. Occasionally, one object may completely hide another object. With Ami Pro, you
can change the order of layered objects so that objects on the bottom are
moved to the top, and objects on the top are moved to the bottom.

To bring an object to the top of the drawing, follow these steps:

1. Select the object.

2. Choose **D**raw, Bring to **F**ront. Ami Pro moves the selected object in
front of all other objects in the drawing.

**If you have
problems...**

To select an object that is completely hidden behind other objects, press and
hold down Ctrl and click in the top object. Each object is selected in turn.
When the object you want is selected, choose **D**raw, Bring to **F**ront.

To move an object behind other objects, follow these steps:

1. Select the object.

2. Choose **D**raw, Send to **B**ack.

Adding Text to a Drawing

You can add text to a drawing created with Draw in Ami Pro in two ways:

■ Use the Text icon to create a text object.

■ Create a frame to hold text, and layer it on top of the frame that holds the drawing.

To learn how to create a frame for text, and to layer the frame on top of the drawing frame, see Lesson 10, "Working with Frames."

If you want to add only a small amount of text, you can create a text object. In Ami Pro, each line of text is a separate object that you can size, move, copy, and rotate like other objects. Text objects are useful when you need to add numbers, labels, or captions to drawings.

To use the Text icon to create a text object, follow these steps:

1. Choose the Text drawing icon.

2. Click the mouse pointer at the location where you want to place the text.

3. Type a line of text.

When you press Enter at the end of a line of text, you can start typing another line of text. However, each line of text is a separate object. You cannot manipulate more than one line of text unless you group them together.

To select a text object, choose the Selection Arrow icon and click the text.

You can manipulate a text object the same way you manipulate other objects. You also can format the text.

To format the text, select the text object, then use the Text menu to select the font and character attributes. Alternatively, you can select text formatting before you type the text. (For information on formatting text, see Lesson 5, "Dressing Up Your Text.")

Note: *You cannot use the alignment, indention, or spacing options on a text object. Text objects must be moved by using the same techniques you used to move other drawing objects.*

Here, two lines of text were grouped, formatted, and rotated.

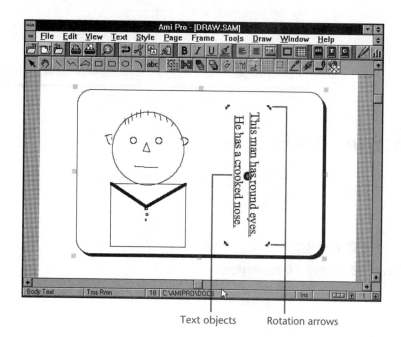

Text objects   Rotation arrows

Lesson Summary

To	Do This
Start Draw	Select an empty frame. Choose Tools, Drawing.
Draw objects	Click the icon. Drag the mouse pointer within the frame to create an object.
Select objects	Click the object you want to select. Press and hold Shift to select additional objects.
Move an object	Point in the selected area and drag the object to the new location.

(continues)

To	Do This
Copy an object	Select the object. Choose **E**dit, **C**opy. Move the copy to the new location.
Resize or reshape an object	Select the object. Drag a handle to increase or decrease the object's size, or to change the object's shape.
Delete an object	Select the object. Choose **E**dit, Cu**t,** or press Del.
Rotate an object	Select the object. Double-click in the selected area. Drag a rotation arrow in the direction you want to rotate the object.
Group objects	Select the objects. Choose **D**raw, **G**roup.

On Your Own

These exercises are designed to help you become familiar with the Draw program.

Create a Drawing
Estimated Time: 10 minutes

1. Create an empty frame large enough to hold a page-sized drawing.

2. Start Draw.

3. Create a round object.

4. Create a rectangular object.

5. Create a multisided object.

Modify the Drawing
Estimated Time: 10 minutes

1. Move the round object to the other side of the frame.

2. Copy the multisided object.

3. Change the line style and use the Line icon to create another object.

4. Elongate the rectangle.

5. Rotate the multisided object.

6. Flip the rectangle either horizontally or vertically.

7. Fill the rectangle with a color or a pattern.

11

Add Text Time
Estimated Time: 10 minutes

1. Add a multiline text description to the drawing.

2. Group the text objects.

3. Copy the text objects.

4. Format each copy of the text objects with different character attributes and fonts.

Here are some additional exercises you can try:

■ Crop the drawing within the frame.

■ Rotate an object or a group of objects exactly 45 degrees.

■ Use a grid to align the objects evenly on a baseline.

■ Extract a line style or fill pattern from one object and apply it to another.

Lesson 12

Working with Tables

In Ami Pro, you can use tables to relate rows and columns of text, numbers, and pictures. With tables, you can create forms, merge documents, create charts, and perform calculations.

In this lesson, you learn the different ways to create, edit, and format tables with Ami Pro.

Specifically, you learn how to

- Create a page table.

- Create a frame table.

- Enter data in a table.

- Edit a table.

- Change the appearance of a table.

Understanding Tables

Table
A combination of related rows and columns that create cells. You enter information into the cells.

In Lesson 8, "Making Your Pages Pretty," you learned to create newspaper-style columns, where text flows from the bottom of one column to the top of the next column. *Tables* also use *columns*, but these columns are not newspaper style. In tables, columns are combined with *rows* to create a grid of *cells*, which contain related information.

Column

A vertical line of cells. For identification, Ami Pro labels columns alphabetically, from left to right.

Cell

A rectangular area in a table where a row and column intersect.

Perhaps the most easily recognizable table is a spreadsheet, but you can use tables for other purposes such as creating a list of words and their definitions, a schedule of monthly meetings, or even a resume.

Choosing a Table Type

In Ami Pro, you can create two kinds of tables—a *frame table* or a *page table*.

A frame table follows all of the rules of other kinds of frames: you can position, flow text around, move, and resize the frame anywhere in the document. You cannot, however, place a page break after a row within the frame table; a frame table must fit on one page. For information on using frames, see Lesson 10, "Working with Frames."

Here, text flows around a frame table in a document.

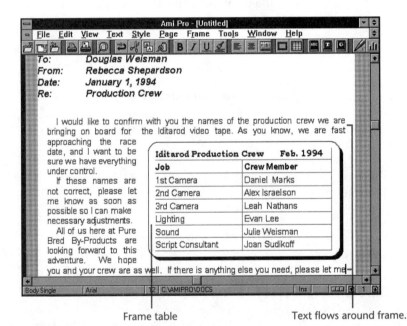

Frame table   Text flows around frame.

Row

A horizontal line of cells. For identification, Ami Pro labels rows numerically, from top to bottom.

Frame table

A frame table is a table that is inserted into a frame.

Page table

A page table is a table that is inserted directly into a document at the insertion point location.

A page table isn't contained in a frame. Existing text at or below the insertion point is moved below the table; existing text before the insertion point is moved above the table. Page tables can contain page breaks between rows, and therefore can span more than one page.

Here, text makes room for a page table.

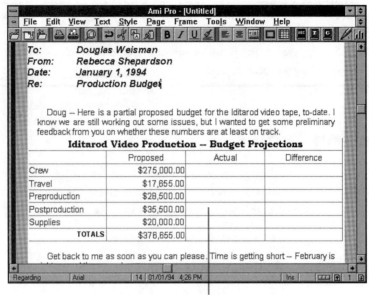

A page table

When you choose whether to create a page table or a frame table, consider the kind of table you are creating and the kind of document that will hold the table. Usually, frame tables are easier to manipulate and can provide some interesting effects in a document, but frame tables must fit on one page.

Viewing Tables

You can use the View Preferences dialog box to display tables with or without column and row headings and with or without table gridlines.

Gridlines

Gridlines are nonprinting dotted lines that indicate the boundaries between cells in a table.

To display *gridlines* choose **V**iew, View **P**references and select **T**able Gridlines. To hide the gridlines, deselect the **T**able Gridlines option. Gridlines do not print. To include lines in your table, you must use the Modify Table Layout dialog box, as described in a following section of this lesson.

To display column and row headings, choose **V**iew, View **P**references and select Table Row/Column **H**eadings. To hide the headings, deselect the Table Row/Column **H**eadings options. Headings are displayed above the columns and to the left of the rows.

If you have problems...	If you selected Table Row/Column **H**eadings in the View Preferences dialog box but the headings do not appear, the insertion point is not inside the table. The headings are displayed only when the insertion point is in a cell in the table.

Creating Tables

Both page tables and frame tables are created by using the same commands. To create a frame table, create the frame in the document and select it before creating the table.

To create a table, follow these steps:

1. Choose Too**l**s, Ta**b**les.

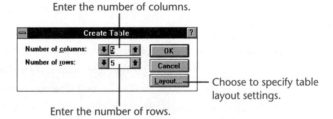

Enter the number of columns.

Choose to specify table layout settings.

Enter the number of rows.

Give some thought ahead of time to how many columns and rows you need in your table. Don't forget rows for titles and, if applicable, column headings.

2. Enter the number of columns and rows you want included in the table.

3. If you want to choose table layout settings now, choose **L**ayout. The Modify Table Layout dialog box appears.

4. In the Default Rows area, check the **A**utomatic check box to adjust the cell size automatically to accommodate as much data as is entered. To set a specific height for rows, deselect the **A**utomatic check box and enter the size in the Height text box.

Set column width and gutter size.

You can modify the table layout at any time by using the Modify Table Layout dialog box.

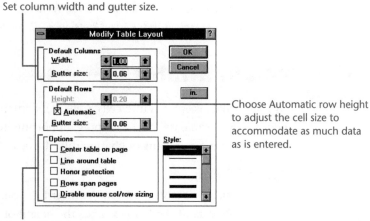

Choose Automatic row height to adjust the cell size to accommodate as much data as is entered.

Choose Table Layout options.

12

5. In the Default Columns area, enter a column width size and a gutter width size.

6. Choose OK to return to the Create Table dialog box.

7. Choose OK to create the table.

Note: *For more information on setting column widths and row heights, see the section "Changing the Size of Columns and Rows," later in this lesson.*

Ami Pro adds a Table menu to the menu bar.

Here a 5-row-by-5-column page table is inserted in the document.

Columns are marked with letters.

Rows are marked with numbers.

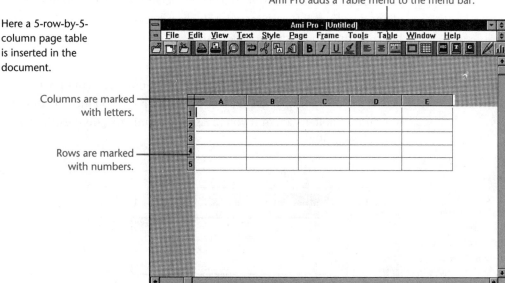

Note: *To display the column and row headings, choose Table Row/ Column **H**eadings in the View Preferences dialog box.*

Entering Data in a Table

In a table, data is entered into cells. Cells can contain text, numbers, or graphics. You can enter data by typing, importing from another application, or creating a drawing or chart within the cell.

Typing Data

To type data into a table, position the insertion point in the correct cell and type. By default, Ami Pro expands the height of the cell to accommodate as much data as you type. To move to the next cell, press Tab or move the insertion point.

If you have problems...

If you set the row to a specific height in the Modify Table Layout dialog box, data that doesn't fit within the cell size is hidden. Select **A**utomatic row height to have Ami Pro adjust the size of the cell to accommodate as much data as you enter and to display hidden data that is already entered.

If a cell contains numbers only, Ami Pro considers it a number cell, and treats the cell differently than a text cell. Ami Pro formats the data according to the table text style setting. By default, in a text cell, Ami Pro aligns data flush left, and includes all characters that you type. In a number cell, Ami Pro aligns the data flush right, adds commas, and removes leading zeros.

For Ami Pro to consider a cell a number cell, it must contain only numbers, a decimal point, a plus sign, or a minus sign. If you include a space, a comma, a dollar sign, or if you press Enter, Ami Pro considers the cell to be a text cell.

Text cells can contain both text and numbers. Number cells must contain numbers only.

Text cells

	A	B	C	D	E
1	Customer	Account #	Credit Limit	Orders	Balance
2	D. Smith	DS1234	2,500	1,050	1450
3	B. Jones	BJ3456	2,000	2,250	-250
4	J. Anderson	JA9876	1,750	650	1,100
5	T. Brown	TB5748	3,000	2,050	950

Number cells

You can format the data in a table by using Ami Pro's character and paragraph formatting commands. For more information on formatting in a table, see the section "Changing the Appearance of a Table," later in this lesson.

Pasting Data

You can paste data from the Windows Clipboard into a table. The data can come from another document, from the same document, or even from another Windows application. (For information on using Ami Pro with other windows applications, see Lesson 16, "Working with Other Windows Applications.")

12

You can paste data into a single cell, or into multiple cells. If data exists in the single cell, Ami Pro adds the new data at the location of the insertion point. If data exists in multiple cells, Ami Pro overwrites the existing data.

Make sure that the table has enough columns and rows before pasting data from the Clipboard. If the data from the Clipboard has tabs in it, Ami Pro considers each tab to indicate a new column. If paragraph marks also exist (if the Enter key was pressed), Ami Pro considers each paragraph mark to indicate a new row.

To paste data from the Clipboard, follow these steps:

1. Select the data in the original document and copy or cut the information to the Clipboard.

2. Open the Ami Pro document that contains the table.

3. Position the insertion point in the cell where you want to place the data.

4. Choose **Edit**, **P**aste.

   Note: *If paragraph marks are present but there are no tabs in the data in the Clipboard, Ami Pro asks if you want to paste all the data in the current cell. Choose **Y**es to add the data to the current cell. Choose **N**o to paste each paragraph in a separate row. Existing data is overwritten.*

Editing Tables

You can edit data in a table by using Ami Pro's editing commands and by using the Table menu commands.

Selecting in a Table

In a table, you can select data within a cell, multiple cells, a column, a row, or the entire table. You can use either the Table menu or the mouse.

Table 12.1 describes mouse techniques to use to select items in a table.

Table 12.1. Mouse Selection Techniques for Use in Tables	
To Select	**Do This**
Data	Drag the mouse pointer from the first character to the last character.
A cell	Double-click within the cell.
A row	Point at the far left edge of the row. When the pointer changes to an arrow pointing right, click.
Multiple rows	Drag the arrow up or down to select the rows.
A column	Point at the top edge of the column. When the pointer changes to an arrow pointing down, click.
Multiple columns	Drag the arrow left or right to select the columns.

Copying and Moving in a Table

In a table, copying and moving are accomplished by using the same cut, copy, and paste commands as in a document.

To copy or move data in a table, use **E**dit, **Cut**; **E**dit, **C**opy; and **E**dit, **P**aste, as shown in the following list:

- To move a column or row, select, and then drag the data to the new location.

- To copy a column or row, select it, press and hold Ctrl, then drag it to the new location.

■ To copy or move a page table, select the table, and then choose **E**dit, Cu**t**; **E**dit, **C**opy; or **E**dit, **P**aste.

■ To move a frame table, drag the frame to the new location.

■ To copy a frame table, select the frame, then use **E**dit, **C**opy and **E**dit, **P**aste and drag the frame to the new location.

For more information on using Frames, see Lesson 10, "Working with Frames."

Inserting Columns and Rows

You can add columns and rows to an existing table.

To add a column or row, follow these steps:

1. Position the insertion point in the column or row beside which you want to insert the new column or row.

2. Choose Ta**b**le, **I**nsert Column/Row.

12

Choose to insert columns or rows.

You can insert columns or rows into an existing table.

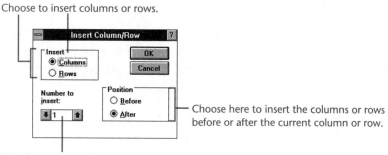

Choose here to insert the columns or rows before or after the current column or row.

Enter how many to insert.

3. Make the selections, and then choose OK. Ami Pro inserts the new columns or rows.

If you have problems...

If the Insert Column option is dimmed in the Insert Column/Row dialog box, not enough room is available on the page to add another column. Try making the existing columns narrower or the page width wider.

You can quickly insert a column or row by using SmartIcons. Choose the Insert Column in Table SmartIcon to insert a column to the left of the column where the insertion point is located. Choose the Insert Row in Table SmartIcon to insert a row below the row where the insertion point is located.

Deleting in a Table

Deleting data in a table is the same as deleting data in a document. Simply select the data and choose **E**dit, **Cu**t, or press Del.

You cannot use **E**dit, **Cu**t, however, to delete a row or column, and you cannot use the **E**dit, **U**ndo command to undo the deletion of a row or column.

To delete a row or column, follow these steps:

1. Position the insertion point within the row or column you want to delete.

 2. Choose Ta**b**le, **D**elete Column/Row. The Delete Column/Row dialog box appears.

3. Select either to delete a row or a column, then choose OK. Ami Pro warns you that deleting rows and columns cannot be undone. To continue, choose **Y**es. To return to the document without deleting the row or column, choose **N**o.

You can quickly delete rows and columns by using SmartIcons. Choose the Delete Selected Rows in Table SmartIcon to delete selected rows, or the row where the insertion point is located. Choose the Delete Selected Columns in Table SmartIcon to delete selected columns, or the column where the insertion point is located.

You can undo the deletion of an entire table.

To delete an entire page table, position the insertion point in it and choose **E**dit, **Cu**t, or press Del. You also can choose Ta**b**le, Delete Entire **T**able.

To delete a frame table, delete the frame.

Changing the Appearance of a Table

You can change the look of a table in many ways. You can format the text in the table, and you can change the width of columns and the height of rows. You can add lines and color to a table, connect adjacent cells, and add headings or leaders.

Note: *In frame tables, you can change the appearance of the table by changing the appearance of the frame. For information on frames, see Lesson 10, "Working with Frames."*

Formatting Text in a Table

To format text in a table, use the character and paragraph formatting commands.

By default, text in a table appears in the Table Text style. You can change the font and apply character attributes such as underlines, italics, and bold face. You can modify the style or create a new style.

To apply formatting, first select the text, the cell, multiple cells, row, or column that you want to format. You can give each cell a different look, or you can select the entire table.

Column heading text cells are center-aligned.

In a table, each cell can be formatted with a different look.

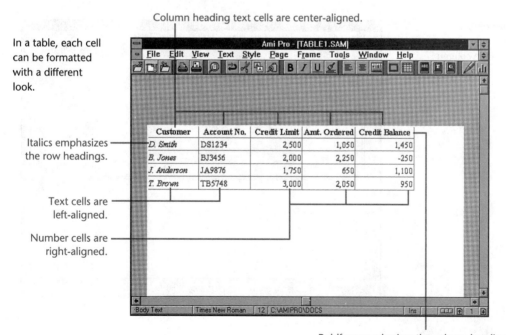

Italics emphasizes the row headings.

Text cells are left-aligned.

Number cells are right-aligned.

Boldface emphasizes the column headings.

Customer	Account No.	Credit Limit	Amt. Ordered	Credit Balance
D. Smith	DS1234	2,500	1,050	1,450
B. Jones	BJ3456	2,000	2,250	-250
J. Anderson	JA9876	1,750	650	1,100
T. Brown	TB5748	3,000	2,050	950

Note: *Text in a table is aligned in relation to the sides of the cell.*

Changing the Size of Columns and Rows

When you create a table, you can set the width of columns and the height of rows in the Modify Page Layout dialog box. You also can change the sizes of rows and columns in existing tables.

- To change the width of all columns equally, choose Table, Modify Table Layout. In the Modify Table Layout dialog box, enter the width of the columns and the column gutters. Choose OK.

To change the width of just one column, do one of the following:

- Position the insertion point in any cell in the column. Choose Table, Column/Row Size. In the Column/Row Size dialog box, enter the width of the columns and the column gutters (the space between columns). Choose OK.

- Point the mouse pointer at one of the column's margin gridlines until the pointer changes to a four-headed arrow. Drag the margin left or right to change the width of the column.

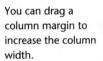

You can drag a column margin to increase the column width.

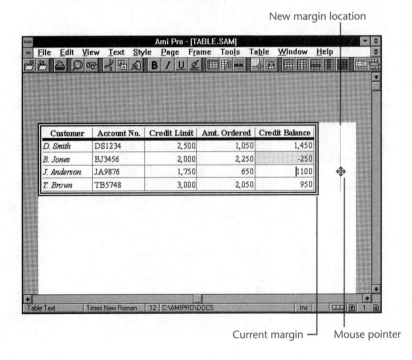

If you select **A**utomatic row height in the Modify Table Layout dialog box, the cells automatically adjust in height to accommodate any amount of data.

To set a specific height for all rows, follow these steps:

1. Choose Ta**b**le, **M**odify Table Layout.

2. In the Default Rows area, deselect **A**utomatic.

3. Enter the row height in the **H**eight text box.

4. Choose OK.

After Automatic is deselected, follow these steps to change the height of just one row:

1. Position the insertion point in any cell in the row.

2. Choose Ta**b**le, Column/Row **S**ize.

3. In the Rows area, enter the height.

4. Choose OK.

Adding Lines and Color

To add a line around the table, follow these steps:

1. Choose Ta**b**le, **M**odify Table Layout.

2. In the Options area, choose the **L**ine Around Table check box.

3. In the **S**tyle area, choose the width or style of the line.

4. Choose OK.

To add lines and color to a cell or group of cells, follow these steps:

1. Position the insertion point within the cell, or select the cells.

2. Choose Ta**b**le, Li**n**es & Color.

In the Lines & Color
dialog box, line
position relates to
each selected cell,
not to the whole
table.

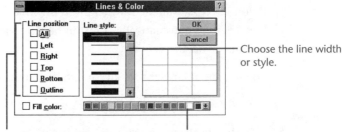

Choose the line width
or style.

Choose on which side of the cell
you want to place the line.

Choose the color or pattern
to use in the cell.

The Fill pattern highlights the
cell with the negative balance.

A double line around the table

Here lines and fill
patterns were
added to enhance
the look of the
table.

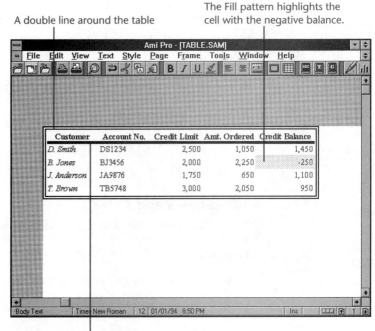

A thick, single line across the
bottom of each cell in the row

**If you have
problems...**

When you print a table, the lines placed between the columns and rows do
not print because no lines exist between the columns and rows—you had
the gridlines displayed in the View Preferences dialog box! Gridlines are
non-printing characters. To add lines between the rows and columns, use
the Lines & Color dialog box.

Connecting Cells

You can connect adjacent cells either horizontally or vertically. This option is useful for functions such as creating a title across the top row of a table.

To connect cells, follow these steps:

1. Select the cells you want to connect.

2. Choose Ta**b**le, **C**onnect Cells. The boundaries between the cells are removed. Existing data in all but the cell on the far left is hidden.

   To replace the boundaries, choose Ta**b**le, **D**isconnect Cells. The hidden data appears again.

Adding Leaders

You can add a leader to data in a cell. A leader is a series of characters, such as dots, dashes, or a solid line that leads from the margin of the cell to the data.

To add a leader, follow these steps:

1. Position the insertion point in the cell or select the cells.

2. Choose Ta**b**le, **L**eaders. The Leaders menu appears.

3. Choose the leader you want. Ami Pro inserts the leader into the cell.

   To remove the leader, choose **N**one on the Leader menu.

Protecting Cells

You can protect cells from accidental editing. This option is useful if you know that others are going to use the table.

To protect a cell, follow these steps:

1. Position the insertion point in the cell, or select the cells.

2. Choose Ta**b**le, **P**rotect Cells.

3. Choose Ta**b**le, **M**odify Table Layout. The Modify Table Layout dialog box appears.

4. In the Options area, choose the Honor **P**rotection check box.

5. Choose OK.

To unprotect a protected cell, first turn off Honor Protection. Click in the protected cell, and choose Ta**b**le, **P**rotect Cells.

Adding Numbers in a Row or Column

You can calculate the sum of numbers in a selected row or column quickly. To do so, you must leave a blank cell at the bottom of the row or at the end of the column, and all the cells in the row or column must be number cells.

To add the numbers, follow these steps:

1. Position the insertion point in the blank cell at the end of the row or column.

2. Choose Ta**b**le, Quick **A**dd. The Quick Add menu appears.

3. Choose to add a row or a column. Ami Pro inserts the total into the blank cell.

If you have problems...

If all the cells in the row or column are not number cells, Ami Pro cannot perform the calculation. Instead, Ami Pro displays REF in the blank cell, indicating that an incorrect reference exists in the table. To remove the REF message, change the data in the incorrect cell.

Using Formulas in Tables

Formula
A mathematical expression used to perform operations on data in cells.

In Ami Pro, you can use *formulas* to add, subtract, multiply, and divide the data in the table cells.

To create a formula in a cell, follow these steps:

1. Position the insertion point in the cell.

2. Choose Ta**b**le, Edit **F**ormula. The Edit Formula dialog box appears.

3. In the **F**ormula text box, type the formula you want to use.

4. Choose OK. Ami Pro makes the calculation and displays the result in the cell that contains the insertion point.

If you change data in one of the cells referenced by the formula, Ami Pro automatically updates the result data.

When you create formulas, keep the following rules in mind:

- ■ Use the + operator to perform addition.

- ■ Use the - operator to perform subtraction.

- ■ Use the * operator to perform multiplication.

- ■ Use the / operator to perform division.

- ■ Use the % operator to calculate percentages.

- ■ Use parentheses to specify the order of operations.

- ■ Use the word *sum* to total the numbers in the specified cells.

- ■ You can use Lotus 1-2-3 syntax.

- ■ You can only create formulas using Number cells.

- ■ Use two periods or a colon to separate the cell addresses when you specify a range of cells.

You can edit a formula in the **F**ormula text box in the Edit Formula dialog box.

You can delete a formula by selecting the cell that contains the formula and pressing Del.

You can copy or move a formula to a different cell by using the **E**dit, Cu**t** or **E**dit, **C**opy and **E**dit, **P**aste commands. When you relocate a formula, Ami Pro automatically changes the cells referenced in the formula to cells in the same relative position to the formula cell.

If you have problems...   If the word REF appears in a text cell, it means you referenced that cell in a formula. Edit the formula to remove the reference to the text cell.

12

Lesson Summary

To	Do This
Create a page table	Choose Tools, Tables. Enter the number of columns and rows.
Create a frame table	Select an empty frame. Choose Tools, Tables. Enter the number of columns and rows.
Display table gridlines	Choose View, View Preferences. Choose the Table Gridlines check box.
Display table column/ row headings	Choose View, View Preferences. Choose the Table Row/Column Headings check box.
Select a cell	Click the cell.
Select a row	Choose Table, Select Row.
Select a column	Choose Table, Select Column.
Select the table	Choose Table, Select Entire Table.
Connect cells	Select the cells. Choose Table, Connect Cells.

On Your Own

These exercises are designed to help you become comfortable when using Ami Pro to create tables.

Create a Table

Estimated Time: 10 minutes

1. Create either a page table or a frame table with at least four columns and four rows, centered on the page.

2. Display the table gridlines and the row and column headings.

3. Enter data in the table. For example, create a table that shows sales figures for the months of January, February, and March for three sales people. Label the cells in the first row with the dates. Label the cells in the first column with the salespeople's names. Fill in the other cells with the sales amounts.

Change the Table
Estimated Time: 15–20 minutes

1. Add another sales person to the table.

2. Change the formatting of the data in the top row. For example, center and boldface the data.

3. Change the formatting of the data in the first row.

4. Add a row to create a title across the top of the table.

5. Add a column on the right. If necessary, change the width of the existing columns to accommodate a new column.

6. Total each salesperson's figures, displaying the totals in the column on the right.

7. Add a double line around the outside of the table.

8. Add printing gridlines to the table.

9. Add a fill pattern to the cell that shows the highest sales figures.

10. Save the table. You can use this information for the chart you create in Lesson 13, "Working with Charts."

Here are some additional exercises you can try:

■ Create a formula to add the data in B2, B3, and B4.

■ Copy the data into a new table.

■ Add a column to the top of the table, connect the cells and type a title for the table.

12

Lesson 13

Working with Charts

In many business presentations, charts are used to display statistical information. Charts are an important visual tool for translating numeric data into a format that most people can easily understand.

With Ami Pro, you can create charts out of existing data, or enter new data. You can edit and enhance charts by adding elements such as clip art pictures and explanatory text.

In this lesson, you learn how to

- ■ Choose a chart type.

- ■ Create a chart.

- ■ Edit a chart.

- ■ Enhance a chart.

Understanding Charts

Chart
A visual or graphic representation of numeric data. Charts come in many types, including bar charts, pie charts, column charts, and line charts.

Charts are useful for enhancing numeric information that may otherwise be boring or difficult to read. However, for a chart to be effective, it is important for you to understand the data you want to display and the information you want to convey before you create a chart.

In Ami Pro, you can select from 12 chart types. Different charts are suitable for displaying information in different ways. For example, a pie chart shows you segments of a whole. It may be useful for displaying different segments of a budget. A line chart shows a progression of segments. It may be useful for displaying growth in market share.

Table 13.1 describes the different charts available in Ami Pro.

Icon	Chart Type	Description
	Column	Displays related data in a group of vertical columns.
	Stacked column	Displays related data stacked in a single vertical column.
	Bar	Displays related data in a group of horizontal bars.
	Stacked-bar	Displays related data stacked in a single horizontal bar.
	Line	Displays the progression of data by using horizontal lines.
	Area	Displays overall data trends for related data sets.
	Line-and-picture	Displays the progression of data by using horizontal lines, with symbols inserted to highlight milestones, segments, or points of interest. You can choose to display like symbols along one line, or you can display each symbol on each line.
	Pie	Displays segments of a whole.
	Expanded pie	Displays segments of a whole, separated by blank space.
	Picture	Displays related data vertically. Each segment is displayed in a different shape.
	Stacked picture	Displays related data stacked in a single column; however, each segment is displayed in a different shape.

Table 13.1. Ami Pro 3 Chart Types

Note: *The icons shown in the first column are used to select the chart type in the Charting dialog box as described in "Changing the Appearance of a Chart," later in this lesson.*

Here, the same data is displayed first in a column chart, then in a stacked column chart. Both charts use a 3D effect, and use legends to identify the data content.

Column chart

Stacked column chart

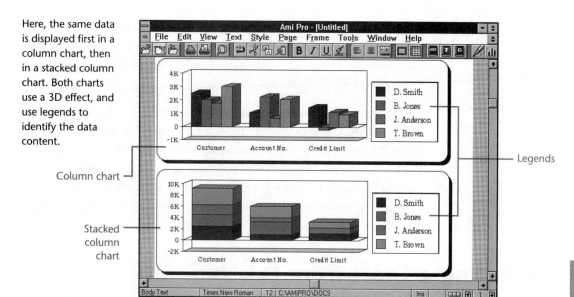

Legends

Here, the data is displayed first in an expanded pie chart, with a 3D effect, then in a line-and-picture chart with a grid and a legend.

Expanded pie chart

Line-and-picture chart

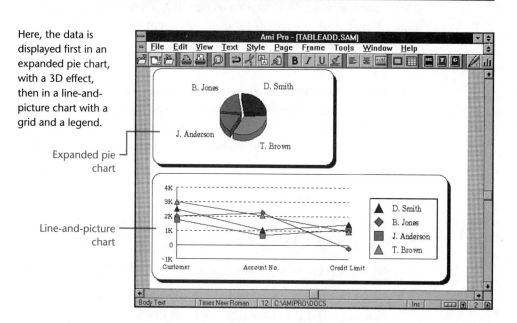

In addition to choosing a chart type, you can choose variations for the charts. For example, you can change the segment groupings or the labels. To choose a variation, simply click the chart type icon again.

Charts can be enhanced with different charting options, such as adding 3D effects or changing colors. You can also use Ami Pro's Draw feature to add objects to a chart. (For information on using Draw, see Lesson 11, "Using Draw.")

Ami Pro places each chart in a frame. You can create the frame before you create the chart, or you can let Ami Pro create it automatically. If you know the size of the chart, it is easier to create the frame first. Ami Pro does not know how big the chart will be, and if you let it create the frame automatically, you will probably end up adjusting the size to accommodate the chart. (For information on creating frames, see Lesson 10, "Working with Frames.")

Creating a Chart from Existing Data

Axis
The length or height of a chart. All charts, except pie charts, have two axes—the x-axis is the bottom, or horizontal, portion of the chart and the y-axis is the side, or vertical, portion of the chart.

Legend
Identifies segments of the chart. Depending on the type of chart, the legend may identify the segments based on color, shape, or both color and shape.

You can use existing data to create a chart in Ami Pro. The data may be entered in an Ami Pro document, or in a different Windows application. (For information on using other applications, see Lesson 16, "Working with Other Windows Applications.")

The data that Ami Pro uses to create a chart must have been entered according to certain guidelines. For example, you must use numeric data, and it must be arranged in columns separated by tabs or spaces. For this reason, data already entered in a table is ideal to use for creating a chart.

If there are text cells in the top row of a table, Ami Pro uses the text to label an *axis* of the chart.

If there are text cells in the left column of a table, Ami Pro can use the text to create a *legend* for the chart.

To create a chart out of an existing table, follow these steps:

1. Select the data in the table that you want to use for the chart. You can select the entire table, or just part of it.

2. Choose **E**dit, **C**opy to copy the data to the Clipboard.

3. Position the insertion point in the document where you want to create the chart.

4. Create and select a frame large enough to hold the chart. (For information on creating frames, see Lesson 10, "Working with Frames.")

If you do not create the frame before creating the chart, Ami Pro creates the frame automatically. You may have to adjust the frame to the right size for the chart.

Table data to use for chart

Empty frame (selected), large enough to hold the chart

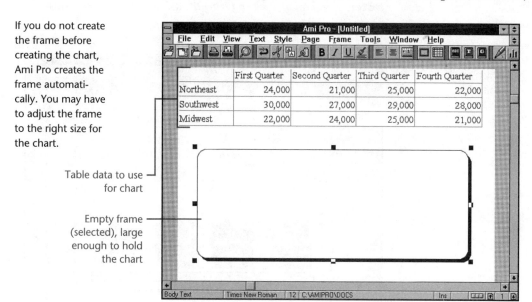

5. Choose Tools, Charting. The Charting dialog box appears.

In the Charting dialog box, you can choose from numerous chart types and variations.

Choose the chart type.

View an example of the chart.

Choose the color set.

Choose options.

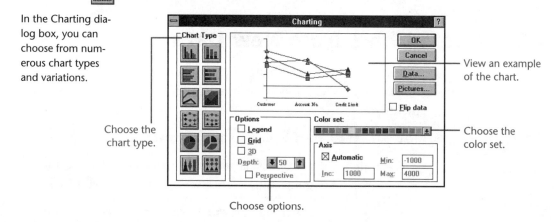

13

6. Choose OK to create a column chart with the default settings.

Note: *For information on changing the default chart settings, see the section, "Changing the Appearance of a Chart," later in this lesson.*

Ami Pro creates the chart and inserts it in the frame.

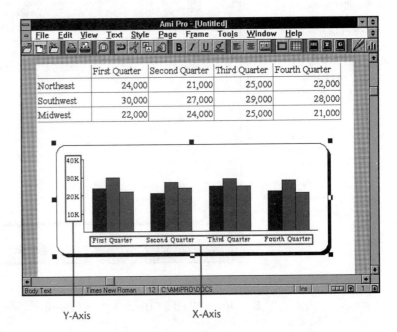

Y-Axis   X-Axis

Creating a Chart from New Data

When the data you want to use for the chart is not already entered in Ami Pro or another Windows application, you can type it in as you create the chart.

To create a chart with new data, follow these steps:

1. Create and select a frame large enough to hold the chart. (For information on creating frames, see Lesson 10, "Working with Frames."

2. Choose Tools, Charting. Ami Pro displays a message box informing you that there is not data available to use to create the chart.

If the Clipboard is empty, Ami Pro asks if you want to enter the data now.

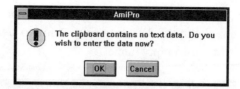

If you have problems...

If Ami Pro displays the Charting dialog box, it means that there was data in the Clipboard that it could use to create the chart. Choose Cancel to return to the document, and replace the contents of the Clipboard with nothing by copying the empty frame.

3. Choose OK. The Charting Data dialog box appears.

Here, budget data is entered and ready for charting.

Multiword labels are separated with underscores.

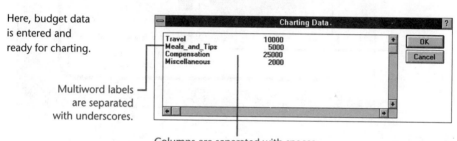

Columns are separated with spaces.

4. Type the data into the box, following these guidelines:

■ Press the space bar to indicate a new column.

■ Do not press Tab.

■ Use an underscore character instead of a space between words.

■ Press Ctrl+Enter to move to the next line (row).

■ Do not press Enter. If you press Enter, Ami Pro accepts the data and closes the dialog box.

5. Choose OK. The Charting dialog box appears.

6. Choose the chart type you want to use, or choose OK to create the chart with the default settings. Ami Pro creates the chart and inserts it into the empty frame.

Here, the budget data is displayed as an expanded pie chart, with a legend identifying each segment.

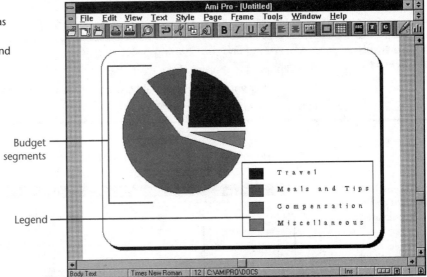

Budget segments

Legend

Changing the Appearance of a Chart

You can modify the appearance of a chart using the options in the Charting dialog box. You can make changes before or after you create the chart.

To make changes to an existing chart, first select the frame that contains the chart. Or, double-click the frame to quickly display the Charting dialog box.

View a sample chart.

In the Charting dialog box, you can select options for modifying the appearance of a chart.

Choose the chart type.

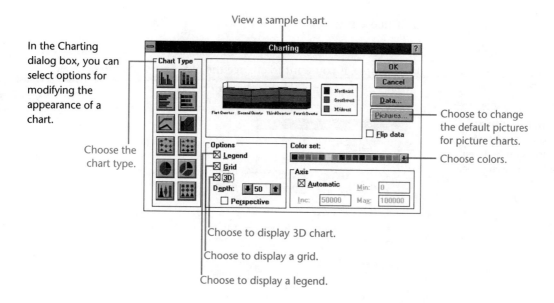

Choose to change the default pictures for picture charts.

Choose colors.

Choose to display 3D chart.

Choose to display a grid.

Choose to display a legend.

13

Note: *The Pictures option is available only if you select a line-and-picture chart, a picture chart, or a stacked picture chart.*

Changing Pictures

By default, when you select a Line-and-Picture, Picture, or Stacked Picture chart, Ami Pro uses a triangle, a diamond, and a rectangle to represent data sets or milestones. If you have more than three data sets, Ami Pro repeats the pictures, using different colors. You can change the pictures by substituting the contents of any AmiDraw file.

Note: *The AmiDraw file must exist before you can substitute it for a charting picture. For information on creating drawings with the Draw feature, see Lesson 11, "Using Draw." For information on importing graphics files, see Lesson 16, "Working with Other Windows Applications."*

To change the pictures, follow these steps:

1. Choose Tools, Charting to create the chart.

   Note: *If the chart already exists, select the frame containing the chart you want to change before you choose Tools, Charting.*

2. Choose one of the chart types that uses pictures—line-and-picture, picture, or stacked picture.

3. Choose **P**ictures.

4. Select the picture assigned to the data set you want to change. For example, if you want to change the picture assigned to data set 1, choose the triangle beside the number 1.

You can change
charting pictures
to a picture stored
in an AmiDraw file.

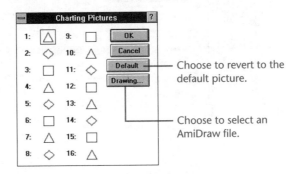

Choose to revert to the default picture.

Choose to select an AmiDraw file.

5. Choose Drawing.

6. In the Drawing dialog box, select the directory that contains the AmiDraw file you want to use. For example, choose the C:\AMIPRO\DRAWSYM directory.

7. In the **F**iles list box, select the file you want to use. A preview of the picture is displayed in the example box.

You can substitute
one of Ami Pro's
clip art pictures for
a charting picture.

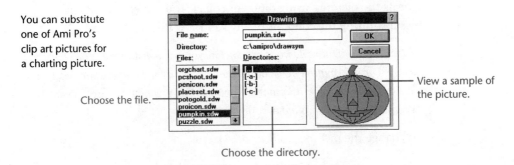

Choose the file.

View a sample of the picture.

Choose the directory.

8. Choose OK. Ami Pro substitutes the file image for the selected charting picture.

9. Continue substituting AmiDraw files for charting pictures until you are done. Then choose OK to return to the Charting dialog box.

Here, clip art files are used for all three segments in a stacked picture chart.

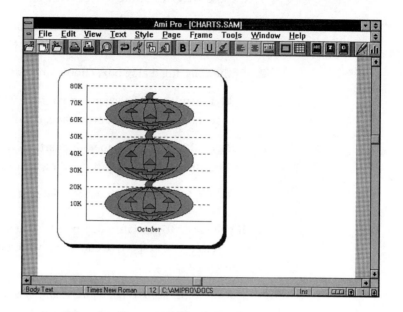

13

Changing Charting Options

You can change the appearance of your chart by adding effects, such as a legend, grid, or 3D depth, and by changing the chart colors.

To change the colors, follow these steps:

1. Choose Tools, **C**harting to create the chart.

   Note: *If the chart already exists, select the frame containing the chart you want to change, before you choose Too**l**s, **C**harting.*

2. In the Charting dialog box, select the Color set you want to use. Click the down arrow beside the color bar to display the different sets.

3. Choose OK.

To add effects, follow these steps:

1. Choose Tools, Charting to create the chart.

   Note: If the chart already exists, select the frame containing the chart you want to change before you choose Tools, Charting.

2. In the Charting dialog box, choose one or more of the following:

   ■ **Legend**, to add a legend to your chart. A legend identifies the data segments by name, shape, or color.

   ■ **Grid**, to add a grid to your chart. A grid extends the Y-axis values across the chart by using a dashed line.

   ■ **3D**, to add three-dimensional depth to your chart.

3. If you select 3D, specify a depth in the Depth text box. You can also select the Perspective checkbox, which may enhance the 3D effect.

   Note: The 3D depth is not a precise unit of measurement. Ami Pro creates the effect by using a percentage of the total depth available.

If you have problems...   If the 3D option is dimmed, it is because you have selected a chart type that cannot be displayed in three dimensions. Either select a different chart type, or forget about using the 3D option.

Here, a 3D column chart is displayed with a legend and a grid.

3D effect

Grid

Legend

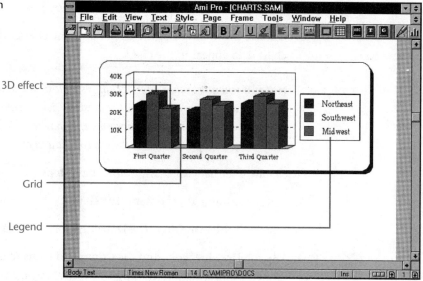

Editing a Chart

After a chart is created, you can make basic editing changes to the data, delete the chart, or use the Draw feature to add enhancements. You can also use the Charting dialog box to change the chart type or chart options, as described in the previous section.

To edit the chart data, follow these steps:

1. Select the frame containing the chart.

2. Choose Tools, Charting.

   Note: *To quickly display the Charting dialog box, double-click the frame containing the chart.*

3. Choose **D**ata. The Charting Data dialog box appears, displaying data from the current chart.

4. Edit the data by inserting or deleting characters. Follow the guidelines for entering new data described earlier in this lesson.

13

5. Choose OK to return to the Charting dialog box.

6. Choose OK to return to the document. The changes made to the chart data appear in the chart.

   Note: *If you must make a lot of changes, editing the data in the Charting Data dialog box may not be the most efficient method to use. If the data was copied from another document, it maybe easier to change the data in the original document, then to copy it and create a new chart.*

To use Draw to enhance a chart, follow these steps:

1. Select the frame that contains the chart.

2. Choose Too**l**s, **D**rawing. The Drawing toolbar appears.

 3. Use the Drawing icons and the Command icons to modify the chart. For information in using Draw, see Lesson 11, "Using Draw."

   Some ways to modify a chart include:

   - Add text for headings, captions, or labels.

   - Format text. Change the size of objects, just as in a legend.

   - Add clip art imported from another program to dress up the chart.

   - Use drawings created with the Draw feature to change the appearance of a plain column or bar chart.

   - Manipulate objects, such as the segments of an expanded bar chart.

Draw can be used to change the size of objects, move objects, and add formatting text.

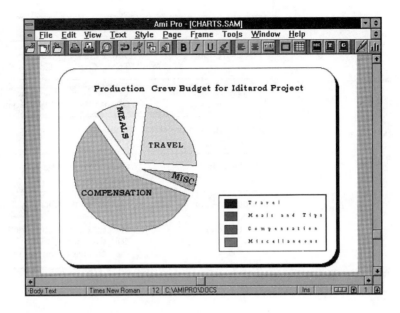

To delete a chart, do one of the following:

- Select the frame containing the chart and choose **Edit**, **Cut**, or press Del. Ami Pro deletes the frame and its contents.

- Use Draw to delete just the contents of the frame.

    Note: *In both cases, Ami Pro does not warn you before deleting the selected frame of objects in the frame. If you delete by accident, choose* **Edit**, **Undo**, *immediately.*

Lesson Summary

To	Do This
Create a chart from a table	Copy the data from table to the Clipboard. Create and select a frame large enough to hold the chart. Choose Tools, **C**harting. Choose the chart type.
Enter new data for a chart	Create and select a frame large enough to hold the chart. Choose Tools, **C**harting. Choose **Y**es to enter data.

(continues)

To	Do This
Edit chart data	Select the frame containing the chart. Choose Tools, Charting. Choose Data. Edit the data.
Choose a chart type	Choose Tools, Charting. Choose the chart type. Choose the chart type again to see variations.
Add a legend to the chart	Choose Tools, Charting. Choose the Legend checkbox.
Display a grid	Choose Tools, Charting. Choose the Grid checkbox.
Display the chart in 3D	Choose Tools, Charting. Choose the 3D checkbox.
Delete a chart	Select the frame containing the chart and choose Edit, Cut, or press Del. Or, use Draw to delete just the contents of the frame.

On Your Own

These exercises are designed to help you understand how to create and use charts. You can start with no data entered, or use data already entered in Ami Pro. If you created a table in Lesson 12, use it to create a chart.

Create a Chart from Existing Data
Estimated Time: 10 minutes

1. Open a document that has data you can use to create a chart. For example, open the document that contains the table created in Lesson 12.

2. Copy the data to the Clipboard.

3. Create a frame large enough to hold the chart.

4. Create the chart.

Create a Chart from New Data
Estimated Time: 10 minutes

1. Create a frame large enough to hold the chart.

2. Copy the empty frame to the Clipboard to be sure there is no data in the Clipboard.

3. Create a chart.

4. Enter the data by following the chart data entry guidelines. Set the chart up into at least three sets with three categories in each set. For example, enter sales figures for three salespeople over three time periods.

13

Change the Chart
Estimated Time: 10 minutes

1. See how the chart looks if you change the chart type.

2. Add a legend to the chart.

3. Add a grid.

4. Display the chart in 3D.

Here are some optional exercises you can try:

■ Edit data in an existing chart to add another set of figures.

■ Use Draw to enhance a chart.

■ Create a chart that uses pictures, and substitute clip art for the default pictures.

Part IV
Advanced Features and Integration

Merging Documents

Merging involves combining variable data with a standard document. Before you can conduct the merge, you create the merge document and a data file that contains the variable data. Then, Ami Pro merges the two into a new document, which you can view, print, and save.

Most often, merging is used to personalize form letters. You can create one letter document, than merge it with different names and addresses. You can also use merge to create standard contracts, proposals, and mailing labels.

In this lesson, you learn how to

- Create a merge data file.

- Manipulate merge data files records and fields.

- Create a merge document.

- Conduct a merge.

Understanding a Merge

Merge
The process of combining information from one document with information from another document to create a new document.

When Ami Pro conducts a *merge*, it takes the variable data from a *data file* and inserts it into a copy of a *merge document*.

For Ami Pro to know which information to take from the data file, and where to put it in the merge document, the information must be organized in a very specific format. Information in a data file is organized into *records*, and each record is organized into *fields*. In the merge document, the location where the variable data is to be inserted is marked by *merge fields*.

Data file
The file that contains the information that changes in each document.

Merge document
The document that contains the information that does not change.

In Ami Pro, there are three basic steps in merging:

- Create the data file.

- Create the merge document.

- Conduct the merge.

However, it is important to consider the finished product before you begin. You should think about how you want the final document to look, what information you want to include in the merge document, and therefore, what information you want to include in the data file.

Creating a Data File

Record
All of the variable information for one entry in the data file.

Field
One item of information in a record.

Merge field
A code used in the merge document to mark the location where variable data information is inserted.

Creating a data file is the first of three steps involved in performing a merge.

In Ami Pro, data files are documents that are specially formatted for use in merges. You can create a data file with new data, or you can use data from a database management program or a spreadsheet. For information on using data from another program, see Lesson 16, "Working with Other Windows Applications."

Each data file consists of a series of records, which contain information entered in fields. To create a new data file, you first define the data fields and then enter the data in the records.

To create a data file, follow these steps:

1. Choose **F**ile, Mer**g**e. The Welcome to Merge dialog box appears.

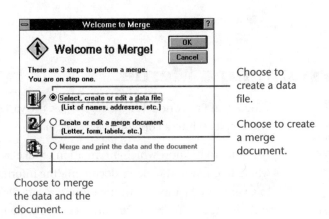

Choose to create a data file.

Choose to create a merge document.

Choose to merge the data and the document.

2. Choose step 1, Select Create or Edit a **D**ata File, then choose OK. The Select Merge Data File dialog box appears.

3. Choose Ne**w**.

In the Create Data File dialog box, enter names for each field.

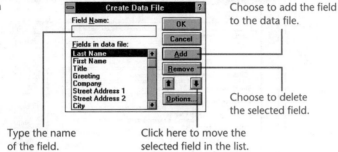

Choose to add the field to the data file.

Choose to delete the selected field.

Type the name of the field.

Click here to move the selected field in the list.

4. In the Field **N**ame text box, enter the name of the first field you want in the data file.

5. Choose **A**dd. Ami Pro adds the name to the **F**ields in Data File list.

6. Continue entering names for all of the fields you want in the data file. Choose **A**dd after each entry. The names appear in the order you enter them. To change the order, select a field, then click the up or down arrow in the dialog box.

14

7. When you have entered all of the fields, choose OK. Ami Pro creates the data file and displays a Data File dialog box showing a data file record that contains all of the field you entered.

Note: *Ami Pro organizes each record according to the first field you enter. If you are creating a data file of names, you probably want the records organized according to last name, so first enter a Last Name field. If you are creating a data file of companies, you first enter a Company Name field.*

Entering Data

The data file records look like index cards with tabs on top. Each tab indicates another record. Each record can have more than one page.

To enter data in a data file record, follow these steps:

1. Position the insertion point in the first field and type the information.

2. Press Tab to move to the next field, and type the information. Continue until you have filled in every applicable field.

3. Choose **A**dd to add the record to the data file. Ami Pro displays a blank record. Continue filling out records until you have added as many as you want to include in the data file.

In the data record, fill in all of the fields that apply. When you add the record to the data file, Ami Pro puts the information from the first field on the tab to identify the record.

Field names

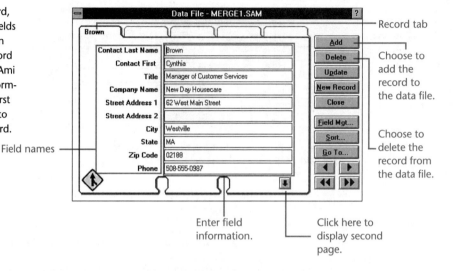

Record tab

Choose to add the record to the data file.

Choose to delete the record from the data file.

Enter field information.

Click here to display second page.

4. Choose Close to close the data file.

5. If you want to save the file, choose **Y**es. Ami Pro displays the Save As dialog box.

6. Enter a file name and choose OK. Ami Pro displays the New dialog box.

Note: *The next step in merging documents, is creating a merge document. That is why Ami Pro displays the New dialog box. You can select the style sheet you want to use to create the merge document, or choose Cancel.*

Manipulating Data Records

Once a data file is created and saved, you can edit and manipulate the data records in several ways. You can scroll through the records, edit them, insert new records, insert new fields, and sort the records into a new order.

To open a data file, follow these steps:

1. Choose **F**ile, Mer**g**e.

2. Choose step 1, Select, Create or Edit a **D**ata File.

3. In the Select Merge Data File dialog box, enter the data file name in the File **N**ame text box. If necessary, choose the correct drive and directory, first.

To edit a merge data file, open it using the Select Merge Data File dialog box.

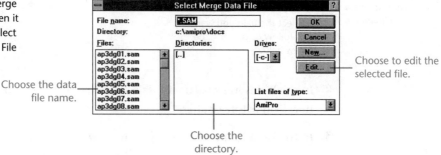

Choose the data file name.

Choose the directory.

Choose to edit the selected file.

4. Choose **E**dit. Ami Pro opens the data file and displays the first record entered.

To scroll through the records, do one of the following:

- ■ To page through the records, click the left or right arrows.

- ■ To move to the first record in the file, click the left double arrow.

- ■ To move to the last record in the file, click the right double arrow.

- ■ To move a specific record to the top, click its tab.

To insert a record after, or on top of, an existing record, display the existing record and choose **N**ew Record. Ami Pro displays a blank record.

To edit an existing record, display the record, make the changes, then choose U**p**date. Ami Pro saves the record with the changes. Choose **N**ew Record to display a blank record.

Adding Fields

To add a field to all records, follow these steps:

1. In a data file record dialog box, choose **F**ield Mgt. Ami Pro displays the Field Management dialog box.

14

You add fields to
every record in the
data base by using
the Field Manage-
ment dialog box.

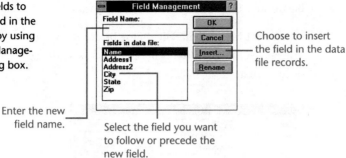

Choose to insert
the field in the data
file records.

Enter the new
field name.

Select the field you want
to follow or precede the
new field.

2. In the Fields in Data File list, select the field you want to place the new field before or after.

3. In the Field Name text box, type the new field name.

4. Choose Insert.

5. In the Insert Field dialog box, choose to insert the field before or after the selected field.

6. Choose OK to return to the Field Management dialog box.

7. Choose OK to insert the field in the data file.

If you have problems...

If it seems like nothing is happening, it's because merge is a very slow procedure. Ami Pro takes a long time to accomplish each task in creating the data file. Wait a little longer. Ami Pro completes the task and you are able to continue.

Sorting Records

You can sort the records in your data file to display them in a particular order.

To sort the records, follow these steps:

1. Open the data file, as described at the beginning of this section.

2. In the Data File dialog box, choose **S**ort. The Sort Records dialog box appears.

You can sort
records by any field.

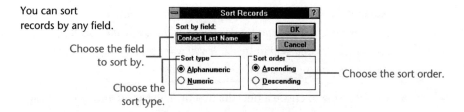

Choose the field
to sort by.

Choose the
sort type.

Choose the sort order.

3. Choose the field to sort, the type of sort, and the sort order.

4. Choose OK. Ami Pro rearranges the records in the data file.

Creating the Merge Document

Once you have created a data file, the second step in merging documents
is creating the merge document. You can create any standard document,
using any style sheet.

Note: *If you have just completed creating and saving the data file, the New
dialog box may be open on your screen. If so, skip to step 5 in the following
step-by-step instructions.*

To create the merge document, follow these steps:

1. Choose **F**ile, Mer**g**e. The Welcome to Merge dialog box is displayed.

2. Choose step 2, Create or Edit a **M**erge Document.

3. Choose OK. The Merge Document dialog box appears.

14

The Merge Docu-
ment dialog box is
similar to the Open
dialog box. You can
select an existing
merge document,
or you can create a
new one.

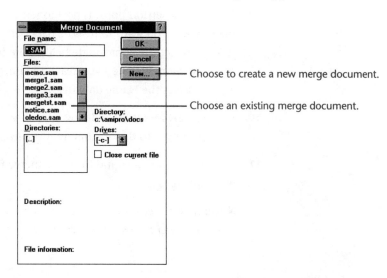

Choose to create a new merge document.

Choose an existing merge document.

Note: *If a document is already open, Ami Pro displays a message asking if you want to use the current document as the merge document. If you do, choose Yes and skip to step 7. If you want to create a new merge document, choose No, and continue with step 4.*

4. Choose New to create a new document. The New dialog box appears.

5. Choose the style sheet to use for creating the merge document. You can create a merge document using any style sheet that is appropriate for the document you are creating.

6. Choose OK. Ami Pro creates a new document and displays the Select Merge Data File dialog box.

7. In the Files list, select the data file you want to use and choose OK.

At this point, a blank merge document is displayed, and the Insert Merge Field dialog box appears in the top right corner of your screen. As you type the document, the Insert Merge Field dialog box remains open on your screen.

If you have problems...   If you accidentally close the Insert Merge Field dialog box, choose **E**dit, **I**nsert, Merge **F**ield, to open it again.

---

8. Begin typing the document text the way you want it to appear in every document created by the merge.

9. When the insertion point is positioned at a location in the document where you want to insert a data field from the data file records, select the appropriate field in the Insert Merge Field dialog box. For example, when you reach the line where a name should appear, select the Name data field.

10. In the Insert Merge Field dialog box, choose Insert. Ami Pro inserts a merge field into the document at the insertion point.

11. Continue typing text and inserting merge fields until the document is complete.

Note: *As you type the document, remember to include all characters before and after the merge data fields, such as commas and spaces.*

Ami Pro inserts the selected merge fields into the document at the insertion point location.

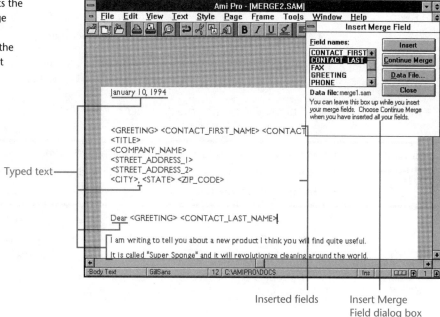

Typed text

Inserted fields

Insert Merge Field dialog box

14

12. Save the document. You can use it again for future merges.

> **Note:** *You can format the document the way you format any document. If merge fields are selected, the formatting changes effect them, as well.*

> **Note:** *To delete a merge field make sure you select the entire field, including the brackets. If you don't select the brackets you may end up deleting the contents of the field, but not the field itself.*

Performing the Merge

When you have created a data file and completed the merge document, the next step is to conduct the merge itself. To begin the merge, you must have the merge document open on your screen.

To merge, follow these steps:

> **Note:** *If you've just completed the merge document, and it is still displayed on your screen, choose* **C***ontinue Merge in the Insert Merge Field dialog box to display the Welcome to Merge dialog box. Then skip to step 6 in the following procedure.*

1. Choose **F**ile, Mer**g**e.

2. Choose step 2, Create or Edit a **M**erge Document.

3. In the **F**iles list in the Merge document dialog box, choose the merge document you want to use.

4. Choose OK to open the document.

If you have problems...

If there is no data file already associated with the document, Ami Pro displays the Select Merge Data file document. Select the data file you want to use for the merge, and choose OK.

Note: To change data files before beginning the merge, choose **D**ata File in the Insert Merge Field dialog box. Ami Pro displays the Select Merge Data file document. Select the data file you want to use for the merge, and choose OK.

5. In the Insert Merge Field dialog box, choose **C**ontinue Merge. Ami Pro displays the Welcome to Merge dialog box.

6. In the Welcome to Merge dialog box, select step 3, Merge and **P**rint the Data and the Document, then choose OK. The Merge dialog box appears.

7. Choose Merge, **V**iew & Print.

In the Merge dialog box, you can select options for merging the document.

Choose to view the documents before printing.

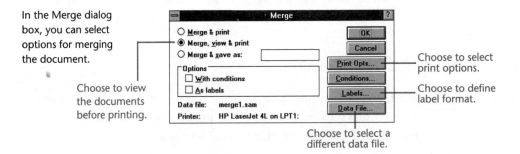

Choose to select print options.

Choose to define label format.

Choose to select a different data file.

8. Choose OK. Ami Pro begins the merge.

When the first document is ready, Ami Pro displays it on-screen. In the upper right corner of the screen, a smaller Merge dialog box appears.

To continue the merge, choose one of the following:

- Choose **P**rint and View Next to print the displayed document and review the next document on-screen.

- Choose **S**kip and View Next to skip the displayed document and review the next document on-screen.

- Choose Print **A**ll to print all of the documents after reviewing only the first one.

- Choose Cancel to stop the merge.

The merge fields in the document have been replaced by data from the data file.

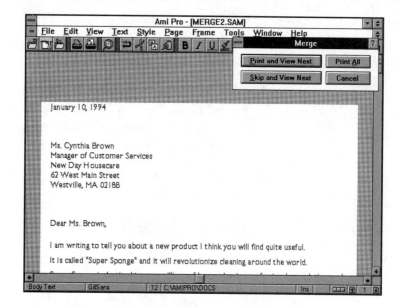

When the merge is complete, Ami Pro displays the merge document. You can save it for future use, create a style sheet from it, or close it without saving.

Creating Labels

You can use merge to print out labels, such as mailing labels. The general procedure is the same as for merging documents, except you must specify the size and format of the labels.

To use merge to print labels, follow these steps:

1. Create a data file that contains the information you want to include in the labels. For information on creating a data file, see the section "Creating a Data File," earlier in this lesson.

2. Create a merge document. For information on creating a merge document, see the section "Creating the Merge Document," earlier in this lesson.

3. Modify the page layout of the merge document to specify a page size equal to the size of *one* label. Do not specify the size of a sheet of labels!

4. Complete the merge document by inserting the merge fields you want to include on the labels.

5. Begin the merge. If the merge document is still displayed on-screen, simply choose **C**ontinue Merge in the Insert Merge Fields dialog box. If the merge document is not displayed, consult the section, "Performing the Merge," earlier in this lesson.

6. In the Merge dialog box, choose **L**abels. Ami Pro displays the Merge Labels dialog box.

Ami Pro prints the labels according to the layout you specify in the Merge Labels dialog box.

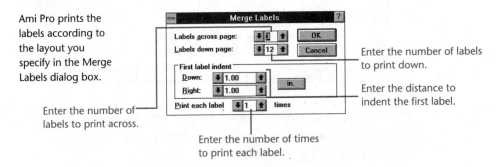

Enter the number of labels to print across.

Enter the number of labels to print down.

Enter the distance to indent the first label.

Enter the number of times to print each label.

7. Look at a sheet of labels on which you are going to print, and fill out the text boxes in the Merge Labels dialog box.

8. Choose OK. Ami Pro returns to the Merge dialog box. The **As** Labels option is selected, and the only print option available is **M**erge & Print.

9. Choose OK to begin the merge. Ami Pro prints the labels.

Lesson Summary

To	Do This
Create a data file	Choose **F**ile, Mer**g**e. Choose Select, Create or Edit a **D**ata file. Choose OK. Choose Ne**w**.
Name data fields	In the Create Data File dialog box, enter a field name in the Field **N**ame text box. Choose **A**dd.
Enter data records	In the Data File dialog box, fill out the data fields. When done, choose **A**dd.
Sort records	In the Data File dialog box, choose **S**ort. Choose the field to sort, the type of sort, and the sort order.
Create a merge document	Choose **F**ile, Mer**g**e. Choose Create or Edit a **M**erge Document. Choose OK. Choose New. Choose a style sheet. Choose OK. Select the data file you want to use. Choose OK.
Insert a merge field	Position the insertion point in the document at the correct location. In the Insert Merge Field dialog box, select the merge field. Choose Insert.
Merge	In the Insert Merge Field dialog box, choose **C**ontinue Merge. Choose Merge and **P**rint the Data and the Document. Choose Merge, **V**iew & Print.

14

On Your Own

These exercises are designed to help you feel comfortable using Ami Pro to merge documents.

Create a Data File
Estimated Time: 15 minutes

1. Create a data file containing records that you can use to send out a form letter. For example, include fields for names, titles, company names, street addresses, cities, states, and ZIP codes.

2. Fill out at least four or five records.

3. Add a new field.

4. Scroll through the records to fill out the new field.

5. Save the data file.

Create a Merge Document
Estimated Time: 15 minutes

1. Create a standard document that you can use as a form letter.

2. Using the data file you just created, insert the merge fields into the document at the correct location.

3. Format the document.

4. Save the merge document.

Merge
Estimated Time: 10 minutes

1. Using the data file and the merge document you just created, begin a merge.

2. View each document before you print it.

3. Go back and correct errors, add fields, or delete records as necessary.

Here are some optional exercises you can try:

■ Change the order of the fields in the data file so that a different field is first.

■ Sort the records in the data file.

■ Create a merge document for generating mailing labels. Use the data file you already created, if possible, or create a new one.

Working with Document Notation

Keeping track of changes when you are editing, reviewing, and revising documents can be a daunting task. When more than one person is involved in the process, the problems of organization become much worse.

Ami Pro provides tools to make on-line reviewing and editing simple. By inserting notes and bookmarks and by using revision marking, you always know whose comments are whose, and you have the option of accepting changes or deleting them. You can even compare two documents to see which changes you like better.

Ami Pro also keeps track of pertinent statistics about each document that you can view and edit.

In this lesson, you are introduced to some of Ami Pro document's notation features. Specifically, you learn how to

- ■ Insert notes.
- ■ Use revision marking.
- ■ Compare documents.
- ■ Add bookmarks.
- ■ Use the Go To command.
- ■ View and edit document information.

Inserting Notes

You can insert *notes* into a document to remind yourself about something you need to add or check in the text, or to communicate with other people who are working on the same document.

More than one person can insert notes into the same document. Ami Pro color codes the notes and includes the writer's initials so that you know who inserted which comments.

You can set Note defaults in the User Setup dialog box. For more information, see Lesson 9, "Customizing Ami Pro."

To insert a note into a document, follow these steps:

1. Place the insertion point where you want the note to appear.

2. Choose **E**dit, **I**nsert.

3. From the Insert menu, choose **N**ote. A blank note window opens on-screen. The background color is the color you selected in the User Setup dialog box.

The note appears as a small box at the insertion point location. To see the note window, double-click the note box.

The note window appears when you double-click the note box.

Note box

4. Type the note in the window, or use the Clipboard to copy and paste text from any document into the note window.

5. To insert the note into the text, click outside the note window, or press Esc.

If you have problems...   If you cannot see the note on-screen, select the Notes check box in the View Preferences dialog box.

To delete the note, position the insertion point on the note box in the text and press Del. Ami Pro displays a message asking if you are sure you want to delete the note. Choose **Y**es.

To remove all notes from the document, open the Note window's control menu and choose Remove All Notes.

If you have problems...   If you delete a note, then decide you want it back, choose **E**dit, **U**ndo immediately.

Using Revision Marking

Revision marking
Identifies insertions and deletions made to an original document.

When a document is subjected to intense editing and rewriting, it is helpful to be able to track the changes. You may forget who suggested a change, or why a change was made, or even what the original text was. Ami Pro provides a *revision marking* feature with which you can easily identify all changes made to a document.

To turn on revision marking, follow these steps:

1. Choose Tools, Revision Marking. The Revision Marking dialog box appears.

To turn on revision marking, choose the Mark Revisions check box in the Revision Marking dialog box.

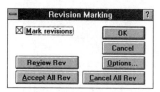

15

2. Choose the **M**ark Revisions check box.

3. Choose OK. All changes made to the document text appear in the default revision marking format.

   Note: *You can quickly turn on revision marking by clicking the Insert/ Typeover button on the status bar. When the word REV appears on the button, revision marking is turned on.*

To return to regular editing, deselect the **M**ark Revision check box in the Revision Marking dialog box.

With revision marking, you can identify changes while still seeing the original document text.

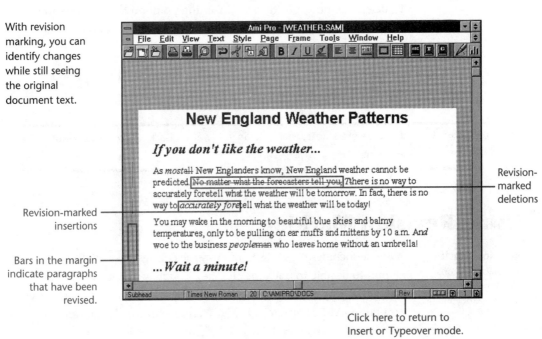

Revision-marked insertions

Bars in the margin indicate paragraphs that have been revised.

Revision-marked deletions

Click here to return to Insert or Typeover mode.

Changing Revision Marking Options

By default, revision marking insertions appear in blue italic and deletions appear in red strikethrough. To change the revision marking options, follow these steps:

1. Choose Too**l**s, Re**v**ision Marking.

2. Choose **O**ptions. The Revision Marking Options dialog box appears.

3. Choose the attributes you want to apply to insertions and the attributes you want to apply to deletions.

If more than one person is editing a document, you can use different revision marking attributes to identify who made which revisions.

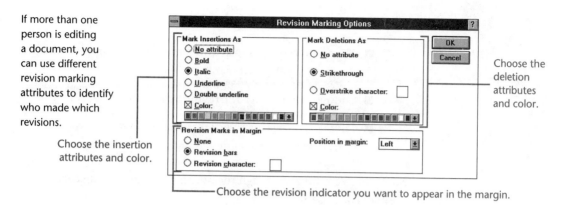

Choose the deletion attributes and color.

Choose the insertion attributes and color.

Choose the revision indicator you want to appear in the margin.

4. Choose OK to return to the Revision Marking dialog box.

5. Choose OK to return to the document.

Checking Revisions

You can check all edits made with revision marking and decide whether to accept or cancel the changes.

To check revision marking, follow these steps:

1. Position the insertion point at the beginning of the document.

2. Choose Tools, Revision Marking.

3. Choose Review Rev. Ami Pro highlights the first marked revision in the document and displays the Review Revision Marking dialog box.

15

Ami Pro highlights each revision in the document so you can accept, skip, or cancel the changes.

Choose to incorporate the revision.

Choose to remove the revision from the document.

Highlighted revision

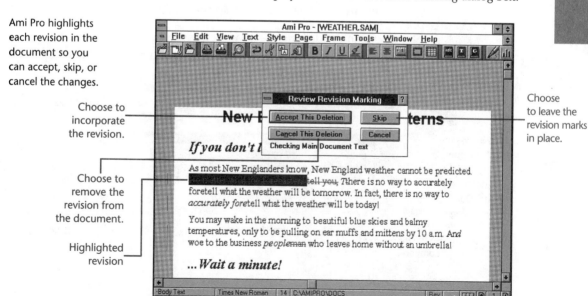

Choose to leave the revision marks in place.

4. Choose one of the following:

- Choose **A**ccept This Insertion/Deletion to incorporate the changes into the document.

- Choose **S**kip to leave the revision marks in the document.

- Choose **C**ancel This Insertion/Deletion to remove the revisions from the document.

5. Ami Pro continues through the document, highlighting each marked revision.

Comparing Documents

Compare
To identify differences between two versions of a document.

You can easily compare differences between two copies of the same document by using Ami Pro's Document *Compare* feature.

Comparing documents is useful for keeping documents up-to-date, and for deciding which of two versions has the most effective edits. For example, if you maintain a copy of a document before anyone has edited it, you can compare the revised version with the original version.

Note: *When you compare documents, the differences between the two are marked with the default revision marking formatting.*

To compare two documents, follow these steps:

1. Open the document you want to use as the source. The source document is the document that you want to be the final, most up-to-date version.

2. Choose Too**l**s, Doc Com**p**are. The Doc Compare dialog box opens.

Ami Pro inserts the name of the open, or source, file into the File name text box of the Doc Compare dialog box.

Choose the file to compare.

3. Choose the file you want to compare to the source file that is already open.

4. Choose OK.

Ami Pro compares the documents and inserts any differences that it finds into the source document, using the default revision marking format.

To identify the differences between the documents, Ami Pro displays text found in the source document as revision-inserted text and text found in the comparison document as revision-deleted text. Text that is the same in both documents is unchanged.

Text as it appears in the source document

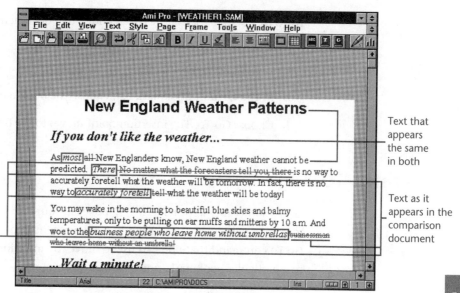

Text that appears the same in both

Text as it appears in the comparison document

To review the differences between the two documents, use the Review Revision Marking dialog box. Choose Tools, Revision Marking, Review Rev, then accept or cancel the differences. For information on using revision marking, see the preceding section.

15

Using Bookmarks

Bookmarks
Nonprinting marks that identify specific locations within a document.

You can add *bookmarks* to your text to indicate specific locations or items of interest. Then, if you or anyone needs to find the spot quickly, all you have to do is go to the bookmark.

To add a bookmark, follow these steps:

1. Position the insertion point at the location of interest.

2. Choose **Edit**, **Bookmarks**.

Bookmark names may be up to 17 characters long, but should not include spaces.

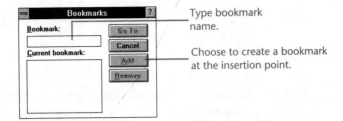

Type bookmark name.

Choose to create a bookmark at the insertion point.

To go to a bookmark that has been added to a document, follow these steps:

1. Choose **E**dit, **B**ookmarks.

2. In the **C**urrent Bookmark list, choose the bookmark you want.

3. Choose Go To. The insertion point moves to the bookmark location.

Using Go To

Go To sometimes appears in dialog boxes in Ami Pro; you choose it to go to a particular place or mark in a document. Ami Pro also has a Go To command that you can use to move the insertion point directly to a particular bookmark, note, footnote, or page.

To use Go To, follow these steps:

1. Position the insertion point at the beginning of the document.

2. Choose **E**dit, **G**o To.

With Go To, Ami Pro moves the insertion point to the next occurrence of the selected item.

Choose to go to the next item.

Choose the item to go to.

3. Choose the item to which you want to go.

4. Choose Go To. Ami Pro moves the insertion point directly to the specified item.

If you have problems...	Go To searches from the insertion point down. If Ami Pro displays a message that it cannot find a match for the item you requested, you probably started the Go To command with the insertion point positioned after the item's location. Choose OK, then move the insertion point to the beginning of the document and try again.

Editing Document Information

Ami Pro stores file information about every Ami Pro document. It keeps track of facts such as when the file was created and revised, how often it has been revised, and how long the file is in bytes, words, pages, and characters.

You can display the document information for a file by displaying the Doc Info dialog box. With the document open on-screen, choose File, **D**oc Info. The Doc Info dialog box appears.

You can edit the information in the Doc Info dialog box, and you can choose options that can help protect your documents from unauthorized editing.

In the Doc Info dialog box, you can enter or edit descriptions and keywords to help you identify the contents of a document, and you can assign locks to control the way the document is revised and annotated.

Enter keywords here.——

Click here to update statistics.

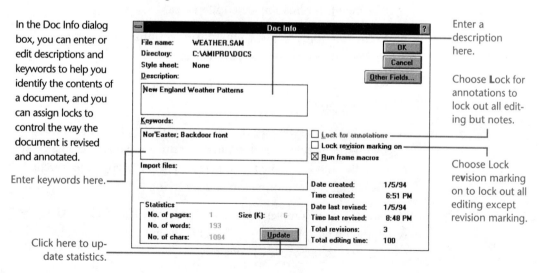

Enter a description here.

Choose **L**ock for annotations to lock out all editing but notes.

Choose Lock revision marking on to lock out all editing except revision marking.

15

With a mouse, you can quickly locate a file using information entered in the Document Information dialog box. This is useful if you don't remember a file name, but you do remember the file description or some of the keywords you entered.

To locate a file using keywords, follow these steps:

1. Choose the Locate Files by Doc Info SmartIcon. Ami Pro displays the Keyword Search dialog box.

You can locate a file based on description or keyword document information.

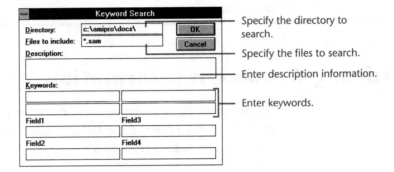

2. In the **D**irectory text box, enter the directory path you want Ami Pro to search.

3. In the **F**iles to include text box, enter the specifications of the files you want to search.

4. In the **D**escription text box, enter text you think appears in the Document Information Description area.

5. In the **K**eywords text box, enter text you think appears in the Document Information Keyword area.

   Note: *You do not have to enter information in both the Description and the Keywords area.*

6. Choose OK. Ami Pro begins searching through all of the specified files in the selected directory. In the status bar, you see the name of each file as it is searched. You may also hear a beep, if the searched file contains the information you are trying to find.

When the search is complete, Ami Pro displays the Files Found dialog box, listing the names of the files. Select a file and choose Open, or choose Cancel to remove the dialog box.

Ami Pro displays a list of all of the files it finds containing the document information you specified.

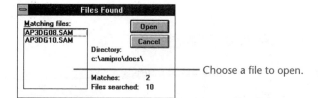

———— Choose a file to open.

Lesson Summary

To	Do This
Insert a note	Choose **E**dit, **I**nsert, **N**ote. Type the note. Click outside the note window.
Display the note text	Double-click the note box.
Turn on revision marking	Choose Too**l**s, Re**v**ision Marking. Choose the **M**ark Revisions check box.
Change revision marking	Choose Too**l**s, Re**v**ision Marking. Choose **O**ptions. Choose the attributes for insertions and the attributes for deletions.
Compare two documents	Open the source document. Choose Too**l**s, Doc Com**p**are. Choose the document to compare to the source file.
Add a bookmark	Choose **E**dit, **B**ookmarks. Type a bookmark name. Choose **A**dd.
Go to a bookmark	Choose **E**dit, **B**ookmarks. Choose the bookmark name. Choose Go To.
Use Go To	Choose **E**dit, **G**o To. Choose the item to go to next. Choose Go To.
Display document information	Choose **F**ile, **D**oc Info.

15

On Your Own

These exercises are designed to help you learn to use Ami Pro document notation features. You can use any document that you have already created, or you can create a new document.

Insert Notes
Estimated Time: 5 minutes

1. Insert a note in a document.

2. Display the note.

Use Revision Marking
Estimated Time: 10 minutes

Note: *Before beginning to use revision marking, save a copy of the document by using the Save As command. You will use this document to practice comparing documents.*

1. Edit your document using revision marking. Make sure to delete some text and insert some text.

2. Review the revisions. Accept some, but reject others.

Compare Documents
Estimated Time: 10 minutes

1. Compare the revised document to the original document.

2. Decide which of the revisions you really want to keep.

Add Bookmarks
Estimated Time: 5 minutes

1. Insert a bookmark into the text.

2. Go to the bookmark by using the Go To command in the Bookmarks dialog box.

View and Edit Document Information
Estimated Time: 10 minutes

1. Save the document you just created.

2. Display the document information for the document.

3. Add keywords to the document information dialog box.

4. Lock the document so that it can be edited only by using revision marking.

Here are some additional optional exercises you can try:

■ Pretend you are more than one person: change the Note defaults so that you can insert notes in different colors.

■ Go back to edit the document information dialog box to allow the document to be edited.

■ Change the attributes and colors for revision marking.

■ Compare two completely different documents just to see what Ami Pro will do with them.

■ Use Go To to go to the notes you have inserted.

15

Working with Other Windows Applications

The capability to import many different file formats is built into Ami Pro. That means you can use files and data created with other programs, including word processing, spreadsheet, database, and graphics applications. You can also export Ami Pro text files so that someone with a different application program can use them.

In fact, in Lesson 10, "Working with Frames," you learned to use Ami Pro's importing capabilities to insert an AmiDraw clip-art file into a frame.

In addition, Ami Pro supports Windows' *Dynamic Data Exchange* (DDE) and *Object Linking and Embedding* (OLE). With DDE and OLE you can link data from other Windows applications into Ami Pro, so that when you update the data in the original application, Windows automatically updates the data in Ami Pro. DDE and OLE make using Windows applications a real timesaver—you can update data in one application without having to update the same information in Ami Pro.

In this lesson, you learn how to

- Import and export text and data.
- Import graphics.
- Copy and paste text, data, and graphics.

■ Link and embed text and data.

■ Learn to use imported data.

Importing and Exporting Text and Data

Applications programs use different file formats. Until recently, a person using one application program could not read, edit, print, or otherwise make use of a file created with another application program.

Filters
Software programs that translate data from one file format to another, preserving formatting whenever possible.

Ami Pro, however, includes *filters* that enable you to convert most application file formats into Ami Pro file formats, and vice versa. The result is that you can *import* files from many programs to use in Ami Pro, and *export* Ami Pro files to use in other programs.

You cannot translate all of the formatting attributes from one application program into other application programs. Don't be surprised if the imported or exported file is not identical to the original file.

Importing

Import
To make a non-Ami Pro file available for use by Ami Pro.

When you import a file into Ami Pro, you can convert it into a new Ami Pro file or insert it into an existing Ami Pro file. Either way, after the file is imported, it is an Ami Pro file. You can edit it, format it, print it, and otherwise manipulate it using all of Ami Pro's features.

Export
To make an Ami Pro file available for use by other application programs.

The steps for importing a file are the same regardless of whether the file is text, such as a word processing file, or data, such as a spreadsheet or database file.

To import a file into Ami Pro, follow these steps:

1. Start Ami Pro.

2. Choose **F**ile, **O**pen. The Open dialog box appears.

Choose the file name.

Choose to insert the file into an existing Ami Pro document.

Ami Pro can import files created with many different applications programs. Click the drop-down arrow in the List Files of Type box to see a list of applications.

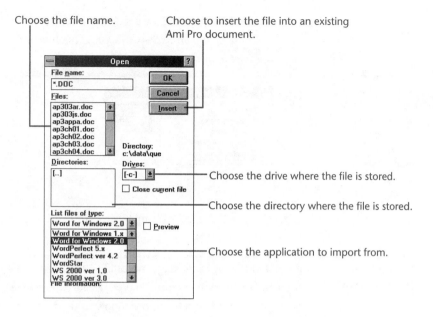

Choose the drive where the file is stored.

Choose the directory where the file is stored.

Choose the application to import from.

Note: *To insert the file into an existing Ami Pro document, open the document and position the insertion point where you want the file's contents to appear before you choose* **F***ile,* **O***pen.*

3. In the List Files of **T**ype list box, choose the format of the file(s) you want to import. The extension associated with the format you select appears in the File **N**ame text box.

4. If necessary, choose the drive and directory where the file is located. Ami Pro lists the files in the **F**iles list box.

5. In the **F**iles list box, choose the file you want to import.

6. Choose OK to open the selected file, or choose **I**nsert to insert the contents of the file into an existing file.

   If you choose **I**nsert, the Import Options dialog box appears. The options in the Import Options dialog box vary, depending on the type of file you are importing.

16

If you have problems...

If the Insert button is dimmed, it means that a document is not open. You can only insert a file into an open document. Before trying to import the file, open a document.

Note: *Some import file types do not require you to specify options. If there are no import options to specify, the Import Options dialog box does not appear.*

Here, a word processing file is being imported, and the options concern how to import style formatting.

7. Choose OK. Ami Pro imports the file and displays it on-screen.

If you have problems...

If Ami Pro displays a message indicating that it cannot convert the file, you probably selected the wrong file type. Make sure the file you are trying to open was created with the application you selected in the List Files of **T**ype box. Then, try again.

Exporting

Exporting means converting an Ami Pro file into another file format. . You might have to export an Ami Pro file if someone who uses a different program needs the file. To export, save the Ami Pro file in the other file format, then store it on a floppy disk and give it to the other person.

To export an Ami Pro file, follow these steps:

1. Start Ami Pro.

2. Open the file you want to export.

3. Choose **F**ile, Save **A**s. The Save As dialog box appears.

Enter the file name.

Choose the application to which you are exporting.

Ami Pro can export files into many different file formats. Click the drop-down arrow in the List Files of **T**ype box to see a list of applications.

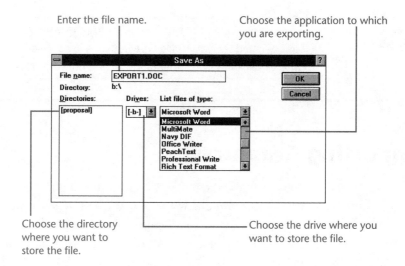

Choose the directory where you want to store the file.

Choose the drive where you want to store the file.

4. In the List Files of **T**ype list box, choose the format in which you want to save the file.

5. If necessary, choose the drive and directory where you want to store the file.

6. In the File **N**ame text box, enter the name you want to give the exported file. Do not forget to enter the correct extension.

7. Choose OK. The Export Options dialog box appears. Options in the Export Options dialog box vary, depending on the type of export file.

Note: *Some export file formats do not require you to select any options. If no options are required, the Export Options dialog box does not appear.*

16

Here, an Ami Pro file is being exported to another word processing application.

8. Choose the options, then choose OK. Ami Pro exports the file and saves it in the specified directory.

<table>
<tr><td>

If you have problems...

</td><td>

If you cannot open the exported file using the other application, you may have selected the wrong file type in the Save As dialog box. Refer to the other application's documentation to find out what file type to select, then try again.

</td></tr>
</table>

Importing Graphics

You can import graphics files from other applications into Ami Pro. In Lesson 10, "Working with Frames," you inserted a clip-art image into a frame using the Import Picture command. You can also use Ami Pro's Draw feature to import drawings you can then edit using all of the Draw tools.

Importing a Drawing

You can import three types of graphics files using Ami Pro's Draw feature:

- AmiDraw files

- Windows bit-map files

- Windows metafiles

You can use all of the Draw capabilities to manipulate files you import as Draw files. For information on using Draw, see Lesson 11, "Using Draw."

To import a file into Draw, follow these steps:

1. Start Draw.

   Note: *You must import a drawing into a frame. Either create and select the frame before you start Draw, or let Draw create and select one automatically. For information on frames, see Lesson 10, "Working with Frames."*

2. Choose File, Import Drawing.

<table>
<tr><td>

If you have problems...

</td><td>

If the Import Drawing option does not appear on the File menu, you are not in the Draw mode. Choose Tools, Drawing to start Draw and select a frame. Then choose File, Import Drawing.

</td></tr>
</table>

Choose the file you want to import in the Import Drawing dialog box.

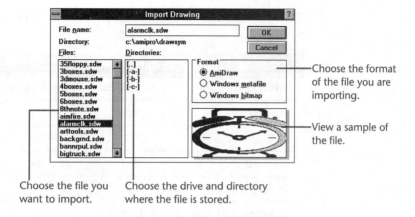

Choose the format of the file you are importing.

View a sample of the file.

Choose the file you want to import.

Choose the drive and directory where the file is stored.

3. Enter the file name in the File **N**ame text box.

4. Choose OK.

Ami Pro imports the file and displays it in the frame on-screen. You can edit it using the drawing and command icons.

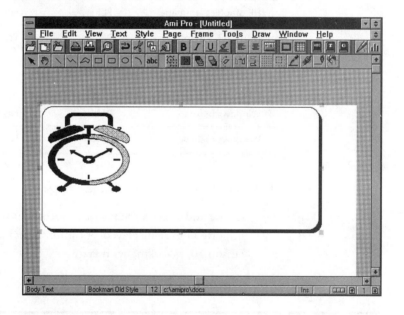

Importing a Picture

You can import pictures from many different file types. Some, such as Freelance and Lotus 1-2-3 graphics files, are imported as Draw files and can be edited using Draw. Others, such as PC Paintbrush PCX files, scanned images, and AutoCAD files, cannot be edited with Draw.

16

Table 16.1 describes the graphics files you can import into Ami Pro.

Table 16.1. Import Graphics Files		
File Type	**File Extension**	**Edit with Draw?**
AmiDraw	SDW	N/A
AmiEquation	TEX	No
AutoCAD	DXF	No
Computer graphics metafile	CGM	No
DrawPerfect/WordPerfect	WPG	Yes
Encapsulated PostScript	EPS	No
Freelance	DRW	Yes
HP graphics language	PLT	No
Lotus 1-2-3 graphics	PIC	Yes
PC Paintbrush	PCX	No
Scanned images	TIF	No
Windows bit-map	BMP	No
Windows metafile	WMF	No

To import a picture file, follow these steps:

1. Create and select a frame in the document where you want the imported image displayed. For information on using frames, see Lesson 10, "Working with Frames."

2. Choose File, Import Picture.

If you have problems... If the Import Picture option is dimmed on the File menu, the selected frame may already contain a Draw graphics image. Follow the instructions in the previous section for importing a drawing.

Choose the picture
you want to import
in the Import
Picture dialog box.

Choose the
File Type.

Choose the Copy
Image check box.

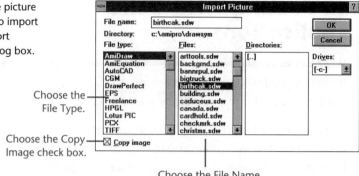

Choose the File Name.

3. Choose the picture you want to import. If necessary, specify the drive and directory where the file is stored.

4. Choose OK.

Ami Pro imports
the picture and
inserts it into the
frame.

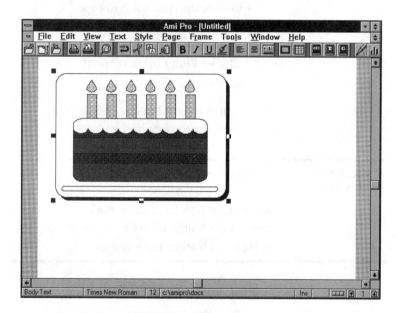

16

Copying and Pasting with Other Windows Applications

Windows was designed to provide a consistent operating environment for varied applications. If you use more than one Windows applications, you know how they use similar menus and commands.

You can use the Windows Clipboard to exchange data between Windows applications. The same copy and paste commands you use within Ami Pro documents also work to copy text, data, and graphics from other Windows applications into Ami Pro.

To copy information from another Windows application into Ami Pro, follow these steps:

1. Start the other application and open the file that contains the information you want to copy.

2. Select the information.

3. Choose **E**dit, **C**opy to copy the information to the Windows Clipboard.

4. Switch to Ami Pro and open the document in which you want to paste the information.

If you have problems...

To switch to Ami Pro from another Windows application, click anywhere within the Ami Pro window. If you cannot see the Ami Pro window on your screen, press Ctrl+Esc to open the Windows Task List. Choose Ami Pro, and then choose Switch To. For more information about using Windows to run multiple applications, consult your Windows documentation.

---

5. Position the insertion point where you want to place the informa-tion. You can insert the information into a frame, into a table, or into a chart.

6. Choose **E**dit, **P**aste. The data is inserted into the Ami Pro document.

Importing Linked Text or Data

Link
To electronically join the data pasted into one application with the data in the original application. Changes made to the data in the original application are automatically made to the pasted data.

Copying and pasting moves data from one Windows application to another—but with Windows, you can do more. You can *link* text or data between applications. Linking ensures that if you modify the text or data in the original application, the changes are made in the other application as well.

Linking is very important if you use data that needs regular updating, such as spreadsheets or databases. If you place linked data into Ami Pro, you do not have to worry about it becoming outdated—when the data is changed in the original application, it is also changed in Ami Pro.

Note: *You can link Ami Pro data with other Windows applications using the same basic procedures you use to link other data to Ami Pro.*

There are two ways to create links between text and data in Windows applications:

Embed
To place data from one application into another application as an object. The embedded object can be edited, displayed, and printed by only the original application.

- *Object linking and embedding*. OLE links or *embeds* the original data into your Ami Pro document as an object. The OLE object contains the original data in the original file format. The original application is responsible for updating, displaying, and printing the linked data.

- *Dynamic data exchange*. DDE links the data in Ami Pro with the data in the original application. When you modify the data in the original application, Windows notifies Ami Pro and asks to update the linked data.

Both applications must support OLE and DDE in order to create the link. Some older Windows applications may not support these features. All the applications in the Lotus SmartSuite support them. For information about whether your applications support OLE or DDE, consult your documentation.

16

Linking and Embedding Data into Ami Pro

You can create an OLE link with an existing object, or you can use OLE to create the object.

To link an existing object, follow these steps:

1. Start the application that contains the data you want to link or embed, open the file, and select the data.

Here, data is
selected in 1-2-3.

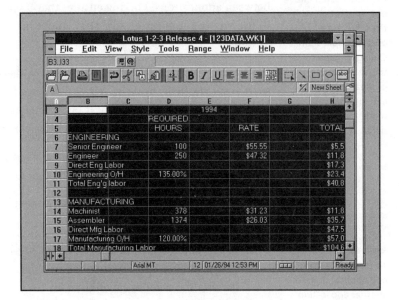

2. Choose **E**dit, **C**opy to copy the selected data to the Windows Clipboard. Do not close the application.

3. Start Ami Pro, open the document where you want the object to appear, and position the insertion point in the correct location.

4. Choose **E**dit, Paste **S**pecial. The Paste Special dialog box appears.

If you have problems...

If Paste Special is dimmed on the Edit menu, there is no data in the Clipboard. Be sure to copy the data in the other application into the Clipboard before choosing **E**dit, Paste **S**pecial in Ami Pro.

Different applications support different OLE formats. OLE Embed provides the most complete OLE support. If OLE Embed is not available, choose OLE Link.

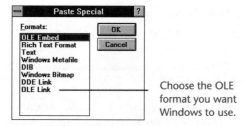

Choose the OLE format you want Windows to use.

5. Choose OK. Ami Pro embeds the data in your document as an object.

> **Note:** *Different applications support different OLE formats. Some of the newer OLE formats provide more sophisticated features than some of the older OLE formats. OLE Embed supports all currently available OLE features. It allows you to embed objects instead of only linking them. OLE Link is not quite as full-featured as OLE Embed.*

Here, data from a 1-2-3 spreadsheet is embedded in an Ami Pro document. You can increase or decrease the size of the frame to display or hide the object's contents.

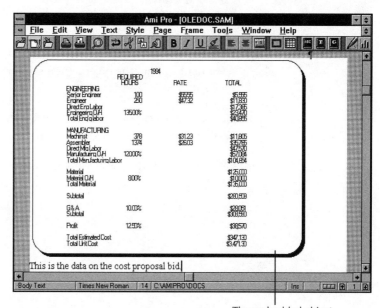

The embedded object

16

Note: *To edit the way the object appears in the frame, use the Frame, Graphics Scaling command. For more information, see Lesson 10, "Working with Frames."*

To create an embedded object, follow these steps:

1. In Ami Pro, open the document where you want to place the object and position the insertion point in the correct location.

2. Choose **Edit**, **Insert**.

3. Choose New **Object**.

In the Insert New Object dialog box, Ami Pro lists all of the Windows applications on your system that support OLE.

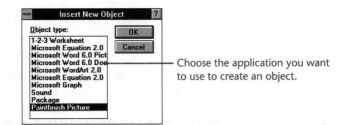

Choose the application you want to use to create an object.

4. Choose the object and choose OK. Ami Pro creates a frame in your document to hold the object, then switches to the application you selected.

5. Create the object you want to embed, then choose **File**, **Update** to paste it into your Ami Pro document.

6. Close the application and switch to Ami Pro.

When you update
the file, it is not
saved to disk.
To save it to disk,
choose File,
Save As.

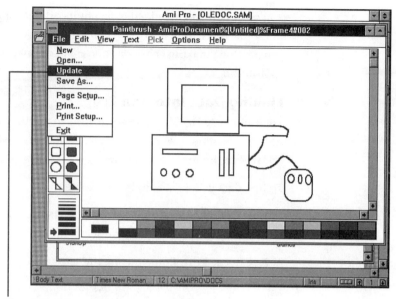

Choose Update.

The object is
embedded in the
frame in your Ami
Pro document.

The frame holding the
object embedded earlier
has been made smaller
to keep the object out of
the way.

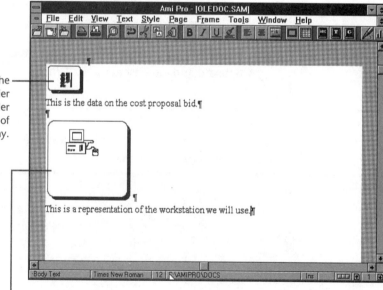

The embedded object

16

You must edit an embedded object in its original application. To start the application, double-click the object in the Ami Pro document. When you are done making changes, choose **F**ile, **U**pdate in the original application.

Linking Data into Ami Pro

You can create DDE links between a file in another application and an Ami Pro document. When data changes in the other application, it is updated in the Ami Pro document.

To link data using DDE, follow these steps:

1. Start the application that contains the data you want to link to Ami Pro, open the file, and select the data.

2. Choose **E**dit, **C**opy to copy the selected data to the Windows Clipboard. Do not close the application.

3. Start Ami Pro, open the document where you want the data to appear, and position the insertion point in the correct location. To insert the data into a table, position the insertion point in the first cell. To insert the data in an empty frame, select the frame.

4. Choose **E**dit, Paste **L**ink. Ami Pro inserts the data from the Clipboard and establishes the DDE link.

If you have problems...   If Paste Link is dimmed on the Edit menu, there is no data in the Clipboard. Be sure to copy the data in the other application into the Clipboard before choosing **E**dit, Paste **L**ink in Ami Pro.

Ami Pro encloses the linked data in brackets in the main document text. To see the brackets, choose **M**arks in the View Preferences dialog box.

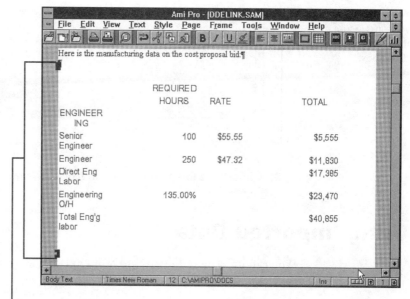

Brackets around linked data

Data edited in the original application is updated automatically as long as Ami Pro is open.

In the future, whenever you open an Ami Pro document that contains a DDE link, Ami Pro asks if you want to update the link. If you answer yes and the other application is running, Ami Pro updates the data. If the other application is not running, Ami Pro tries to start it.

To update the data manually, follow these steps:

1. Start the other application.

2. In Ami Pro, choose **E**dit, Link **O**ptions. The Link Options dialog box appears.

16

You can manage
your links by using
the Link Options
dialog box.

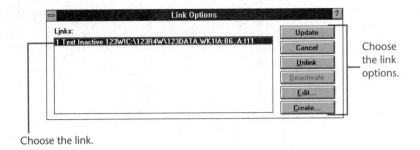

Choose
the link
options.

Choose the link.

3. Choose the link you want to update, then choose Update.

Using Imported Data

You can use data imported into Ami Pro to augment and enhance Ami
Pro documents, or to save you time you might otherwise spend reenter-
ing existing data.

Here are just a few ways you can use imported data in Ami Pro:

- You can use database records to generate a mail merge or create a
  monthly schedule.

- You can use slide graphics files from a presentation program to
  illustrate a presentation handout.

- You can use spreadsheet data to create tables and charts.

To use an imported data base file in a mail merge, select the file name
in the Select Merge Data File dialog box. For more information, see
Lesson 14, "Merging Documents."

To create a chart using data from a spreadsheet, follow these steps:

1. Start the spreadsheet application and select the data you want
   to use.

2. Choose **E**dit, **C**opy to copy the data to the Windows Clipboard.

3. Switch to Ami Pro and open the document where you want to
   create the chart.

4. Select an empty frame to hold the chart.

5. Choose Too**l**s, **C**harting.

6. Choose the chart type and options that you want to use. For more information, see Lesson 13, "Working with Charts."

7. Choose OK. Ami Pro creates the chart and inserts it in the frame.

Here, a column chart has been created using the same 1-2-3 spreadsheet data seen in an earlier example.

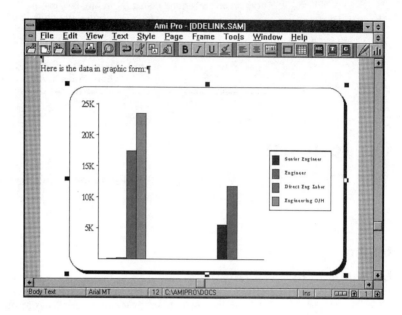

Lesson Summary

To	Do This
Import a file	In Ami Pro, choose **F**ile, **O**pen. Choose the import file format, and then choose the import file. Choose OK. After choosing the import options, choose OK.
Export a file	In Ami Pro, choose **F**ile, Save **A**s. Choose the export file format, and then enter the file name. Choose OK. After choosing the export options, choose OK.
Import a drawing	Start Draw. Choose **F**ile, Import Drawing. Enter the file name, and then choose OK.
Import a picture	Select a frame. Choose **F**ile, **I**mport Picture. Choose the file, and then choose OK.
Use Copy and Paste	In the other application, select the data. Choose **E**dit, **C**opy. In Ami Pro, choose **E**dit, **P**aste.

16

(continues)

To	Do This
Embed an existing object	In the other application, select the data. Choose **E**dit, **C**opy. In Ami Pro, choose **E**dit, Paste **S**pecial. Choose the OLE format, and then choose OK.
Create an embedded object	In Ami Pro, choose **E**dit, **I**nsert, New **O**bject. Choose the other application, and then choose OK. In the other application, create the object to embed. Choose **F**ile, **U**pdate.
Link data	In the other application, select the data. Choose **E**dit, **C**opy. In Ami Pro, choose **E**dit, Paste **L**ink.

On Your Own

These exercises are designed to help you practice using Ami Pro with other Windows applications.

Import a File
Estimated Time: 10 minutes

1. Import a file from any other Windows application.

2. Edit the file using Ami Pro and save it with a new name.

Export a File
Estimated Time: 5 minutes

1. Export an Ami Pro document for use in another application.

2. Open the file with the other application.

Import Graphics
Estimated Time: 10 minutes

1. Import one of Ami Pro's clip-art pictures into a document using Draw.

2. Import one of Ami Pro's clip-art pictures into a document without using Draw.

Paste Data
Estimated Time: 10 minutes

Copy and Paste data from another application file into an Ami Pro document.

Embed Data
Estimated Time: 15 minutes

1. Embed data from another application file into an Ami Pro document. If necessary, create the object.

2. Start the other application from Ami Pro to edit the object.

Link Data
Estimated Time: 10 minutes

16

1. Link data from another application file into an Ami Pro document.

2. Edit the data in the other application and update the changes in Ami Pro.

Here are some optional exercises you can try:

- Link spreadsheet data into an Ami Pro table.

- Create a chart using the spreadsheet data.

- Import a database file to use as a merge data file.

- Conduct a merge using the imported data file.

Managing Your Files and Documents

Planning and organizing a document is often the most difficult part of writing. That's why Ami Pro provides many tools to help you construct and keep track of documents.

In this chapter, you learn to outline a document, create a table of contents, and insert footnotes into your text. You also learn to use Ami Pro's file management utility to organize your files and documents on disk.

Specifically, you learn how to

- Outline a document.

- Generate a table of contents.

- Add footnotes.

- List files in the File Manager.

- Copy, move, delete, and rename files in the File Manager.

- Change file attributes in the File Manager.

Using Outline Mode

Outline mode is an editing environment structured specifically for creating an outline. It provides options for assigning and changing *heading levels*, for expanding and contracting the outline, and for editing the text.

Outline mode

An editing mode in Ami Pro that you use to create an outline by assigning heading levels to paragraphs and text.

You can create a document in Outline mode, or you can use Outline mode to edit an existing document.

To change to Outline mode, choose **V**iew, **O**utline Mode.

To create a document in Outline mode, change to Outline mode before you select **F**ile, **N**ew. In the New dialog box, choose the _DEFAULT.STY or the _OUTLINE.STY style sheet.

In Outline mode, Ami Pro adds an Outline toolbar, an Outline menu option, and Outline buttons to your screen display.

Outline buttons

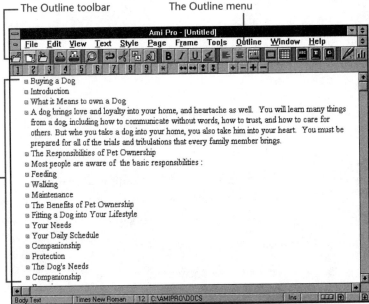

— The Outline toolbar   The Outline menu

If you have problems...

If the Outline buttons are not displayed on your screen, choose **V**iew, View **P**references and choose the Outline Buttons check box.

Setting Outline Levels

Heading level

A position assigned to a paragraph or text to create an outline in Outline mode.

To create an outline, you organize paragraphs into progressive levels. You can assign paragraphs to levels 1 through 9, with level 1 being the highest, or top, and level 9 being the lowest. All body text is assigned to level none, which means no level at all. You assign levels by *promoting* and *demoting* the paragraph.

Promoting
Moving a paragraph to a higher level in the outline.

You can tell at what level a paragraph is, compared to the other paragraphs, by its position on the page: Level 1 paragraphs are flush left, and subsequent levels are indented.

At first, all of the paragraphs in a document in Outline mode are the same level. You use the icons, buttons, and commands to structure your outline into levels.

Demoting
Moving a paragraph to a lower level in the outline.

To promote a paragraph, follow these steps:

1. Position the insertion point within the paragraph.

2. Choose **O**utline, **P**romote.

3. Repeat until the paragraph is at the level you want.

To demote a paragraph, follow these steps:

1. Position the insertion point within the paragraph.

2. Choose **O**utline, **D**emote.

3. Repeat until the paragraph is at the level you want.

Here the outline has been structured in levels.

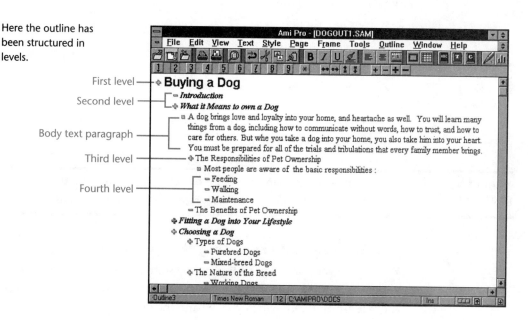

Note: *Within the outline, Body Text paragraphs remain at level 0, or none. This text may become part of the document text or may be used to explain or clarify the outline headings.*

Understanding Level Hierarchy

Levels are hierarchical: each level is subordinate to the level above. You can tell whether a heading has subordinates by looking at its outline button:

- A plus sign indicates that the heading has subordinates.

- A filled plus indicates that the heading has subordinates, but that they are hidden because the heading has been contracted.

- A minus sign indicates that the heading has no subordinates.

- A box indicates an outline level of 0, or none.

Actions performed on one level directly affect all subordinate levels in that section. If you select a level 1 heading and its subordinate paragraphs and then delete the level 1 heading, you also delete all the subordinate headings.

To promote or demote a section, follow these steps:

1. Select all of the levels in the section.

2. Choose **O**utline, **P**romote or **O**utline, **D**emote.

   Note: *To quickly select an entire section, click the Outline button beside the highest level heading.*

If you have problems...   If you promote or demote paragraphs by accident, choose **E**dit, **U**ndo immediately. Ami Pro reverts the paragraphs back to their previous level.

Contracting and Expanding the Outline

You can contract and expand the outline so that only certain levels are displayed. When you contract the outline, the selected level and all levels above it are displayed; when you expand the outline, the hidden levels are also displayed.

To contract the entire outline, choose the Outline level icon corresponding to the level you want to display. For example, to display only level 2 and 1 paragraph, choose the Level 2 icon.

To expand the entire outline, choose the Asterisk icon.

To contract or expand only one section of the outline, do one of the following:

- Position the insertion point within the highest-level paragraph of the section, and choose **O**utline, **C**ontract, or **O**utline, **E**xpand.

- Double-click the highest-level paragraph's Outline button.

Note: *To expand or contract the next subordinate level of a section one level at a time, click the Expand One Level or Contract One Level icon.*

Here the outline has been contracted to show level 1, 2, and 3 paragraphs.

Solid plus signs indicate hidden subordinate paragraphs.

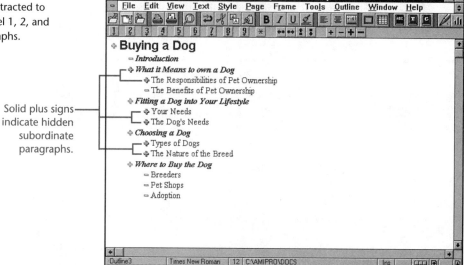

Note: *When you print a document in Outline mode, only the displayed paragraphs print. By using expand and contract, you can easily print different variations of the outline.*

17

Editing the Outline

In Outline mode, you can use Ami Pro's editing commands to format, copy, and delete text and headings. You can also change the outline by promoting and demoting paragraphs, and by moving the paragraphs up and down to rearrange the outline.

 To move a paragraph to the line above the previous paragraph (no matter what the level), position the insertion point in the paragraph you want to move and choose **O**utline, Move **U**p.

 To move a paragraph to the line below the following paragraph (no matter what the level), position the insertion point in the paragraph you want to move and choose **O**utline, Move **D**own.

If you have problems...

Moving a paragraph up or down in the outline does *not* change its assigned level. If you find that all your levels are out of order, it's because you moved paragraphs without paying attention to the level of the paragraphs you were putting them between. Use **E**dit, **U**ndo, or promote and demote the paragraphs until they are the correct level.

To move a paragraph and all of its subordinate paragraphs, click its Outline button to select the section, then drag it to the new location.

Note: *It is easier to drag an entire section if you contract it first.*

Numbering the Outline

To quickly add numbers to your paragraphs, follow these steps:

1. Choose **S**tyle, **O**utline Styles.

The Outline Styles dialog box displays style names corresponding to the levels in the document outline.

Quick Numbering buttons

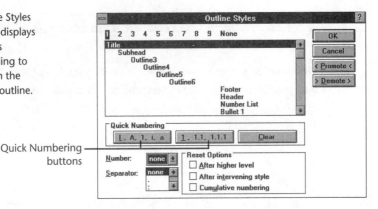

2. Choose one of the Quick Numbering buttons. Ami Pro numbers the styles in the dialog box.

3. Choose OK. Ami Pro numbers your outline.

Note: *To see the outline with the numbers but without the Outline buttons, deselect Outline buttons in the View Preferences dialog box.*

Outlining with an Outline Style Sheet

Instead of creating an outline in Outline mode, you can use an outline style sheet. With an outline style sheet, you choose styles to organize the document into levels of headings and text, instead of using the Outline buttons, icons, or menu. An added benefit of the style sheet is that paragraph numbers are assigned automatically.

Ami Pro comes with four outline style sheets. The first three provide typical outline page layouts and styles, including indents, numbers, letters, and Roman numerals. The fourth, _OUTLINE.STY, is the style sheet used in Outline mode. It provides none of the page layout features that the other style sheets have, but it has styles you can apply to each level of heading and text.

To use an outline style sheet, follow these steps:

1. Choose **F**ile, **N**ew.

2. Choose one of the outline style sheets: _OUTLINE1.STY, _OUTLINE2.STY, _OUTLINE3.STY, or _OUTLINE.STY.

3. Choose the **W**ith Contents check box. To see how to structure the outline, you have to display the new document with the outline style sheet contents.

4. Choose OK. Ami Pro creates a new document using the selected style sheet.

Note: *Before you select a style sheet, choose the **P**review check box in the New dialog box so you can see the different page layouts.*

17

Using the style sheet contents as a guide, you can easily type the outline text. Use the styles to assign or change levels.

Enter the document title.

To enter a text paragraph within the outline, use Body Text.

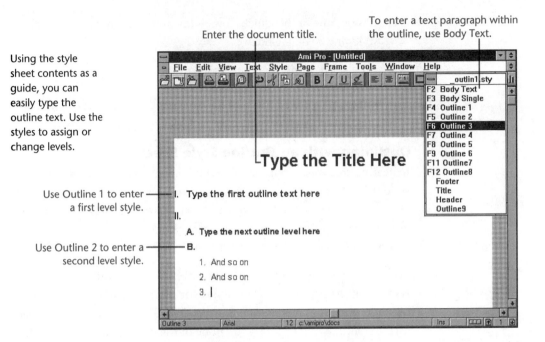

Use Outline 1 to enter a first level style.

Use Outline 2 to enter a second level style.

As you type, select the style appropriate for the current level. You might have to modify paragraph formatting or create a new style to correctly align text under a heading.

First level

Body text

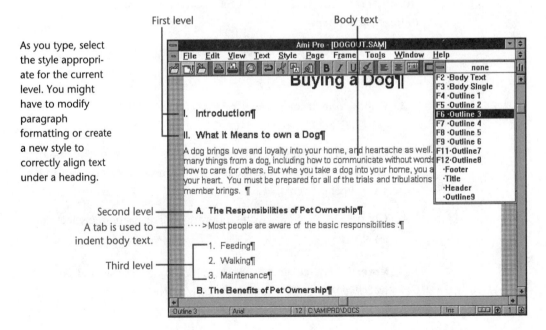

Second level

A tab is used to indent body text.

Third level

To use the outlining tools described in the previous section, choose **V**iew, **O**utline Mode to change to Outline mode.

In Outline mode, the fonts and numbering scheme are carried over from Layout mode and heading levels are set automatically.

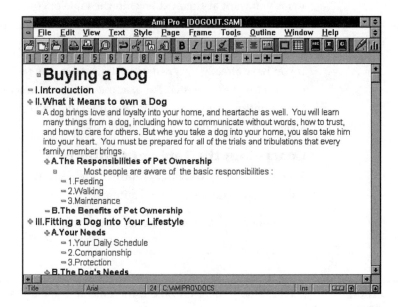

Creating a Table of Contents

Including a table of contents with a document helps readers find the information they need. With Ami Pro, you can automate the creation of a table of contents.

To create a table of contents, simply identify the styles in the document you want to include in the table, and Ami Pro does the rest. You can include page numbers, and select a leader character (an ellipsis, for example) to separate the text from the page number.

Note: *Text appears in the table of contents exactly as it appears in the document. Make sure it is formatted the way you want it (and spelled correctly) before you create the table of contents.*

17

Identifying the Table of Contents Styles

The first step in creating a table of contents is identifying the styles you want to include. To identify the styles, you simply make sure that each item you want in the table of contents is formatted with a paragraph style corresponding to its level in the table of contents.

For example, all of the items you want at the first level in the table of contents should be formatted with one style, such as Title. All of the items you want at the next level in the table of contents should be formatted with another style, such as Subhead. You can include up to nine levels in the table of contents.

If you have already assigned consistent styles, the task of creating a table of contents is even easier. For example, if the document was created using an outline, all the paragraphs at the same level should have the same style. You do not have to change the styles.

Generating the Table of Contents

When you're sure you have identified the items with consistent styles, you can generate the table of contents.

To generate the table of contents, follow these steps:

1. Choose Tools, TOC, Index.

If you have problems...   If TOC, Index is dimmed on the Tools menu, you may be in Outline or Draft mode. You must be in Layout mode in order to create a table of contents. Choose view, layout mode. Then choose Tools, TOC, Index.

---

2. Choose TOC Options.

In the TOC Options dialog box, assign levels to the paragraph styles you want to appear in the table of contents.

Levels

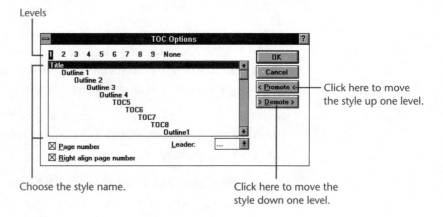

Click here to move the style up one level.

Choose the style name.

Click here to move the style down one level.

3. Choose a style you want to appear in the table of contents.

4. Choose **P**romote or **D**emote until the correct level number is high-lighted at the top of the dialog box. For example, if you want the Title style to be the first level in the table of contents, highlight it, then choose **P**romote until the number 1 is highlighted. Continue until you have assigned a level to every style.

5. Choose the **P**age Number check box to include page numbers. Choose **R**ight Align Page Number to align the page numbers on the right margin. Choose a leader character for the page number.

6. Choose OK to return to the TOC, Index dialog box.

7. Choose the Generate Table of **C**ontents check box.

8. Choose OK.

Ami Pro generates the table of contents and places it on a new page at the beginning of the document.

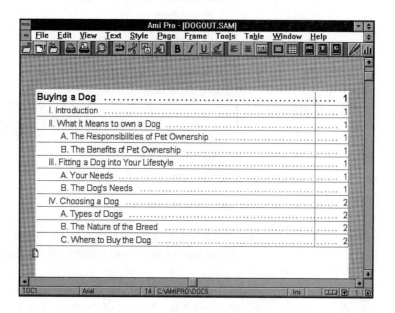

17

Using Footnotes

Footnote
Reference text that is displayed at the bottom of the page that contains the reference mark.

You use *footnotes* to reference information in a text. When you insert a footnote, Ami Pro inserts a reference number in superscript at the inser-tion point location. You type the footnote text at the bottom of the page.

To add a footnote, follow these steps:

1. Position the insertion point in the text where you want the reference number to appear.

2. Choose Tools, **F**ootnotes.

3. Verify that the **I**nsert Footnote option is selected, and choose OK. Ami Pro inserts the footnote number and moves the insertion point to the footnote area at the bottom of the page.

Type your footnote text in the footnote area at the bottom of the page.

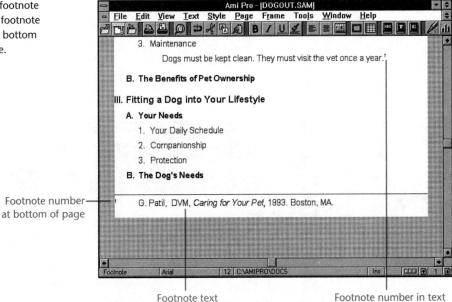

Footnote number at bottom of page

Footnote text

Footnote number in text

4. When you have finished typing the footnote text, click outside the footnote area to continue editing the document.

Ami Pro insert footnotes from the bottom margin up. If you don't have enough room at the bottom of the page, Ami Pro splits the last footnote across multiple pages.

If you insert or delete a footnote, Ami Pro automatically renumbers all of the reference numbers. To remove a footnote, delete the reference number in the document text. Ami Pro asks if you are sure you want to delete the footnote. Choose **Yes**.

Ami Pro also provides options for customizing footnotes. You can create endnotes (where the explanatory text appears at the end of the chapter instead of on each page), reset the numbers on each page, start with any number you want, and change the length of the line separating the footnotes from the document text.

To select footnote options, choose **O**ptions in the Footnotes dialog box.

Note: *To quickly move a footnote, drag the reference number to the new location. Ami Pro automatically renumbers other footnotes, if necessary.*

Using the Ami Pro File Manager

Ami Pro's File Manager offers many of the same features as the Windows File Manager, but it is designed specifically for use with Ami Pro files. The Ami Pro File Manager understands that Ami Pro files are usually associated with other files, such as style sheets. To manage your Ami Pro files effectively, you should always use the Ami Pro File Manager, not the Windows File Manager.

Note: *The Ami Pro File Manager can run independently from Ami Pro, which means it can stay open even if you close Ami Pro. As a rule, however, use the File Manager only while you are using Ami Pro.*

 To open the File Manager, choose **F**ile, **F**ile Management. The Ami Pro File Manager opens in a window on your screen.

17

File Manager menu   Current directory

File list in the
File Manager in
alphabetical order.
By default, only Ami
Pro documents and
Ami Pro macros are
displayed in the file
list.

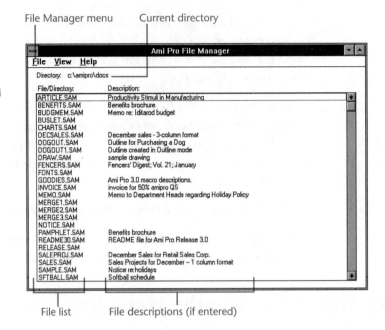

File list   File descriptions (if entered)

To close the File Manager, choose **F**ile, E**x**it.

Changing the Directory

The File Manager lists the files stored in the default document directory.

To list the files stored in a different directory, follow these steps:

1. Choose **F**ile, **Ch**ange Directory.

2. Type the path to the directory you want to change to, and choose OK.

   Note: *All drives available on your system are listed at the end of the file list. You can quickly display the files stored on another drive by scrolling to the end of the list, and choosing the drive.*

Modifying the File List

Wild-card characters
Special characters you use to represent other characters.

You can limit the number of files displayed in the file list, by using *wild-card characters* to specify a select group of files.

With wild-card characters, you can specify a specific file or a series of files. Wild-card characters can also help you locate a file even if you're not exactly sure of its file name. To specify the files to display, follow these steps:

1. Choose **V**iew, **P**artial to specify the files you want to display.

2. Use the wild-card characters ***** and **?** to specify the files you want to list. The **?** stands for any character. The ***** stands for any character and all of the characters that follow it.

To list only the document files that begin with the letter S, type **S*.SAM** in the Partial dialog box.

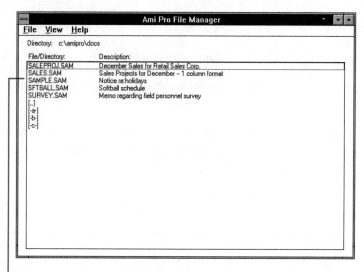

Only files starting with the letter S are listed.

> **Note:** *To list all Ami Pro documents and macros again, choose *.S?M Files from the **V**iew menu.*

Copying Files

You can use the File Manager to quickly copy one file, or many files to a destination directory. The original file remains intact, and an exact copy goes in the destination directory.

To copy files, follow these steps:

1. Choose the file or files you want to copy. To select a file, click it. To deselect it, click it again.

2. Choose **F**ile, **C**opy.

17

Files to copy

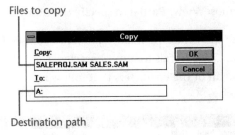

Copying is useful
for backing up files
onto floppy disks.

Destination path

3. In the **T**o text box, enter the path to the destination directory.

4. Choose OK. The File Copy Options dialog box appears for each file you selected to copy.

5. In the File Copy Options dialog box, choose whether or not to include any associated graphics or styles sheet files along with the copied file.

6. Choose OK to copy the file.

If you have problems...   Ami Pro cannot copy a file onto itself. If the destination directory is the same directory where the original file is stored, Ami Pro displays a message informing you that the source and destination file are the same. Choose OK, then specify a different destination directory, or give the copy a new file name.

Moving Files

You can quickly move one file or many files from one directory to another.

To move files, follow these steps:

1. Choose the files in the file list.

2. Choose File, **M**ove.

3. In the **T**o text box, enter the path to the destination directory.

4. Choose OK. The File Move Options dialog box appears for each file you selected to move.

Verify the source file and the destination path, and choose File Move options in the File Move Options dialog box.

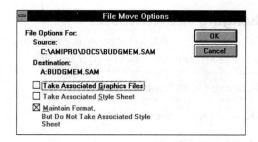

5. In the File Move Options dialog box, choose whether to include any associated graphics or styles sheet files along with the moved files. If you do not include these files, Ami Pro may not be able to find them when they are needed.

6. Choose OK. Ami Pro moves the files to the destination directory and removes them from the original, or source, directory.

Renaming Files

To quickly rename a file, follow these steps:

1. Choose the file in the file list.

2. Choose **F**ile, **R**ename.

3. In the **T**o text box, enter the new file name.

4. Choose OK.

Deleting Files

To quickly delete a file, follow these steps:

1. Choose the file in the file list.

2. Choose **F**ile, **D**elete.

3. Verify that the file in the **D**elete text box is the one you want to delete, then choose OK.

   Note: *Ami Pro does not warn you before deleting the file! Make sure that the selected file is the one you want to delete.*

17

Changing File Attributes

With the Ami Pro File Manager, you can change the *read-only* and *read-write* attributes of one file or many files.

To change file attributes, follow these steps:

1. Choose the files in the file list.

2. Choose **F**ile, **A**ttributes.

3. Choose either Read **O**nly or **R**ead-Write.

4. Choose OK.

Viewing Document Information

With the Ami Pro File Manager, you can display a Doc Info dialog box that provides statistics about a selected file. The dialog box displays such information as the file description, when the file was created, when the file was revised, and how long the file is.

To display document information, follow these steps:

1. Choose the file in the file list.

2. Choose **V**iew, **D**oc Info.

The Doc Info dialog box displays statistics about the selected file. The statistics cannot be edited.

Doc Info	

File name: DOGOUT1.SAM
Directory: c:\amipro\docs
Style sheet: None
Description:

Outline created in Outline mode

□ Lock for annotations
☒ Run frame macros

Keywords:

Import files:

Statistics			
No. of pages:	1	Size (K):	0
No. of words:	0		
No. of chars:	0		

Date created: 1/4/94
Time created: 1:38 PM
Date last rev: 1/26/94
Total revisions: 4
Total editing time: 131

OK
Cancel
Other Fields...

Note: *You cannot edit information displayed in the Doc Info dialog box in the File Manager. For information on editing document information, see Lesson 15, "Working with Document Notation."*

Lesson Summary

To	Do This
Promote or demote an outline heading	Choose **O**utline, **P**romote, or **O**utline, **D**emote.
Contract an outline	Choose the Outline level icon corresponding to the level you want to display.
Expand an outline	Choose the asterisk icon.
Generate a table of contents	Choose Too**l**s, TOC, **In**dex. Choose **T**OC Options. Promote or demote styles to the correct level. Choose OK. Choose the Generate Table of **C**ontents check box. Choose OK.
Add a footnote	Choose Too**l**s, **F**ootnotes. Choose OK. Type the footnote text in the footnote area at the bottom of the page.
Open the File Manager	Choose **F**ile, **F**ile Management.
Copy or move files	Choose the files. Choose **F**ile, **C**opy, or **F**ile, **M**ove. Enter the path to the destination directory.
Rename a file	Choose the file. Choose **F**ile, **R**ename. Enter the new file name.
Delete a file	Choose the file. Choose **F**ile, **D**elete.
Display document information	Choose the file. Choose **V**iew, **D**oc Info.

17

On Your Own

These exercises are designed to help you learn to manage your documents and files with Ami Pro.

Outline a Document
Estimated Time: 10 minutes

Use either Outline mode or an Outline style sheet.

1. Enter heading paragraphs for a document outline.

2. In Outline mode, promote and demote the headings to three or four levels.

3. Contract the outline to only first and second headings.

4. Expand the outline.

5. Number the outline.

Generate a Table of Contents
Estimated Time: 10 minutes

1. Use the document created while creating an outline, or use any document of your choice.

2. Identify the items you want to include.

3. Generate the table of contents.

Add Footnotes
Estimated Time: 5 minutes

1. Add three footnotes to the document.

2. Move one of the footnotes.

3. Delete one of the footnotes.

List Files in the File Manager
Estimated Time: 10 minutes

1. Start the File Manager.

2. List only documents that start with the letter M.

3. List all Ami Pro documents.

4. Copy the outline document you created to a backup diskette.

5. Rename the original.

6. Delete the original. Then copy the backup to the \Ami Pro\Docs directory.

7. Change the file attributes so you cannot delete the file again.

Here are some optional exercises you can try:

- Rearrange your outline by moving headings and sections.

- Add paragraphs of text to the outline.

- Create a table of contents for another document.

- See how many footnotes you can fit on a page.

- In the File Manager, list only style sheets.

Note: *All style sheets have the extension STY.*

17

Installing Ami Pro 3

This appendix provides instructions for installing Ami Pro 3 on a single-user computer system. For information on installing Ami Pro 3 on a network, consult the *Ami Pro 3 User's Guide*.

This appendix also covers the installation of the Adobe Type Manager and the WordPerfect SwitchKit, two optional programs you can install in addition to Ami Pro.

To install Ami Pro 3, Windows 3.0 or higher must already be installed on your computer. If Windows 3.0 or higher is not installed, consult either the Windows documentation or *Using Windows 3.1*, Special Edition, published by Que Corporation.

Installation Requirements

To install Ami Pro, you need a minimum of 5M of available hard disk space. To install all Ami Pro options, you need approximately 15M of hard disk space, and at least 3M of additional space for holding temporary Windows and Ami Pro files.

In addition, you need the following system requirements:

- A 286-, 386-, or 486-based computer.

- Microsoft Windows version 3.0 or higher, running in Standard or Enhanced mode.

- A minimum of 2M of RAM.

- An EGA, VGA, SVGA, or Hercules Graphics Adapter and monitor, compatible with your version of Windows.

- DOS version 3.0 or higher.

- A minimum of one 1.2M 5 1/4-inch disk drive, one 1.44M 3 1/2-inch disk drive, or one 720K 3 1/2-inch disk drive.

A Windows-compatible mouse is strongly recommended, but not required. Some features, such as SmartIcons, cannot be used without a mouse.

Using Install

Ami Pro comes with six 3 1/2-inch or six 5 1/4-inch disks and one ATM Program disk. Some packages also contain a Working Together Bonus Pack. If your system requires double-density 3 1/2-inch disks rather than high-density disks, contact Ami Pro by using the Media Conversion form included with the Ami Pro documentation.

Through the installation procedure, you can choose **H**elp to display on-screen information about installing Ami Pro. You can choose **E**xit Install to quit the installation. If you choose **E**xit Install, Ami Pro will not be installed correctly on your system. You have to start from the beginning to complete the installation.

Note: *The following installation instructions assume that you are installing from a disk in drive A. If you use drive B, just substitute drive B for drive A throughout this Appendix.*

To install Ami Pro, follow these steps:

1. Start Windows. The Program Manager screen is displayed.

2. Insert Ami Pro Disk 1 into drive A.

3. Choose **F**ile, **R**un. The Run dialog box appears.

4. In the **C**ommand Line text box, type: **A:INSTALL**.

5. Choose OK. A dialog box appears, informing you that Ami Pro is copying its installation files onto your hard disk. After a moment, the Welcome to Install dialog box appears.

6. Choose Continue. The Company Name dialog box appears.

7. Type your company name and choose OK. The Name and Initials dialog box appears.

8. Type your name. Ami Pro enters your initials automatically.

   Note: *The Company Name and Name and Initials dialog boxes only appear the first time you install Ami Pro.*

9. Choose OK. The installation Main Menu appears.

From the Main Menu, you can choose to install Ami Pro, install Ami Pro on a network server, or view information about what's new in this version of the program.

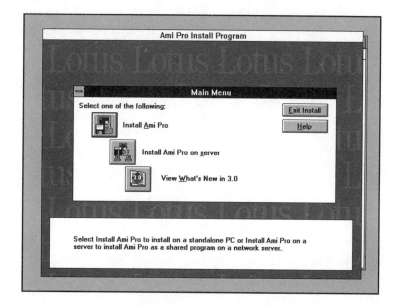

10. Choose Install **A**mi Pro. The Install Choices dialog box appears.

11. Choose one of the following:

   ■ **C**omplete Ami Pro Install to install all program features. If this is the first time you are installing Ami Pro, and you have enough disk space, choose this option.

A

- **L**aptop Ami Pro Install to install just the basic features and the spell checker. If you have limited disk space, choose this option. You can use this option on any computer, not just on a laptop.

- **Cu**stom Ami Pro Install to install the basic features and other options you select. Choose this option to select from a list of Ami Pro features.

- **O**ptions Install, to install just the features you select. To use Options Install, the basic Ami Pro features already must be installed on your system.

12. No matter which installation option you choose, the Windows or NewWave Installation dialog box appears next. These instructions assume that you are installing Ami Pro as a Windows application. Choose Windows.

After you select either NewWave or Windows, the installation selected in the Install Choices dialog box begins.

Using the Complete Install

After you select to install Ami Pro in Windows, the Specifying the Program Directory dialog box appears.

To complete the installation, follow these steps:

1. Make sure that the name of the directory where you want to install Ami Pro is correct and choose OK. Ami Pro begins the installation.

2. When the time comes to insert a new disk, Ami Pro beeps and displays a message box. Follow the instructions that appear on-screen, making sure you insert the correct disk at the correct time.

    During the installation, Ami Pro displays a status bar that shows the progress of the installation procedure.

3. When installation is complete, Ami Pro asks if you want to install the WordPerfect SwitchKit. When this installation is complete, Ami Pro displays the Main Menu.

4. From the Main Menu, choose **E**xit Install. Ami Pro prompts you to begin installation of the Adobe Type Manager.

Using the Laptop Custom or Options Install

After you choose to install Ami Pro in Windows, the Specifying Options and Directories dialog box appears.

The recommended options for the installation you chose are selected; the others are dimmed, but you can select them if you want.

```
┌────────────────────────────────────────────────────────────────┐
│ ─              Specifying Options and Directories                │
│                                                                  │
│                                              ┌──────────┐        │
│                                              │    OK    │        │
│                                              ├──────────┤        │
│                                              │Main Menu │        │
│ Program directory:                           ├──────────┤        │
│ ┌──────────────────────────┐                 │   Help   │        │
│ │C:\AMIPRO                  │                 └──────────┘        │
│ Options to install:      Space needed:  Options to install:      Space needed: │
│ ☒ Ami Pro basics . . . . . .    3807 K  ☐ Choose text filters . . . .  upto 1258 K │
│ ☐ QuickStart tutorial . . . . . 1245 K  ☐ Choose graphic import filters . upto 224 K │
│ ☐ Drawing . . . . . . . . . . .  285 K  ☐ Macro documentation . . . . . .  622 K │
│ ☐ Charting . . . . . . . . . . .  228 K  ☐ Dialog editor . . . . . . . . . .  151 K │
│ ☐ Image processing . . . . . .  248 K  ☐ Sample macros . . . . . . . . .  930 K │
│ ☐ Equation editor . . . . . . .  899 K  ☐ Style sheets/sample documents .  1314 K │
│ ☐ Thesaurus . . . . . . . . . .  402 K  ☐ Clip art . . . . . . . . . . . . .  430 K │
│ ☐ Grammar checker . . . . . .  1181 K  ☐ Help . . . . . . . . . . . . . . .  821 K │
│ ☒ Spell checker . . . . . . . .  364 K  ☐ ATM . . . . . . . . . . . . . . .  568 K │
│                                                                  │
│                              Total disk space needed:   4171 K   │
│                              Disk space available:     15237 K   │
└────────────────────────────────────────────────────────────────┘
```

These numbers show the amount of disk space (in kilobytes) required to install the selected options and the space available on the hard disk.

To complete the installation, follow these steps:

1. In the Specifying Options and Directories dialog box, type the program directory name in the Program Directory text box.

2. Select the options that you want to install.

   Note: *You must install the Ami Pro basics files in order to run the program.*

3. Choose OK. Ami Pro begins installation. When you need to insert a new disk, Ami Pro beeps and displays a message box. Follow the instructions that appear on-screen.

   During the installation, Ami Pro displays a status bar that shows you the progress of the installation procedure.

4. When installation is complete, Ami Pro asks if you want to install the WordPerfect SwitchKit. When this installation is complete, Ami Pro displays the Main Menu.

5. From the Main Menu, choose **E**xit Install. Ami Pro prompts you to begin installation of the Adobe Type Manager.

A

Table A.1 summarizes the available options.

Table A.1. Ami Pro Custom or Options Install Choices	
Option	**Explanation**
Ami Pro Basics	Installs the basic Ami Pro features.
QuickStart Tutorial	Installs the on-line tutorial for Ami Pro.
Drawing	Installs the Drawing program features.
Charting	Installs the Charting program features.
Image Processing	Installs the Image Processing tool used for processing imported TIFF images.
Equation Editor	Installs the scientific and mathematical equation editor. This option requires a symbol font.
Thesaurus	Installs the 1.4 million-word thesaurus.
Grammar Checker	Installs the on-line grammar checking feature.
Spell Checker	Installs the on-line spelling checking feature and the 115,000-word dictionary.
Text Import and Export Filters	Installs the text import and export filters. You can select from a list of filters, the ones you want to install.
Graphic Import Filters	Installs the graphic import filters. You can select from a list of filters, the ones you want to install.
Macro Documentation	Installs on-line macro documentation. The documentation also is available in a 700-page hard copy manual.
Dialog Editor	Creates custom dialog boxes when used with the macro language.
Sample Macros	Installs sample macros that you can use.
Style Sheets/Sample Documents	Installs all of Ami Pro's style sheets and sample documents.
Clip Art	Installs more than 100 clip art images for use with the Drawing program.
Help	Installs the on-line help system.
ATM	Installs the Adobe Type Manager.

Installing the WordPerfect SwitchKit

If you are upgrading from WordPerfect to Ami Pro, you can install the WordPerfect SwitchKit. With the SwitchKit installed, you can convert old WordPerfect files to Ami Pro format and learn Ami Pro functions while using WordPerfect keystrokes.

When Ami Pro installation is complete, the WordPerfect SwitchKit Installation dialog box appears.

To install the SwitchKit, choose **I**nstall SwitchKit. Choose Do **N**ot Install SwitchKit to return to the Main Menu.

Installing the Adobe Type Manager

Ami Pro doesn't install the Adobe Type Manager automatically. Before returning you to the Program Manager, however, Ami Pro gives you the opportunity to start the ATM installation.

To install the Adobe Type Manager, follow these steps:

1. In the Ami Pro Install Program dialog box, choose OK to complete the installation. The Main Menu appears.

2. Choose **E**xit Install. The Insert New Install Disk dialog box appears, instructing you to insert the ATM disk in the appropriate disk drive.

    Note: *If you don't want to install the Adobe Type Manager, choose Cancel to return to the Windows Program Manager.*

3. Insert the ATM Program disk and choose OK. The ATM Installer dialog box appears.

4. The directories shown for PostScript outline fonts and the font metrics files are the default directions. In most cases, you want to install the fonts and files in these directories.

5. Choose **I**nstall. The ATM Installer begins transferring files. A status bar indicates on-screen how the installation is progressing.

A

> **Note:** *If you are using The Lotus SmartSuite program disks, ATM Installer prompts you when you need to insert the ATM Fonts disk in the floppy drive.*

6. When installation is complete, choose **R**estart Windows.

Using the WordPerfect SwitchKit

If you installed the QuickStart Tutorial, the first time you start Ami Pro, the QuickStart Tutorial Main Menu displays. You can select any topic, or choose E**x**it Tutorial.

Note: *For complete instructions about starting Ami Pro, refer to Lesson 1, "Learning the Basics."*

If you installed the WordPerfect SwitchKit, the Ami Pro SwitchKit Loading Options dialog box appears after the QuickStart Tutorial.

In the dialog box, choose one of the following options:

- Automatically Run with Ami Pro if you want Ami Pro to load the SwitchKit every time you start the program. Ami Pro also adds the For **W**ordPerfect Users option to the Help menu.

- Add Menu Item if you want Ami Pro to add the SwitchKit to the Help menu. To turn on the SwitchKit, choose **H**elp, For **W**ordPerfect Users.

- Start SwitchKit Manually if you want to use the SWITCH.SMM macro to start the SwitchKit.

  Note: *To start the WordPerfect SwitchKit, a document must be open on-screen. For information on opening a new document, refer to Lesson 2, "Creating a Document."*

Starting the WordPerfect SwitchKit

To manually start the SwitchKit, follow these steps:

1. Choose Too**l**s, **M**acros. The Macros submenu appears.

2. Choose **P**layback. The Play Macro dialog box appears.

3. In the **M**acros list, choose the SWITCH.SMM macro, then choose OK. Ami Pro adds the For **W**ordPerfect Users option to the Help menu.

To start the SwitchKit, choose **H**elp, For **W**ordPerfect Users, **O**n. The WordPerfect SwitchKit instruction window appears in the lower right corner of the screen.

Using the Instruction Window

Ami Pro displays the SwitchKit instruction window as long as the SwitchKit is activated. You can use the instruction window SmartIcons to navigate in the SwitchKit.

To find out what functions are performed by the icons displayed at the bottom of the instruction window, click the "i" in the instruction window, the i SmartIcon, or press Ctrl+Shift+I.

The "i" in the instruction window

The i SmartIcon

Ami Pro displays information about using Ami Pro commands in the instruction window. Use the Print SmartIcon to print the information. Use the Help SmartIcon to display more help.

To get help with Ami Pro commands, press a WordPerfect key combination. In the instruction window, Ami Pro displays information about how to perform this function with Ami Pro.

A

To close the instruction window, click the Close SmartIcon.

Converting WordPerfect Documents to Ami Pro

To convert WordPerfect documents to Ami Pro format, follow these steps:

1. Choose **F**ile, **O**pen.

2. In the List Files of Type text box, choose WordPerfect.

3. In the **F**iles list box, choose the file you want to convert.

    Note: *To convert WordPerfect files, you must have installed the appropriate text import and export filters.*

To convert more than one WordPerfect document at a time, follow these steps:

1. Make sure that the SwitchKit is turned on.

2. Choose **F**ile, **N**ew, OK to open a new document.

3. Choose **H**elp, **F**or WordPerfect Users, Batch **C**onvert. The Batch Convert dialog box appears.

4. In the Convert From list box, choose the filter that represents the version of WordPerfect under which you created the files.

5. In the Files list box, select all the files that you want to convert. If necessary, first choose the drive and directory that contain the WordPerfect documents.

6. Choose OK. The Import Options dialog box appears.

7. Choose Apply Styles, Ignore Styles or Import a Style Sheet.

8. Choose OK. Ami Pro imports the files into Ami Pro format.

Index

354 pages

GO AHEAD. PLUG YOURSELF INTO
PRENTICE HALL COMPUTER PUBLISHING.

Introducing the PHCP Forum on CompuServe®

Yes, it's true. Now, you can have CompuServe access to the same professional, friendly folks who have made computers easier for years. On the PHCP Forum, you'll find additional information on the topics covered by every PHCP imprint—including Que, Sams Publishing, New Riders Publishing, Alpha Books, Brady Books, Hayden Books, and Adobe Press. In addition, you'll be able to receive technical support and disk updates for the software produced by Que Software and Paramount Interactive, a division of the Paramount Technology Group. It's a great way to supplement the best information in the business.

WHAT CAN YOU DO ON THE PHCP FORUM?

Play an important role in the publishing process—and make our books better while you make your work easier:

- Leave messages and ask questions about PHCP books and software—you're guaranteed a response within 24 hours

- Download helpful tips and software to help you get the most out of your computer

- Contact authors of your favorite PHCP books through electronic mail

- Present your own book ideas

- Keep up to date on all the latest books available from each of PHCP's exciting imprints

JOIN NOW AND GET A FREE COMPUSERVE STARTER KIT!

To receive your free CompuServe Introductory Membership, call toll-free, **1-800-848-8199** and ask for representative **#597**. The Starter Kit Includes:

- Personal ID number and password

- $15 credit on the system

- Subscription to CompuServe Magazine

HERE'S HOW TO PLUG INTO PHCP:

Once on the CompuServe System, type any of these phrases to access the PHCP Forum:

GO PHCP   **GO BRADY**
GO QUEBOOKS   **GO HAYDEN**
GO SAMS   **GO QUESOFT**
GO NEWRIDERS   **GO PARAMOUNTINTER**
GO ALPHA

Once you're on the CompuServe Information Service, be sure to take advantage of all of CompuServe's resources. CompuServe is home to more than 1,700 products and services—plus it has over 1.5 million members worldwide. You'll find valuable online reference materials, travel and investor services, electronic mail, weather updates, leisure-time games and hassle-free shopping (no jam-packed parking lots or crowded stores).

Seek out the hundreds of other forums that populate CompuServe. Covering diverse topics such as pet care, rock music, cooking, and political issues, you're sure to find others with the sames concerns as you—and expand your knowledge at the same time.

Que—The World's Leading 1-2-3 Experts!

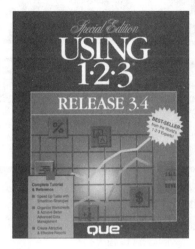

Windows Word Processing Is Easy When You're Using Que!

Count on Que for the Latest in DOS Information!

Using MS-DOS 6, Special Edition

Que Development Group
Version 6

$29.95 USA
1-56529-020-8, 1,000 pp., 7³/₈ x 9¹/₈

Easy DOS, 3rd Edition

Shelley O'Hara
Through Version 6.2

$19.95 USA
1-56529-640-0, 240 pp., 8 x 10

More DOS Titles from Que

DOS 6 SureSteps

Que Development Group
Version 6

$24.95 USA
1-56529-262-6, 300 pp., 7³/₈ x 9¹/₈

Killer DOS Utilities

Que Development Group
Version 6

$39.95 USA
1-56529-115-8, 1,000 pp., 7³/₈ x 9¹/₄

MS-DOS 6 QuickStart

Que Development Group
Version 6

$21.95 USA
1-56529-096-8, 420 pp., 7³/₈ x 9¹/₈

I Hate DOS

Bryan Pfaffenberger
Version 6

$16.95 USA
1-56529-215-4, 384 pp., 7³/₈ x 9¹/₈

MS-DOS 6 Quick Reference

Que Development Group
Version 6

$9.95 USA
1-56529-137-9, 160 pp., 4³/₄ x 8

Complete Computer Coverage

Only Que gives you the most comprehensive programming guides!

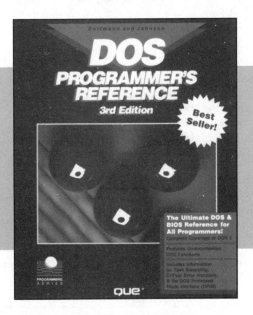

Ami Pro 3 QuickStart: Exercises and Disk

This section includes exercises that build upon the examples presented in the lessons and Visual Index of *Ami Pro 3 QuickStart*. With "hands-on" exercises, you can further your understanding of Ami Pro by practicing with existing documents rather than creating new documents from scratch.

The *Ami Pro 3 QuickStart Disk* is a 720K double-density 3 1/2" disk that contains the following items:

- Sample files used in the lessons of *Ami Pro 3 QuickStart*. These include the examples shown in the Visual Index at the beginning of *Ami Pro 3 QuickStart*.

- Practice files you use in the exercises in this section.

Installing the Disk Files

Before you can complete the exercises in this section or use any of the files on the accompanying disk, you must first install the files onto your hard disk. The disk includes an installation program to make this process simple.

Note: *To avoid overwriting the files on this disk, make a backup copy of the disk files before you install them.*

To install the disk files, follow these steps:

1. In the Windows Program Manager, choose **F**ile, **R**un.

2. Type **B:INSTALL** in the **C**ommand Line text box and choose OK.

Note: *If your Ami Pro QuickStart disk is in a drive other than B, substitute that letter for B in step 2.*

A welcoming screen appears, followed by the Select Installation Drive dialog box.

In most cases, you should
install the files to drive C.

3. In the Select Installation Drive dialog box, select a drive to install the files to and choose OK. The drive you select should be your hard drive.

The Install dialog box appears.

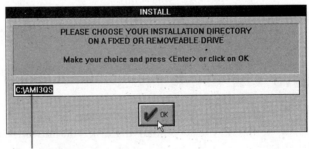

The installation directory

4. If you want to install the files to a directory other than AMI3QS, type a new directory in the Install dialog box, and then choose OK. Otherwise, just choose OK.

When the installation is complete, you return to the Program Manager.

The installation program copies files to the AMI3QS directory (or the directory you specified in step 4, if you changed this default). The program also creates three subdirectories and copies to those subdirectories the Visual Index files, the practice exercise files, and some additional samples.

Using the Disk Files

As mentioned previously, the disk files include sample files from the lessons and Visual Index of *Ami Pro 3 QuickStart* and files for use with the exercises in this section. The following sections discuss how to use these files and include listings of the files on the disk.

Files from QuickStart Lessons and Visual Index

The following table lists (in alphabetical order) sample files pertaining to the lesson examples and Visual Index documents in *Ami Pro 3 QuickStart*. Beside each file name is the associated lesson number.

Files that were used to print documents shown in the Visual Index of *Ami Pro 3 QuickStart* include page number references to the appropriate Visual Index page. To use these files, start Ami Pro and choose **F**ile, **O**pen to open the document file you want to use. Make any desired changes to the file. If you have not made a backup copy of the disk, use a different file name to save the file containing your changes. For more information on opening a file, see Lesson 3 in *Ami Pro 3 QuickStart*, "Revising a Document."

Note: *Depending on the type of printer you use, you may need to make adjustments to the page setup in order to get the look you want when you print the files.*

File Name	Lesson	Page # in Visual Index (if applicable)
123DATA.WK1	16	
ALIGN.SAM	6	
AP3DG01.SAM		8
AP3DG02.SAM		9

(continues)

File Name	Lesson	Page # in Visual Index (if applicable)
AP3DG03.SAM		10
AP3DG04.SAM		11
AP3DG05.SAM		12
AP3DG06.SAM		13
AP3DG07.SAM		14
AP3DG08.SAM		15
AP3DG09.SAM		16
AP3DG10.SAM		17
AP3DG11.SAM		18
AP3DG12.SAM		19
AP3DG13.SAM		20
AP3DG14.SAM		21
CHARTS.SAM	13	
COMPARE.SAM	15	
CUSTOM.SAM	9	
DDELINK.SAM	16	
DRAWING.SAM	11	
FONTSAMP.SAM	5	
FRAMES.SAM	10	
FRTABLE.SAM	12	
IMPGRAF.SAM	16	
MRGEDAT.SAM	14	
MRGEDOC.SAM	14	
NEWDOC.SAM	2	
NEWLINES.SAM	3	

File Name	Lesson	Page # in Visual Index (if applicable)
NEWSLETT.SAM	7	
OLEDOC.SAM	16	
OUTMODE.SAM	17	
OUTSTYLE.SAM	17	
PGTABLE.SAM	12	
PRETTY.SAM	8	
PROOFING.SAM	4	
REVISE.SAM	3	
REVMARKS.SAM	15	
RULERS.SAM	8	
SETPAGE.SAM	7	
STYSAMPS.SAM	2	
TABLE.SAM	12	

Files for Exercises

Use the remaining sample files on the accompanying disk with the exercises covered in the following sections.

Each of these files is named using the format CH*nn*AP#.SAM, where *nn* is the lesson number, and # is the exercise number within that lesson. For example, use the CH04AP2.SAM file with Lesson 4, Exercise 2.

To use these files, start Ami Pro, open the file, and then follow the instructions in the exercises. If you want to save the modified document after completing an exercise, save the file with a different name to avoid overwriting the original file (in case you want to follow the exercise again).

Lesson 1 Exercises

The following exercises are based on Lesson 1, "Learning the Basics."

Exercise 1.1: Using Windows
Estimated Time: 5 minutes

The disk has no file for this exercise. Follow these steps:

1. Start Windows.

2. Open the Lotus Application Group window.

3. Start Ami Pro.

4. Minimize the Ami Pro window to an icon.

5. Restore the Ami Pro window.

6. Use the File menu to exit Ami Pro.

7. Start Ami Pro again.

8. Use the Application Control menu to exit Ami Pro.

Exercise 1.2: Getting Help
Estimated Time: 10 minutes

The disk has no file for this exercise. Follow these steps:

1. Start Ami Pro.

2. Use the Help menu to find Help information on using the mouse in Ami Pro.

3. Maximize the Help window.

4. Print the information in the Help window.

5. From the open Help window, search for information on SmartIcons.

6. Go to the topic "Using SmartIcons."

7. Print the information in the Help window.

8. View a history of the current Help session.

9. Close the Help window.

10. Use the Help pointer to display Help information about the File Exit command.

11. Exit Ami Pro.

Lesson 2 Exercises

The following exercises are based on Lesson 2, "Creating a Document."

Exercise 2.1: Choosing a Style Sheet
Estimated Time: 5 minutes

The disk has no file for this exercise. Follow these steps:

1. Choose to open a new document.

2. In the New dialog box, display style sheet descriptions.

3. Preview sample style sheets.

4. Choose to open a document without contents or macros.

5. Choose a style sheet to create a memo document.

Exercise 2.2: Entering Text
Estimated Time: 5 minutes

Open CH02AP2.SAM in the \AMI3QS\Practice directory and follow these steps:

1. Type your name on the From line in the memo.

2. Insert a paragraph before the closing line and type the following text: **If we continue to learn of this problem, we will have to take drastic measures.**

3. Go back and change the date.

4. Add another paragraph before the closing line and type the text: **We consider this to be a very serious matter. If it continues, you can expect to witness some of the following actions:.**

Exercise 2.3: Choosing a New Style
Estimated Time: 5 minutes

Open CH02AP3.SAM in the \AMI3QS\Practice directory and follow these steps:

1. Position the insertion point on the line above the closing line. Choose the Bullet 1 style. Type the following text, putting each sentence in its own paragraph: **We will rope off the visitors spots between 8:30 and 9:00 a.m. We will place notices in violators' permanent records. We will revoke parking privileges.**

2. Start a new paragraph in the Body Text style and type the text: **We are prepared to take the following steps to ensure that further action is not necessary:.**

3. Start a new paragraph in the Numbered List style and type the following text, putting each sentence in its own paragraph: **Guarantee that the parking lot will be plowed by 8:00 a.m. after a snowfall. Escort employees to their cars after dark. Place a guard in front of the building between 8:30 and 9:30 a.m. and between 5:00 and 6:00 p.m.**

4. Start a new paragraph in the Body Text style and type the text: **We hope these conditions are satisfactory.**

5. Save the document with a new name.

Exercise 2.4: Printing the Document
Estimated Time: 5 minutes

Open CH02AP4.SAM in the \AMI3QS\Practice directory and follow these steps:

1. View the document in full page mode.

2. Change back to Custom view.

3. Check the printer setup to be sure it is correct for the printer you are using.

4. Print the document.

5. Close the document.

Lesson 3 Exercises

The following exercises are based on Lesson 3, "Revising a Document."

Exercise 3.1: Basic Editing
Estimated Time: 5 minutes

Open CH03AP1.SAM in the \AMI3QS\Practice directory and follow these steps:

1. Close the document.

2. Open the document again, directly from the File menu.

3. Type your name on the From line in the memo.

4. Delete the existing date and insert tomorrow's date.

5. Change the style of the bullet list to Bullet 2.

Exercise 3.2: Manipulating Selected Text
Estimated Time: 10 minutes

Open CH03AP2.SAM in the \AMI3QS\Practice directory and follow these steps:

1. Select the fourth paragraph and the bullet list.

2. Move the selected text below the numbered list.

3. Copy the selected text back to its original location.

4. Delete the selected text.

5. Undo the deletion.

6. Revert to the last saved version of the document.

7. Replace all occurrences of the word "visitors" with the word "executives."

Exercise 3.3: Using Multiple Windows
Estimated Time: 10 minutes

Open CH03AP3.SAM in the \AMI3QS\Practice directory and follow these steps:

1. Open CH03AP4.SAM.

2. Arrange the windows so you can see both documents.

3. Copy the numbered list and its introductory paragraph from CH03AP3.SAM to CH03AP4.SAM.

4. Move the bullet list and its introductory paragraph from CH03AP3.SAM to CH03AP4.SAM.

5. Close CH03AP4.SAM.

6. Maximize CH03AP3.SAM.

Lesson 4 Exercises

The following exercises are based on Lesson 4, "Proofreading Your Document."

Exercise 4.1: Using Spell Check
Estimated Time: 5 minutes

Open CH04AP1.SAM in the \AMI3QS\Practice directory and follow these steps:

1. Check the spelling in the document.

2. Add the word "Kane" to your user dictionary.

3. Skip all occurrences of the word "Kleaning."

4. Add the names to your user dictionary.

5. Correct all misspelled words.

Exercise 4.2: Using Grammar Check
Estimated Time: 5 minutes

Open CH04AP2.SAM in the \AMI3QS\Practice directory and follow these steps:

1. Check the document using the Business Writing grammar and style settings. Be sure to check all parts of the document. Display the Readability Statistics when the check is complete.

2. Select the correct options for replacement.

Exercise 4.3: Using the Thesaurus
Estimated Time: 5 minutes

Open CH04AP3.SAM in the \AMI3QS\Practice directory and follow these steps:

1. Look up a synonym for the word "regret."

2. Look up a synonym for the word "sorrow."

3. Replace the word "regret" with the word "anguish" in the letter.

Lesson 5 Exercises

The following exercises are based on Lesson 5, "Dressing Up Your Text."

Exercise 5.1: Working with Fonts
Estimated Time: 5 minutes

Open CH05AP1.SAM in the \AMI3QS\Practice directory and follow these steps:

1. Change the font of the title to 42-point Arial.

2. Change the font for all the recipient information to 16-point Times New Roman.

3. Change the font for the return address to 16-point Courier.

Exercise 5.2: Applying Character Attributes
Estimated Time: 5 minutes

Open CH05AP2.SAM in the \AMI3QS\Practice directory and follow these steps:

1. Make the title bold.

2. Make the No. of Pages line italic.

3. Underline the Subject line.

4. Double-underline the return address information.

5. Copy the formatting from the return address information to the sender and date information.

Lesson 6 Exercises

The following exercises are based on Lesson 6, "Lining Up Your Paragraphs."

Exercise 6.1: Aligning Text
Estimated Time: 5 minutes

Open CH06AP1.SAM in the \AMI3QS\Practice directory and follow these steps:

1. Right-align the five lines that display the company address information.

2. Center the headline.

3. Justify all body text in the press release.

Exercise 6.2: Indenting Text
Estimated Time: 5 minutes

Open CH06AP2.SAM in the \AMI3QS\Practice directory and follow these steps:

1. Indent all text .30 inches from the right margin.

2. Create a hanging indent in the first paragraph by indenting all but the first line by .70 inches.

3. Indent the second and third paragraphs .70 inches from the left.

4. Indent both quotes 1.5 inches from both the left and right margins.

5. Center the names of the people being quoted.

6. Double-underline the return address information.

7. Copy the formatting from the return address information to the second paragraph.

Exercise 6.3: Setting Line Spacing
Estimated Time: 5 minutes

Open CH06AP3.SAM in the \AMI3QS\Practice directory and follow these steps:

1. Single-space the company address information.

2. Single-space the quotes.

3. Use custom spacing set at .25 to bring body text lines closer together.

Lesson 7 Exercises

The following exercises are based on Lesson 7, "Setting Up Pages."

Exercise 7.1: Modifying the Page Layout
Estimated Time: 5 minutes

Open CH07AP1.SAM in the \AMI3QS\Practice directory and follow these steps:

1. Increase the left margin from 1 inch to 1.25 inches.

2. Add a line around the whole page, along the inside edge of the margin.

Exercise 7.2: Inserting a Page Layout
Estimated Time: 10 minutes

Open CH07AP2.SAM in the \AMI3QS\Practice directory and follow these steps:

1. Insert a two-column page layout with 1-inch margins all around.

2. Place a double line between the columns.

Exercise 7.3: Using Rulers
Estimated Time: 10 minutes

Open CH07AP3.SAM in the \AMI3QS\Practice directory and follow these steps:

1. Display the horizontal ruler on-screen.

2. Insert a ruler for the first article in the newsletter.

3. Set a left-aligned tab at 2 inches.

4. Indent all text .25 inches from the left margin and .25 inches from the right margin.

5. Tab the heading in to the tab stop.

6. Insert a ruler for the bullet list at the bottom of the first page.

7. Set a decimal tab stop at 6.25 inches.

8. Align the salary figures at the decimal tab stop.

Lesson 8 Exercises

The following exercises are based on Lesson 8, "Making Your Pages Pretty."

Exercise 8.1: Adding Headers and Footers
Estimated Time: 15 minutes

Open CH08AP1.SAM in the \AMI3QS\Practice directory and follow these steps:

1. Add a header beginning on the second page. Flush left, type: **Mark Lee**. Flush right, type: **The Weekend Gardener**.

2. Add a footer beginning on the first page. In the center, type: **February 17, 1994**.

3. In the footer, insert a page number flush right. Precede the number with the word "Page" and a hyphen.

Exercise 8.2: Adding Borders and Lines
Estimated Time: 5 minutes

Open CH08AP1.SAM in the \AMI3QS\Practice directory and follow these steps:

1. Add a heavy line down the left margin.

2. Make the line red.

Lesson 9 Exercises

The following exercises are based on Lesson 9, "Customizing Ami Pro."

Exercise 9.1: Creating and Modifying Styles
Estimated Time: 10 minutes

Open CH09AP1.SAM in the \AMI3QS\Practice directory and follow these steps:

1. Modify the Title style so that it is underlined and has a larger font size.

2. Modify the subhead style so that it is all capital letters and indented .20 inches from the left margin.

3. Add a square bullet to the body text style. Indent the text beside the bullet .20 inches.

4. Format the word "Meats" so that it is underlined and only its initial letter is capitalized.

5. Select the word "Meats" and use it to create a new style, called Subhead 1.

6. Apply the Subhead 1 style to the words "Meats," "Fish," and "Pasta."

Exercise 9.2: Creating a Style Sheet
Estimated Time: 5 minutes

Open CH09AP2.SAM in the \AMI3QS\Practice directory and follow these steps:

1. Modify the page layout to include a line around the margins.

2. Use the modified styles and the modified page layout to create a new style sheet. Call the style sheet Menus.

3. Create a new document using the Menus style sheet.

Exercise 9.3: Customizing SmartIcons
Estimated Time: 5 minutes

The disk has no file for this exercise. Follow these steps:

1. Create a SmartIcon set that consists of the SmartIcons for:

    Open an Existing File

    Create a New File

    Save the Current File

    Close a File

    Toggle Draft/Layout View

    View Preferences

    Exit Ami Pro

    Bold Text

    Italic Text

    Underline Text

    Print

    Delete

2. Display your new SmartIcon set along the left side of your screen.

3. Display your new SmartIcon set along the bottom of your screen.

4. Display your new SmartIcon set as a floating set and move it anywhere on the screen.

Exercise 9.4: Changing Program Defaults
Estimated Time: 5 minutes

The disk has no file for this exercise. Follow these steps:

1. Set Ami Pro to save your documents every 5 minutes.

2. Set Ami Pro to Undo up to four levels.

3. Set Ami Pro to display on the File menu only three of the most recently opened files.

4. Enter your name, initials, and note color of choice.

5. Set Ami Pro to list style sheets by description in the New dialog box.

Lesson 10 Exercises

The following exercises are based on Lesson 10, "Working with Frames."

Exercise 10.1: Inserting Text and Graphics in a Frame
Estimated Time: 10 minutes

Open CH10AP1.SAM in the \AMI3QS\Practice directory and follow these steps:

1. Insert a frame on the right side of the menu.

2. Using the Subhead style, type the following text in the frame: **Today's Specials Are:**.

3. Center the text in the frame.

4. In the Body Text style, flush left, type the following items: **Meat Loaf**; **Lobster**; **Veal Marsala**; **Mud Pie**.

5. Create another frame on top of the existing frame.

6. Insert the FOOD.SDW clip art file in the top frame.

Exercise 10.2: Manipulating a Frame
Estimated Time: 5 minutes

Open CH10AP2.SAM in the \AMI3QS\Practice directory and follow these steps:

1. Move both frames together to the bottom of the page.

2. Adjust the size of the frames so that the picture is half-on and **half-off** the text frame.

3. Modify the layout of the graphics frame by removing all borders and shadows.

Lesson 11 Exercise

The following exercise is based on Lesson 11, "Using Draw."

Exercise 11.1: Using Draw
Estimated Time: 20 minutes

Open CH11AP1.SAM in the \AMI3QS\Practice directory and follow these steps:

1. Select the frame and start Ami Pro's Drawing feature.

2. Use the drawing tools to create three or four objects of different shapes.

3. Change the size of the objects.

4. Use a text object to title your drawing.

5. Format the text.

6. Move the objects around the frame, individually.

7. Move two or three of the objects together.

8. Add color to a solid object.

9. Rotate an object one-half turn to the left.

10. Use a different line style to create another object.

Lesson 12 Exercises

The following exercises are based on Lesson 12, "Working with Tables."

Exercise 12.1: Creating Tables
Estimated Time: 5 minutes

Open CH12AP1.SAM in the \AMI3QS\Practice directory and follow these steps:

1. In the frame, create a table with six columns and four rows.

2. In the document below the frame, create a table with four columns and six rows.

3. Display the table gridlines and table row/column headings on-screen.

Exercise 12.2: Entering and Editing Data in a Table
Estimated Time: 5 minutes

Open CH12AP2.SAM in the \AMI3QS\Practice directory and follow these steps:

1. In the Frame table, fill in the cells as follows:

    B2 - 2500

    C2 - 2000

    D2 - 2200

    E2 - 2400

    B3 - 4000

    C3 - 3800

    D3 - 3900

    E3 - 4100

    B4 - 3300

C4 - 3400

D4 - 3700

E4 - 3500

2. In the Page table, fill in the cells as follows:

B2 - 25000

B3 - 20000

B4 - 22000

B5 - 24000

C2 - 40000

C3 - 38000

C4 - 39000

C5 - 41000

D2 - 33000

D3 - 34000

D4 - 37000

D5 - 35000

3. In the Frame table, calculate the totals for all three rows.

4. In the Page table, calculate the totals for all three columns.

Exercise 12.3: Changing the Look of Tables
Estimated Time: 10 minutes

Open CH12AP3.SAM in the \AMI3QS\Practice directory and follow these steps:

1. Change the size of the frame to fit neatly around the table.

2. Format the text in the frame table. Use boldface for the column labels and italics for the row labels.

3. Format the table so that the cells are separated by gridlines that will print.

4. In the Page table, center the column headings in their cells.

5. Add a heavy line underneath the top row of cells.

6. Align the word "Total" flush right and make it all caps.

7. Find the highest total in each table and add a fill pattern to the cell.

Lesson 13 Exercise

The following exercise is based on Lesson 13, "Working with Charts."

Exercise 13.1: Creating and Enhancing a Chart
Estimated Time: 10 minutes

Open CH13AP1.SAM in the \AMI3QS\Practice directory and follow these steps:

1. Use the data from the table to create a column chart.

2. Add a legend to the chart.

3. Add a grid to the chart.

4. Use Draw to add a title to your chart. Type the following text: **Sales Commissions: January through April**.

Lesson 14 Exercises

The following exercises are based on Lesson 14, "Merging Documents."

Exercise 14.1: Creating a Merge Data File
Estimated Time: 15 minutes

Follow these steps:

1. Start the merge process and choose to edit a data file.

2. Choose to edit CH14AP1.SAM.

3. Add a field for Contact Name.

4. Enter sample names in the Contact Name field on the **existing** records.

5. Add a record for the LMN Corp., located at 65 Union Ave., Somewhere, RI, 04000.

6. Close the data file.

Exercise 14.2: Creating a Merge Document
Estimated Time: 15 minutes

Open CH14AP2.SAM in the \AMI3QS\Practice directory and **follow** these steps:

1. Choose to edit a merge document.

2. Choose CH14AP2.SAM.

3. Choose CH14AP1.SAM as the merge file.

4. Beneath the date, insert the Company Name field.

5. Beneath the company name, insert the Address 1 field.

6. Beneath the Address 1 Field, insert the Address 2 field.

7. Beneath the Address 2 field, insert the City, State, and ZIP Code fields.

8. Leave a space, then insert the Contact Name field.

9. Continue the merge.

10. Choose to merge, view, and print the data.

11. Choose to print or skip each document as it is displayed.

Lesson 15 Exercises

The following exercises are based on Lesson 15, "Working with Document Notation."

Exercise 15.1: Using Notes and Bookmarks
Estimated Time: 5 minutes

Open CH15AP1.SAM in the \AMI3QS\Practice directory and follow these steps:

1. Go to the note already in place in the document, and read it.

2. Insert a new note at the end of the first paragraph. Type this text: **Remember to find out exactly how many miles long the race will be this year — final costs depend on this.**

3. Go to the first bookmark in the document.

4. Go to the bookmark called SPECS.

5. Insert a bookmark named WILDCALL at the title "The Call of the Wild."

Exercise 15.2: Using Revision Marking
Estimated Time: 10 minutes

Open CH15AP2.SAM in the \AMI3QS\Practice directory and follow these steps:

1. Turn on Revision Marking.

2. Change the Revision Marking options so that inserted text appears in pink italics and deleted text appears in blue strikethrough.

3. Edit the final paragraph to read as follows:

   The production will require three crews, with five people each. One crew will follow the selected musher and team; one crew will provide color material; and one crew will follow the race as a whole.

4. Review the revisions and accept only those in the final paragraph.

Exercise 15.3: Comparing Documents
Estimated Time: 10 minutes

Open CH15AP3.SAM in the \AMI3QS\Practice directory and follow these steps:

1. Compare CH15AP3.SAM to CH15AP1.SAM.

2. Review the differences.

3. Accept the text as it appears in the CH15AP3.SAM version.

Exercise 15.4: Editing Document Information
Estimated Time: 5 minutes

Open CH15AP4.SAM in the \AMI3QS\Practice directory and follow these steps:

1. Display the document information for CH15AP4.SAM.

2. Enter a description of the file. Type the text: **Proposal for Iditarod video production**.

3. Enter Keywords for the file. Type the text: **Mushers, Alaska**.

4. Update the file statistics.

Lesson 16 Exercises

The following exercises are based on Lesson 16, "Working with Other Windows Applications."

Exercise 16.1: Importing and Exporting Data
Estimated Time: 10 minutes

The disk has no file for this exercise. Use your own data files from the application installed on your computer system.

1. Open another application file using Ami Pro.

2. Export an Ami Pro file for use with another application.

Exercise 16.2: Copying Data from Another Application
Estimated Time: 10 minutes

Open CH16AP2.DOC in the \AMI3QS\Practice directory and follow these steps:

1. Start another application.

2. Copy data from the other application into the Windows Clipboard. If you have 1-2-3, you can use the 123DATA.WK1 worksheet provided on this disk.

3. Copy the data into CH16AP2.DOC.

Exercise 16.3: Linking Data
Estimated Time: 10 minutes

Open CH16AP3.SAM in the \AMI3QS\Practice directory and follow these steps:

1. Start another application.

2. Copy data from the other application into the Windows Clipboard. If you have 1-2-3, you can use the 123DATA.WK1 worksheet provided on this disk.

3. Link the data into CH16AP3.SAM.

4. Close Ami Pro.

5. Modify the data in the original application; for example, change a number in the 1-2-3 worksheet.

6. Start Ami Pro.

7. Update the linked data in the Ami Pro document.

Exercise 16.4: Embedding Data
Estimated Time: 10 minutes

Open CH16AP4.SAM in the \AMI3QS\Practice directory and follow these steps:

1. Start another application.

2. Copy data from the other application into the Windows Clipboard. If you have 1-2-3, you can use the 123DATA.WK1 worksheet provided on this disk.

3. Embed the data into CH16AP4.SAM.

4. From Ami Pro, start the original application to edit the embedded object.

5. Switch back to Ami Pro.

Lesson 17 Exercises

The following exercises are based on Lesson 17, "Managing Your Files and Documents."

Exercise 17.1: Creating and Modifying an Outline
Estimated Time: 10 minutes

Open CH17AP1.SAM in the \AMI3QS\Practice directory and follow these steps.

1. Change to Outline mode.

2. Promote line 5 to level 2.

3. Promote line 6 to level 3.

4. Promote lines 7 and 8 to level 4.

5. Promote line 9 to level 3.

6. Promote line 10 to level 3.

7. Demote line 9 to level 4.

8. Promote and demote the remaining headings to complete the outline.

Exercise 17.2: Creating a Table of Contents
Estimated Time: 5 minutes

Open CH17AP2.SAM in the \AMI3QS\Practice directory and follow these steps:

1. Select two levels of headings for creating a Table of Contents.

2. Generate the Table of Contents on a separate page at the beginning of the document.

Exercise 17.3: Adding Footnotes
Estimated Time: 5 minutes

Open CH17AP3.SAM in the \AMI3QS\Practice directory and follow these steps:

1. Go to footnote 1 in the Market Share body text paragraph.

2. Edit the footnote by changing the date from January 1994, to July 1994.

3. Add a footnote to the Profits heading. Type this text: **Acme Accounting, 1994 Audit**.

Exercise 17.4: Using the File Manager
Estimated Time: 15 minutes

The disk has no file for this exercise. Follow these steps:

1. Start the Ami Pro File Manager.

2. Display only the documents that begin with the letter C.

3. Change to the CHAP17 directory.

4. Copy the file CH17AP4.SAM. Name the copy CH17AP4A.SAM.

5. Rename CH17AP4A.SAM with the name CH17AP4B.SAM.

6. Make CH17AP4B.SAM a read-only file.

7. Delete CH17AP4B.SAM.